Joinings and Disjoinings

T0168243

Joinings and Disjoinings

The Significance
of Marital Status
in Literature

Edited by
JoAnna Stephens Mink
and
Janet Doubler Ward

Bowling Green State University Popular Press
Bowling Green, Ohio 43403

Contents

Introduction

That we have long been interested in the topic of marital status is not surprising. After all, almost everyone is interested in marital status, our own and that of others. Practically every time we complete a form, whether it be for auto or life insurance, for a card to the local public library, or for a credit card, we need to check the blank next to "marital status." Our childhoods were probably not much different from those of other little girls growing up in American culture of the 1950s and 60s. We played "mommy and daddy" with other neighborhood children, mimicking our own parents as well as the television parents we grew up with. And if our own families weren't quite like the Andersons, the Nelsons, or the Cleavers, we were certain that one day we would find our own handsome prince, who would sweep us off our feet, take us to the senior prom and into that never-never land of marital bliss. After all, it worked for Cinderella.

We "went steady" in high school, "dated around" in college, and "had relationships" in adulthood. As we grew older, like our childhood friends whom we had since forgotten, we became disillusioned with these relationships. We broke up, we married, we divorced, we remarried. Throughout these joinings and disjoinings, however, we continued to define our existence—perhaps our very identity—through our marital status. In fact, whether we are willing to admit it or not, marriage has remained an integral part of our lives, not only as individuals but also as a society. We could not forget it, even if we wanted to. It is all around us; every time we pick up a newspaper, a magazine, or a novel, we are confronted with the significance of marriage. Influenced by the sexual revolution of the 1970s, we have individually and collectively considered the importance of marriage in our own lives. Finally, as we enter the 1990s, we must consider the opinion offered by Barbara Ehrenreich in the May 1989 issue of *Ms.* magazine that "Fundamentally, men and women need each other less than they used to." Whether we disagree or agree with Ehrenreich's statement, we must acknowledge that marriage remains an important issue in our culture and is one that touches our lives.

As readers of literature and teachers of literature, in our private reading and in our classrooms, we frequently focus on the importance of marriage or singleness as by ourselves and with our students we ponder the plethora of short stories and novels which discuss this important phenomenon. Consequently, it is not surprising that as thinking and feeling, and sexual, American women, we are interested in the idea of marital status. Only now,

1

however, have we been able to consider this all-important topic in a scholarly way, in a collection of essays focusing on the significance of marital status in literature. Given the many responses to and statements of interest in our project, the topic appears to be of wide interest. Indeed, it touches all of us in one way or another.

We have tried to assemble here a collection of critical essays which reflect the multitude of literary works that discuss the significance of marital status, and in this Introduction we touch upon the unifying threads which form the woof and warp of the tapestry of images about marriage. Although some of the essays deal with familiar works, we have endeavored to provide a forum for lesser-known works as well, and our contributors have provided social, historical, and literary context to form a touchstone for their discussions. In their essays, written expressly for this anthology, our contributors have provided expertise from their particular fields which, when taken as a whole, expands our investigation of the issue of marital status.

Our organization is chronological, beginning with Patricia Prandini Buckler's essay, "Love and Death in Chaucer's *The Book of the Duchess*." Our readers are undoubtedly familiar with Chaucer's marriage theme in *The Canterbury Tales*, especially in "The Wife of Bath's Tale" and "The Merchant's Tale." Buckler's discussion illuminates one of his less-anthologized works as a response to the general devastation of the Black Death. *The Book of the Duchess*, Chaucer's earliest major poem, offers comfort to his patron, John of Gaunt, on the death of his wife Blanche, but it also shares the potential for consolation with all spouses who must mourn in their widowhood. Perhaps we should account for the great chronological gap between Buckler's essay and the subject of Christopher K. Brooks's, which takes us into the eighteenth century. One would expect that a discussion of marital status would include at least passing reference to the many marriage plots in Shakespeare's plays and other Renaissance dramas. There are, however, many such discussions in various journals and collections of essays which focus specifically on these plays, and we wished in this anthology to include discussions which are otherwise unobtainable.

In the eighteenth century, as Brooks points out in "Marriage in Goldsmith: The Single Woman, Feminine Space, and 'Virtue'," marriage became increasingly a legislative and economic concern. Oliver Goldsmith voices strong dislike for the political and mercantile attitudes that had begun to dominate the reasons for marriage in the 1760s and 1770s by attacking the Hardwicke Marriage Act of 1753. By examining Goldsmith's varied marital couples through his use of virtue, Brooks both recontextualizes the term "virtue" and reevaluates Goldsmith as a political thinker. Finally, virtue allows a woman to maintain her identity within marriage by establishing a balance of power between her and her often powerful suitors.

Patrick Bizzaro transcends gender boundaries and marriage conventions in "The Symbol of the Androgyne in Blake's *The Four Zoas* and Shelley's *Prometheus Unbound*: Marital Status Among the Romantic Poets." By looking at the way in which Blake and Shelley, as representatives of the

Romantic Period, use the myth of the androgyne, Bizzaro shows that this unification can come about only when gender-distinction polarities are overcome. This essay is somewhat different from the others in our collection because it pushes the scope of our topic, and the issue of marital status, beyond male-female parameters into a new political-social mythology based on equality.

Our next essay focuses on American literature and explores the interpretative and methodological problems posed by antebellum marital fiction. In his discussion of works by Catharine Sedgwick and Alice Cary, Thomas H. Fick shows in "Real Lives: Didactic Realism in Antebellum Marital Fiction" that these authors go beyond the romantic idealizations of marriage which were popular at the time. Instead, by describing the realities of marriage, they provide a practical vision of marriage. One of the unfortunate realities of marriage, especially at mid-nineteenth century, was the plight of the widow. Oftentimes destitute and powerless, women were subject in their viduity to the whim—and even, the cruelty—of their more economically secure male relatives. In "Text and Context in Fanny Fern's *Ruth Hall*: From Widowhood to Independence," Joyce W. Warren describes just such a woman. In this largely autobiographical novel Fern (pseudonym for Sara Willis Parton) defiantly describes the restrictions that conventional nineteenth-century American society imposed upon women writers. By describing the courageous stand which Fern takes in her novel, Warren provides valuable insight not only into one of the lesser-known works of American literature but also into the constraints placed upon widows.

Richard D. McGhee, on the other hand, shows how Dorothea Brooke's widowhood is liberating, rather than constraining. In " 'To Be Wise Herself': The Widowing of Dorothea Brooke in George Eliot's *Middlemarch*" McGhee traces the development of Dorothea's subjectivity through the stages of melancholia, mourning, and reality testing. Informed by post-Freudian and feminist theories, he demonstrates that Dorothea's mourning of Casaubon frees her energies and allows her to accept Will Ladislaw's love. Eliot was one of many nineteenth-century authors and thinkers who were concerned with philosophical and psychological issues; the emerging images of bifurcation and parallelism apply not only to these concerns but to social concerns—class struggle and gender inequality—as well. Because men and women were considered inherently different, marriage was a union of complementary opposites—the rational male and the emotive female. Laurie Buchanan shows that in Elizabeth Gaskell's novels, androgyny becomes a solution not only to class unrest but also to the male's acknowledgement of his "feminine" side. Buchanan's "Marriages of Partnership: Elizabeth Gaskell and the Victorian Androgynous Ideal" points out the importance of marriage to this ideal understanding between individuals and between classes.

Like many of today's women, many turn-of-the-century women considering marriage had to take into account parental authority and involvement, especially when, though adults, they were still living at home.

4   Joinings and Disjoinings

In " 'The Web of Self-Strangulation': Mothers, Daughters, and the Question of Marriage in the Short Stories of Mary Wilkins Freeman," Mary R. Reichardt discusses Freeman's many tales detailing the conflict between a daughter and a mother over the daughter's decision concerning marriage. A woman writer who devoted nearly sixty years to perfecting her craft, Freeman recorded the thoughts, feelings, and circumstances of an entire generation of American women; Reichardt's essay sheds light on Freeman's artistic themes and concerns about marriage in relation to her personal life. A real-life person who could have been a fictional character is Peter Altenberg, one of a number of turn-of-the-century Viennese (Freud was, of course, another) to write on "the woman question." As the title of Pamela S. Saur's essay hints, Altenberg urged men to reject both the bourgeois role of husband and the insensitive role of conquering Don Juan, and to develop themselves instead into idealists like himself—"Peter Altenberg: The Radical Bachelor."

As a counterpoint and another view of bachelors and men in general, in "Proving One's Worth: The Importance of Marriage in the World of Barbara Pym," Katherine Anne Ackley says that Pym portrays men as privileged beings, pampered, spoiled, and self-centered, who validate women by marrying them. Ten of the central characters in Pym's thirteen novels are unmarried, a condition which affects their self-esteem, claims Ackley; widows, having the status of marriage but the freedom of the single state, are in the best position.

Our last two essays are particularly significant because of the way in which the authors use the vehicle of marital status to open up their texts, to provide an interpretation that goes far beyond their focus of marriage. Mary F. Catanzaro examines Samuel Beckett's use of language in "The Dismembered Couple: *Krapp's Last Tape* and *Happy Days*" as it relates to marriage. Thus, she expands the scope of the topic of this anthology by applying the theme of marriage to the very language and form of the text. Even when communication fails or when the partner disappears, the memory of the couple is preserved (in his/her absence) through objects—Krapp's tape player, Winnie's fetish objects. His subjects' attempts to triumph over memory in order to reconstruct the other, claims Catanzaro, is paradoxical and only the voice or the objects remain. Beckett assures us that the couple will not vanish; however, he posits no remedy for the problem of one's own relation to an indifferent universe.

Stefanie Dojka explores how South African writer Nadine Gordimer scrutinizes the institution of marriage in order to show racial and political exploitation. By examining the marriage of two white middle-class liberals, Bam and Maureen Smales, in *"July's People*: She Knew No Word," Dojka compares the disintegration of their partnership when gender roles are overturned to the disintegration of the morally oppressive racially-based economic system. When their former servant July hides them in his house during the futuristic South African revolution, the institution of marriage, as it reflects that system, is scrutinized. As a result, Dojka points out,

Gordimer's depiction of marriage reveals the nature of the social and economic forces of racial exploitation.

It was our intent to assemble a collection of essays which illustrate not only the common threads which unite discussion of the significance of marital status in literature, but also the diverse perspectives which such a topic can shed upon various works and, indeed, upon our own analysis of the importance of marriage and marital status in our lives and our society. The essays, all written solely for this collection, give voice and shape to our search because they approach the issue from a variety of viewpoints. In this way, our contributors evolve a continuing dialogue which transcends gender, class, and historical distinctions. We hope that the essays in this collection, taken both individually and together, provide a framework for further discussion and exploration of this pervasive concern. We note, for example, that this collection does not address the role of marriage in the lives and fiction of Black writers. Indeed, our own search of the criticism indicates a sad omission in this important area, deserving of future consideration. May this collection serve, then, as an impetus for further exploration of an issue which affects us all. As we journey through the varying stages or aspects of marriage and our lives, may we come to an understanding and, perhaps, a resolution of our selves and the world around us. This greater understanding is, of course, our ultimate goal, and we welcome and encourage this exploration.

We take this opportunity to acknowledge and thank those who helped us in the various stages of this project. We would like to thank Atlantic Christian College for the postage and office help which they provided.

We thank those who sent us drafts, manuscripts, and messages of encouragement.

Most important, our sincere thank you to those whose essays form this anthology and without whose cooperation our task would have been insurmountable.

JoAnna Stephens Mink
Janet Doubler Ward

Love and Death in Chaucer's
The Book of the Duchess

Patricia Prandini Buckler

Like the continent, Chaucer's England experienced death in its most hideous and macabre shape—that imposed by the bubonic plague. In an age when infections or ailments considered routine today were often fatal, the plague devastated a population already weakened by famine and reduced by war. The living struggled to keep up with the amassing dead bodies, trying to dispose of them in a Christian and reverent fashion while avoiding contagion. The ghastly spectacle undoubtedly numbed the survivors, and many understandably became hardened to the deaths of their most beloved relatives and friends. In the opening pages of *The Decameron*, Giovanni Boccaccio chronicles the callous, even ruthless behavior of Florentine citizens during the epidemic of 1348, "where things had reached such a pass that people cared no more for dead men than we care for dead goats" (35). Many reacted to the epidemic by turning to hedonism and promiscuity, while others were attracted to the opposite pole, that of extreme religious fervor and harsh penance.

Boccaccio's detailed description of conditions during the plague is probably the most gruesome contemporary account, but it should not be considered the final word on the range of human reactions to the medieval pestilence. Chaucer composed another and far different work, partly in response to the Black Death, which represents a more moderate and rational reaction to the epidemic's horrors. His earliest major poem, *The Book of the Duchess* is Chaucer's compassionate, tender, and courtly memorial to one who died of the plague in 1369—Blanche, Duchess of Lancaster, wife of John of Gaunt.

The life of Blanche would probably have been reduced to a few sentences in the larger history of fourteenth century England if the young Geoffrey Chaucer had not composed *The Book of the Duchess*. Blanche died on 12 September 1369, (possibly 1368), before she was thirty, after a decade of marriage to John of Gaunt and the births of their five children, one of whom was to become King Henry IV. She died just a month after her mother-in-law, Queen Philippa, had also succumbed to the pestilence. (Her father, Henry of Lancaster, and her only sibling, her sister Maud, had perished in the epidemic of 1361-62.) John of Gaunt learned that he had lost both his wife and mother when he returned from the war in France, where he had been engaged at Calais, some weeks later. He provided Blanche with a lovely and dignified resting place in St. Paul's, saw to it that priests regularly said masses for her soul, and paid for commemorative services annually until his death. Although he married twice more, John of Gaunt himself was buried at his own request at the side of his "most dear companion," Blanche.[1]

The Duke's most lasting memorial to his wife, however, was to be found not in her alabaster tomb which has long since disappeared, but in the words of Geoffrey Chaucer's poem, *The Book of the Duchess*, which was probably written at the Duke's request and read publicly at one of the annual anniversary services. The poem is more than a personal commemoration or private expression of mourning; it is also a work intended to comfort and lighten the spirits of all who suffered such terrible losses during the plague years. In this regard, it becomes an elegy for all deceased loved ones and a consolation for all bereaved survivors.

Although much scholarship has tended to minimize the influence of the Black Death on Chaucer's work, an historical event of such cataclysmic social and psychological impact must have affected the poet deeply, just as it did Boccaccio and the well-known French poet, Guillaume de Machaut, whose works Chaucer copied and imitated. Like the *Decameron*, Machaut's poem, *Le Jugement dou Roy de Navarre*, a source for *The Book of the Duchess*, begins with a description of the epidemic. Since Chaucer wrote *The Book of the Duchess* during the plague years for a court from whom the pestilence had taken a heavy toll, it merits a closer look in the context of the epidemic.[2]

Certainly, the poem richly bears numerous layers of connotation, many of which remain to be unveiled. Considered an elegy by some, a consolation poem by others, a Christian allegory by still others,[3] *The Book of the Duchess* yields a variety of interpretations, none wholly satisfactory. Critics have tended to focus on it either as historical artifact (occasional poem) or work of the imagination, when in truth *The Book of the Duchess*, more than most poems, is both. Its private meanings as courtly elegy and agent of consolation for John of Gaunt's bereavement are enlarged and surpassed by its public significance as a curative distraction or source of healing delight for all who have suffered similar losses.

The poem presents three tales of melancholy whose meanings are intertwined. The first is the story of the narrator, who suffers from insomnia, due to a sickness he cannot explain. One night he reads himself to sleep with the story of Ceyx and Alcyone from Ovid's *Metamorphoses* which becomes the second narrative of the poem. After reading the story, the narrator falls asleep and dreams about a hunt and an encounter in the woods with a Black Knight who tells a tale of true love and the death of his cherished lady and wife. The narrator's dialogue with the Black Knight constitutes the longest and clearly primary segment, yet the other two episodes imbue it with its fullest meaning. The poem ends almost immediately, with the Knight's return to his castle, and the narrator's awakening to find himself still in bed with his book, whereupon he resolves to record his dream in rhyme.

My interpretation of the poem will first examine its handling of the ideas of illness, grief, bereavement and death, after which I will show how the context of the plague expands its meaning.

The first panel of the triptych, the narrator's own tale, shows him suffering from melancholy in its classic form—his symptoms include sleeplessness, irrational fear and worry, despondency, lack of attention to external stimuli:

> Al is ylyche good to me—
> Joye or sorowe, wherso hyt be—
> For I have felynge in nothyng,
> But, as yt were, a mased thyng,
> Alway in poynt to falle a-doun;
> For sorwful ymagynacioun
> Ys alway hooly in my mynde.[4](9-15)

The narrator describes himself as having "melancolye" and "drede...for to dye" (11. 22-3). His illness seems both chronic and severe. He has suffered for eight years, and only one physician (apparently not available) can cure him. He is living against nature and believes death is inevitable. The hallmarks of this sickness coincide with the mental and physical deterioration of a frustrated courtly lover, an interpretation which would identify the "phisicien but oon" as a lady, possibly a real lady in Chaucer's life. The same symptoms could also indicate grief over the death of a loved one, or, in a Christian interpretation, sorrow over sin or alienation from God. Boethius' Lady Philosophy could heal the narrator in the former case; Christ himself might be the physician in the latter. Given the bereavement suffered by Alcyone in the book and by the Black Knight in the dream sequence, as well as the occasion for the work, consistency would favor diagnosing the narrator's illness as grief over a deceased lover (Lumiansky 7-9). (Machaut's narrator has shut himself up in his chamber to isolate himself from infection.)

Whatever the cause of the sickness, the narrator follows common medieval medical advice when he turns to a book of tales to distract himself. Insomnia was one of the symptoms of illness caused by an excess of emotion, usually anger, fear, sorrow, or grief. Physiologically, excessive emotion caused heat to rush to the aching heart, a movement which weakened the rest of the body and often proved fatal. Delightful conversation, music, listening to stories, reading, chess, or other games distracted the patient, getting the mind off the cause of the excess emotion, permitting the off-balance humors to re-settle, returning the patient to a more desirable and healthful emotional state.[5]

The reading does cure the narrator's insomnia, although the tragic story itself might seem conducive to developing more, rather than less, sorrow. The tale from Ovid tells of the deep love between Queen Alcyone and her husband, King Ceyx. Ceyx fails to return from a sea voyage, throwing the faithful Alcyone into a state of severe anxiety and grief. Her condition is described in words similar to those used earlier in reference to the narrator:

> Ful ofte she swouned, and sayed "Alas!"
> For sorwe ful nygh wood she was,
> Ne she koude no reed but oon;
> But doon on knees she sat anoon
> And wepte, that pittee was to here. (103-7)

Juno answers the queen's piteous prayers by arranging a dream in which the god of sleep, Morpheus, having entered the dead body of Ceyx, appears to his widow, affirming the king's death by drowning. In spite of divine advice (in the voice of Ceyx) to " 'Awake! let be your sorwful lyf! / For in your sorwe there lyth no red' " (202-3), Alcyone dies of grief within three days.

This second episode demonstrates more than the fatal fruitlessness of excessive grief, however. Its glimpse into the sterile realm of Morpheus, "Ther never yet grew corn ne gras, / Ne tre, ne [nothing] that ought was, / Beste, ne man, ne noght elles," (156-8) shows the deathlike condition of those sleeping in the cave "as derk/ As helle-pit" (170-1). Even Juno's messenger with his horn is hard-pressed to stir its occupants to listen or act. Although the narrator doesn't mention it explicitly, the danger of too much sleep, a state which is as worthless and unproductive as the illness of insomnia, becomes apparent. Sleep may be necessary to good physical and emotional health, but in excess it becomes an escape from life's hassles or withdrawal from the world. In this sense, Alcyone's death from grief is a way of succumbing to eternal sleep and therefore contrary to nature's impulse toward light and life. In the Christian world, the queen's despair would have placed her beyond redemption in death.

As the panel which connects the narrator's sorrowful state with that of the Black Knight, the story of Ceyx and Alcyone bears important adumbrations of meaning for the rest of the work. Alcyone suffers from lack of information—she is desperate to know whether her husband is alive or dead—but when the worst is confirmed, she can't cope with it. Her only response to the truth is to die herself. Stephanie Hollis makes the cogent point that the narrator, too, lacks courage to face completely the truth about death:

> What is to the dreamer an exemplum concerning the power of the gods of sleep, is in fact an exemplum which demonstrates human inability, in even the most favourable circumstance, to confront and accept the actuality of death...
>
> It is surely the dreamer's refusal to face this fundamental fact of life that accounts for his patent misconstruction of the point of the story. Ironically, the story is to him a source of consolation, rescuing him from his own death, which he fears greatly will be the consequence of his sleeplessness (5).

Because the narrator can neither confront death nor accept its reality, he draws from the story the eccentric conclusion that by praying to the gods of sleep and offering them the prize of a cozy and beautifully crafted featherbed, he can buy or beg healing rest. And so he falls asleep, and dreams "so ynly swete a swevene" (276) that even the most skilled interpreters of dreams in history, Joseph and Macrobius, could not adequately explain it.

The sweet repose enjoyed by the narrator has offered him a new beginning, another opportunity to come to grips with the reality of death. His dream begins with a fresh awakening into a lovely morning with birds singing a solemn service of great beauty. His chamber itself has been transformed into a kind of church or illuminated manuscript, lined with stained glass windows depicting the story of Troy, and walls decorated with "bothe text and glose, / Of al the Romaunce of the Rose" (333-4). Even in his dreams, he lives in the bookish world of heroes and romance rather than in the "real" world where death is a natural part of life.

Outside the day is perfect—cloudless blue sky, bright clear air, ideal temperature. A hunting horn sounds and the narrator, with a touch of Chaucerian humor, rides his horse out of his bedroom to join the pursuit, which he learns is under the leadership of Octavian. His despondency apparently cured, the dreamer willingly embraces the joy of the bright May morning. The quarry escapes, and the narrator is distracted by a puppy who leads him into a glorious meadow, thick with green grass and every conceivable flower, more blossoms than there are stars in the heavens. The verdancy of nature, the narrator says, "had forgete the povertee/ That wynter, thorgh hys colde morwes, / Had mad hyt suffre, and his sorwes" (410-12). In the nearby primeval forest, animals too numerous to count engulf him. Eventually he discovers a dark figure sitting alone beneath a powerful oak. This idyllic rural setting is so conventionally romantic that the only possible explanation for the presence of the Man in Black is that he is a lover.

Thus begins the narrator's dialogue with the Man in Black, the longest section of the poem and the third panel of the triptych. The verdant environment, the courtly language, the Knight's encomium to his lady, his apparent love-sickness, all characterize romance in the French tradition. Yet as many have pointed out before, the episode is more than a simple love debate: it uses the conventions of courtly love to eulogize Blanche and comfort John of Gaunt (seen by most as the lady and knight of the story), to offer the consolation of philosophy or the comfort of Christian redemption— in other words to become more than it at first seems to be.[6]

The focus of the tale begins shifting from the dreamer to the sorrowful Knight, who is so preoccupied with his internal condition that he is oblivious to everything around him. The dreamer's words describing the stranger's state echo his earlier self-characterization, and also bring to mind the sorrowful suffering of Alcyone:

For-why he heng hys hed adoun,
And with a dedly sorwful soun

He made of rym ten vers or twelve
Of a compleynte to hymselve,
The most pitee, the moste rowthe,
That ever I herde; for by my trowthe,
Hit was gret wonder that Nature
Myght suffre any creature
To have such sorwe, and be not ded. (461-9)

The Black Knight's suffering from melancholia seems far more severe than
the narrator's, however, because in addition to bloodless extremities and
lack of sensation or attention, the green tinge of his complexion—"Hys
hewe chaunge and wexe grene/ And pale" (497-8)—according to medical
belief indicated illness so serious that a cure was unlikely (Grennen 134).
The dreamer concludes correctly that the Knight has "wel nygh lost hys
mynde" (511).

   After he does attract the Knight's attention, the dreamer begins to probe
his own thoughts for a strategy by means of which he might help this poor,
sorrowful soul:

   Anoon ryght I gan fynde a tale
   To hym, to loke where I myght ought
   Have moore knowynge of hys thought. (536-8)

The dreamer initiates a conversation by commenting on the hunt, but then
invites the Man in Black to reveal his sorrow promising

   ... "to make yow hool,
   I wol do al my power hool.
   And telleth me of your sorwes smerte;
   Paraunter hyt may ese youre herte,
   That semeth full sek under your syde." (553-7)

As the Knight's appearance has been a living catalogue of symptoms for
fatal melancholy, his response to the dreamer's invitation is a list of the
customary remedies:

   "May noght make my sorwes slyde,
   Nought al the remedyes of Ovyde,
   Ne Orpheus, god of melodye,
   Ne Dedalus with his playes slye;
   Ne hele me may no phisicien,
   Noght Hypocras, ne Galyen;
   Me ys wo that I lyve houres twelve." (567-72)

Compared to the Black Knight's affliction, the dreamer's illness, cured by
the first device—Ovid's story—seems simple.

The Knight rails especially against death because, though he would welcome it, it continually eludes him. His pain is so bad, he says, that Sisyphus in hell is better off, " 'For whoso seeth me first on morwe/ May seyn he hath met with sorwe,/ For y am sorwe and sorwe ys y' " (595-7).

Several points can be made about this early part of the dialogue. In addition to the medical accuracy of the Knight's description, Chaucer has given it moral urgency as well. The bereaved knight is both in danger of death and desiring it. Although the exact nature of his sorrow is still somewhat ambiguous, the dreamer cannot miss the despair in his statements. (Whether or not the dreamer actually knows that the Black Knight is grieving over a dead lady at this point is a hotly contested issue. The narrator has overheard the Knight chant a lay in which he states his lady bright " 'Is fro me ded and ys agoon' " (479), yet he and the Knight continue to talk as though the fact of the lady's death has not yet been disclosed. Whether this is because of the narrator's slowness or politeness or denial or preoccupation with himself, or whether it is a slip on Chaucer's part, or whether the narrator pretends ignorance in order to facilitate the Knight's therapy, is irrelevant to the present discussion. The first audience for the poem knew, just as we know, that Blanche was dead.) When the dreamer volunteers to listen to the Knight's woes, he is offering himself as a *confabulator*, identified in medieval medical guides as a conversationalist whose particular purpose is to tell stories or lead quiet discussions that pleasurably distract a prince or other important personage, usually before bed, to induce sleep and cause other physiological and psychological benefits. Such diversion of the mind would aid the digestion, clear the brain of troubling thoughts, and sharpen the memory (Olson 82-5).

The Black Knight's situation appears so severe that the success or failure of the dreamer's plan would surely make the difference between life and death. Urging the Knight to unburden himself, the dreamer responds only at strategic intervals, so that the Knight's conversation with the dreamer is more like a soliloquy with periodic interruptions. He describes how the ruthless turning of Fortune's wheel has changed all his good into bad, his happiness into sorrow, his life into death. He played a game of chess with Lady Fortune, he complains, and she won by taking his queen:

> "For Fortune kan so many a wyle
> Ther be but fewe kan hir begile,
> And eke she ys the lasse to blame;
> Myself I wolde have do the same,
> Before God, hadde I ben as she;
> She oghte the more excused be." (673-8)

In spite of his misery, however, the Black Knight reaffirms his own moves. Given the opportunity, he would do the same again, because " 'through that draughte I have lorn/ My blisse' " (686-7). But now that he has lost his bliss, the Knight sees no future for himself:

> "For evermore, y trowe trewly,
> For al my wille, my lust holly
> Ys turned; but yet, what to doone?
> Be oure Lord, hyt is to deye soone." (687-90)

These statements of despair evoke the dreamer's first interruption, in which he advises the Knight to be as philosophical as Socrates who " 'counted nat thre strees/ Of noght that Fortune koude doo' " (718-9), and to beware of the damnation which is the eternal fate of suicides. The love-debate model emerges again as the dreamer, after citing several traditional examples of great lovers who killed themselves after having been betrayed by their partners, says " 'ther is no man alyve her/ Wolde for a fers make this woo!' " (739-40). The Black Knight counters this provocative statement with a caution, which will operate somewhat like a refrain through the remainder of the Knight's soliloquy:

> "Why so?" quod he, "hyt is nat soo.
> Thou wost ful lytel what thou menest;
> I have lost more than thou wenest." (742-4)

The Knight's combative reaction here marks an important turning point in the poem. He finally accepts the narrator's offer to hear the details of his woe, and the story from here on becomes fully the Knight's.

First he describes his petulant youth, devoted to love's service but without focus or compass. Eventually Fortune caused him to glimpse a lady whose perfections outshone his dreams. More than 200 lines of the soliloquy are spent in praise of the lady, Fair White. It is of course this description of the lady's beauty, charm, and virtue which constitutes primarily the elegy for Blanche of Lancaster. Perfection meets ideal love in her, and her qualities, as described by the grieving husband, outshine every star in the firmament:

> "Ryght on this same, as I have seyd,
> Was hooly al my love leyd;
> For certes she was, that swete wif,
> My suffisaunce, my lust, my lyf,
> Myn hap, myn hele, and al my blesse,
> My worldes welfare, and my goddesse,
> And I hooly hires and everydel." (1035-41)

Again the dreamer interrupts, with lukewarm praise ("'I not how ye myghte have do bet'" (1044)) for the lady, made even more equivocal by his declaration,

> "Yow thoghte that she was the beste,
> And to beholde the alderfayreste,

Whoso had loked hir with your eyen." (1049-51)

And again the Black Knight argues, asserting that everyone who saw her agreed and swore that she was the fairest lady anywhere. With this statement the circle of mourners is expanded so that the bereavement which had belonged to the Black Knight alone begins to be shared with all who knew and loved her, and now miss her. As the Knight continues, he describes the depth and feeling of his love for the lady, but is interrupted yet again by the dreamer, who wants to hear less praise and more facts:

> "Ye han wel told me herebefore,
> Hyt ys no nede to reherse it more,
> How ye sawe hir first, and where.
> But wolde ye tel me the manere
> To hire wich was your firste speche,
> Therof I wolde yow beseche;
> And how she knewe first your thoght,
> Whether ye loved hir or noght.
> And telleth me eke what ye have lore,
> I herde yow telle herebefore." (1127-36)

The Black Knight repeats his refrain, " 'Thow nost what thow menest;/ I have lost more than thou wenest' " (1137-8). As Georgia Ronan Crampton has so well argued, each repetition of this formula marks a shift in attitude and progression in the narrative (493). Indeed, the tension tightens at this particular juncture, with the dreamer becoming even more insistent and the Black Knight more determined to get the whole story out.

He begins " 'to telle shortly' " his first, frustrated attempt to gain her favors, and his successful effort some time later, which was followed by incomparable married bliss:

> "Therwyth she was alway so trewe,
> Our joye was ever ylyche newe;
> Oure hertes wern so evene a payre,
> That never nas that oone contrayre
> To that other, for no woo.
> For sothe, ylyche they suffred thoo
> Oo blysse, and eke oo sorwe bothe;
> Ylyche they were bothe glad and wrothe;
> Al was us oon, withoute were.
> And thus we lyved ful many a yere
> So wel, I kan nat telle how." (1287-97)

The dreamer interrupts one last time, to bring the conversation to its inevitable climax. " 'Where is she now?' " he asks, and the Black Knight falls silent, becoming "ded as stoon" (1298-1300):

> "Bethenke how I seyde here-beforn,

'Thow wost ful lytel what thou menest;
I have lost more than thow wenest'—
God wot, allas! ryght that was she!"
    "Allas, sir, how? what may that be?"
    "She is ded!" "Nay!" "Yis, be my trouthe!"
    "Is that youre los? Be God, hyt ys routhe!" (1304-10)

These are the last words of the dialogue, and twenty-four lines later, *The Book of the Duchess* comes to a close. Clearly the entire conversation between the dreamer and the Man in Black has been moving inexorably toward these final words in which the bereaved lover and husband of Fair White comes to grips with the actuality of his loss. His confession to the dreamer has resulted in a therapeutic rebalancing of his inner world, and he is now able to cope with an outer world without Blanche.

In a far more businesslike tone, the narrator says that this king headed home to "a long castel with walles white,/ Be seint Johan! on a ryche hil" (long recognized as a word play for John of Gaunt who was "King of Castile," "Lancaster," "Blanche," "St. John" the Duke's patron saint, and "Richmond," another of his titles). The dreamer then awakens, and also resumes life's normal routines by planning a new poem based on the dream.

In this final panel of the triptych, Chaucer has depicted with more colors, better details, and finer workmanship the themes already portrayed in the first two, concerning the nature of love and the meaning of death. At first the narrator, isolated in his room and ill with anxiety, resisted the experiences of life, which may indeed include unfulfilled love, loss of one's beloved, or even death. He sought escape from the harsh lesson by entering a fictional world, only to have his fears confirmed by the sad tale of Ceyx and Alcyone. The true love they shared actually led to Alcyone's death, since she could not face life without her husband. The narrator still could not face the moral of this story and so denied it by focusing on the gods of sleep. He couldn't avoid the truth for long, however, because it presented itself to him again in his dream, with much greater elaboration. Finally he is compelled to acknowledge that the great happiness of love fulfilled, even when blessed by marriage, can ultimately result in grief and possibly even death. The dreamer and the Man in Black come to this realization together, because it is too much for a person alone to bear. The final truth, acknowledgement of which allows both griefstricken characters to return to civilization—in effect to the "real world" of daily life—is that death, like perfect love, does not deny life, but enriches and affirms it. Although Blanche of Lancaster is dead, the world is a better place because she lived in it, and her mourners are better people for having known her.

Such a work seems to be particularly suited to the world in which it was created. In addition to the horrifying reality of the Black Death itself, medieval Europe was confronted with the religious belief that the epidemic was a punishment from God, although even the good seemed to die. Furthermore, medical thinking held that corrupt air caused the pestilence, so that the very breath of life could bring death. Individuals isolated themselves from the plague-stricken, which often denied nursing care to the ill, spiritual comfort to the dying, and decent burial to the dead. Anyone living in such times undoubtedly wondered if the world possessed any virtue or if God possessed any mercy.

The depression and alienation expressed by Machaut in the introduction to *Le Jugement dou Roy de Navarre* reflect these same terrors. The plague was seen in moral as well as physical and social dimensions. Besides the Black Death, the narrator here reflects on other worldy evils—war, water poisoned by Jews, hypocritical flagellants, which were bound to call down God's wrath. Machaut's narrator, like Chaucer's, is shut up in his room fearful and anxious, and emerges only in springtime after the epidemic is over. The dreamer's words about the green fields which had forgotten the harshness of winter clearly allude to the wintertime of pestilence in *Navarre*. The Black Knight's diatribe against Fortune, in which he recites the evil inversion of every previously known good, captures the vivid sense of a world out of balance conveyed in Machaut's prologue. When all creation seems upside down, chaos and catastrophe reign. Chaucer's use of the Machaut poem as one of his sources is particularly significant because the allusions to the *Navarre* provide a dark undertone for the grief in *The Book of the Duchess* (Machaut 137-54).

Colin Wilcockson's introduction to this poem in the third edition of *The Riverside Chaucer* mentions the plague background, suggesting that "the recollection of the countless thousands who mourned their dead was intended to provide Gaunt with the consolation of companionship in grief" (330). I think the connection was much stronger and less one-sided than that, however, since although John of Gaunt alone might have been Chaucer's patron, he was by no means an audience of one. The poet undoubtedly wrote with an eye to pleasing the holder of the purse, but he would not have ignored the rest of his listeners. Everyone at Blanche's public memorial must have suffered losses from the plague, even the two dozen poor men who were paid to stand around her tomb holding burning torches. Although they wore the blue and white livery of the Lancaster household provided for the occasion (Lewis 179-80), they were surely not personal friends of the late Duchess. Yet everyone who heard *The Book of the Duchess* would certainly have experienced some degree of personal grief and anxiety because of the pestilence; surely Chaucer meant his poetry to speak to them as well as to John of Gaunt. Ann Middleton says that Ricardian poetry in general,

speaks "as if" to the entire community—as a whole, and all at once rather than severally— rather than "as if" to a coterie or patron.... What common understanding—that is, "we," each of us in the presence of others—can see about our common condition, the world we share *as a people* becomes the poetic subject (98).

One cannot doubt that Chaucer's public tribute to John of Gaunt and his late wife Blanche addressed the common human condition of horror, shock, and bereavement resulting from the devastation of the Black Death.

Returning to Glending Olson's excellent discussion of the medicinal uses of literature, one must conclude that if Chaucer's depiction of the therapeutic applications of literature and conversation do reflect actual contemporary practice, then *The Book of the Duchess* itself becomes the means for healing:

If we think of the playfulness as a therapeutic response to melancholy induced by the delights of fiction, its curative nature makes it a fitting part of the preparation for the dream itself. For if Ovid is Chaucer's *confabulator*, then the narrator is the Black Knight's, and Chaucer John of Gaunt's. The narrator's role in the dream is to lead the knight to wholeness, to let him "ese [hys] herte" by telling of his sorrow (553-7), and he does not speak except to further that end. But the work as a whole is Chaucer's speech, and it is meant to comfort a prince. (88)

I wish to extend this conclusion a bit further, and point out that the work of literature must in fact heal whomever it can reach, just as the plague could kill all it touched. From this perspective, every reader becomes both the dreamer and the prince. Chaucer invites each of us to come out of our locked chambers and, through the transforming ministrations of literature, to face even the darkest truths about life. *The Book of the Duchess* allows everyone to confront and reject the despair of Alcyone, to share the mortal grief of the Man in Black, and finally, in the company of the dreamer and the Knight, to face up to our own mortality, accepting as we do so the fact that we are all living at risk of dying. But ultimately we must throw off grief and return to the business of life, whose value a better understanding of death has reaffirmed.

Notes

[1]Details of Blanche of Lancaster's life, death, and burial are found in N.B. Lewis, "The Anniversary Service for Blanche, Duchess of Lancaster, 12 September, 1374." *Bulletin of the John Rylands Library* 21 (1937): 176-92; Bradford B. Broughton, "Chaucer's 'Book of the Duchess': Did John [of Gaunt] love Blanche [of Lancaster]?" in *Twenty-Seven to One: A Potpourri of Humanistic Material Presented to Dr. Donald Gale Stillman on the Occasion of His Retirement from Clarkson College of Technology by Members of the Liberal Studies-Humanities Department Staff, 1949-1970*. Ogdensburg, N.Y.: Ryan Press, Inc. n.d.; Marjorie Anderson, "Blanche, Duchess of Lancaster." *Modern Philology* 45 (1947-1948): 152-59, among others.

[2]See Norman Hinton's discussion in "The Black Death and the *Book of the Duchess*" for a fuller account of the plague background.

[3]For examples of these various interpretations, see: Charles P.R. Tisdale, "Boethian 'Hert-Huntyng': The Elegiac Pattern of *The Book of the Duchess*." *The American Benedictine Review*, (1973): 365-380; Stephen Manning, "Rhetoric as Therapy: The Man in Black, Dorigen, and Chauntecleer." *Kentucky Philological Association Bulletin*. (1978): 19-25; John Lawlor, "The Pattern of Consolation in *The Book of the Duchess*." *Speculum* 21 (1956): 626-48; Jerog O. Fichte, "*The Book of the Duchess*—A Consolation?" *Studia Neophilologica* 45 (1973): 53-67; D.W. Robertson, Jr., "The Historical Setting of *The Book*

of the Duchess." Mediaeval Studies in Honor of Urban Tigner Holmes, Jr.. Ed. John Mahoney and John Esten Keller. Chapel Hill: U. of N. Press, 1965. 170-95.

⁴All quotations from Chaucer come from the F.N. Robinson 2nd ed., Cambridge: Riverside Press, 1957.

⁵A thorough and most persuasive discussion of the medical uses of literature is found in Glending Olson, *Literature as Recreation in the Later Middle Ages,* Ch. 2, "The Hygienic Justification."

⁶For Chaucer's use of French sources in *The Book of the Duchess,* see James Wimsatt, *Chaucer and the French Love Poets.* Chapel Hill: Univ. of N. Carolina Press, 1968; B.A. Windeatt, ed. & tr., *Chaucer's Dream Poetry: Sources and Analogues.* Cambridge: D.S. Brewer/Rowman & Littlefield, 1982.

Works Cited

Boccaccio, Giovanni. *The Decameron.* Tr. Richard Aldington. N.Y.: Dell, 1975.

Chaucer, Geoffrey. *Works.* Ed. F.N. Robinson. 2nd ed. Cambridge: Riverside Press, 1957.

────── *The Riverside Chaucer.* Ed. Larry D. Benson. 3rd ed. Boston: Houghton Mifflin, 1987.

Crampton, Georgia Ronan. "Transitions and Meaning in *The Book of the Duchess." Journal of English and Germanic Philology* 62 (1963): 486-500.

Grennen, Joseph E. "Hert-Huntyng in *The Book of the Duchess." Modern Language Quarterly,* 25 (1964): 131-9.

Guillaume de Machaut. *Oeuvres.* 3 vols. Paris: Ernest Hoeppfner, Librairie de Firmin-Didot, 1906. Johnson reprint. 1965. Vol. 1.

Hinton, Norman. "The Black Death and *The Book of the Duchess." His Firm Estate: Essays in Honor of Franklin James Eikenberry.* Ed. Donald E. Hayden. Tulsa: University of Tulsa Press, 1967. 72-8.

Hollis, Stephanie. "The Ceyx and Alceone Story in the Book of the Duchess." *Parergon: Bulletin of the Australian and New Zealand Canberra* 12 (1977): 3-9.

Lumiansky, R.M. "The Bereaved Narrator in Chaucer's *The Book of the Duchess." Tulane Studies in English* 9 (1959): 5-17.

Middleton, Anne. "The Idea of Public Poetry in the Reign of Richard II." *Speculum* 53 (1978): 94-114.

Neaman, Judith. "Brain Physiology and Poetics in *The Book of the Duchess." Res Publica Litterarum: Studies in the Classical Tradition* 3 (1980): 101-13.

Olson, Glending. *Literature as Recreation in the Later Middle Ages.* Ithaca: Cornell U. Press, 1982.

Marriage in Goldsmith:
The Single Woman, Feminine Space, and "Virtue"

Christopher K. Brooks

Oliver Goldsmith, novelist, historian, playwright, essayist, poet, and biographer, succeeded in these many genres because his works were so contemporary and palatable to a wide audience. His most pervasive canonical themes include economics, politics, and the role of marriage in eighteenth-century English society. It is this later theme that permeates Goldsmith's "greatest" works, including *She Stoops to Conquer* and *The Good Natur'd Man* (his plays), *The Vicar of Wakefield* (his novel), and *The Citizen of the World* (his immensely popular "eastern tale"/essay collection). In each of these works, commentary on and depictions of marriage—especially marriages between persons of different social orders—is common and critical to Goldsmith's political and economical ethics. Each potential marital partner represents an aspect of society or an economic ethic that is a direct reflection of Goldsmith's sense of a balanced and natural world in which marriage represents a sacred union between man and woman. The most interesting aspect of Goldsmith's recurring marital ethic involves the roles that his young women must play: teachers, women of "virtue," quiet or secretive heroines.

For example, in what might be perceived as a pre-feminist attitude, Kate Hardcastle decides to "teach" her would-be seducer "a little confidence" in order to restore his manly virtue. Meanwhile, Sophia Primrose must remain sensible and virtuous, never speaking for herself, to secure the love (and accompanying fortune) of Sir William Thornhill. And Miss Richland, her name revealing her status, must secretly rescue her profligate future husband from his misguided virtues by imposing her own sense of *economic* virtue onto him. In all three cases, the woman, in essence, "gets her man" by representing the goodness that the male character lacks and by maintaining some sort of "virtue." The successes that Goldsmith's women gain may vindicate, in a subtle way, Barbara Schnorrenberg's large assertion: "Modern feminism, like modern society, begins in the eighteenth century" (in Kanner, 205). This is not today's feminism by any means, for it is still passive, often silent, and at times invisible: but the positive changes made in the worlds of Goldsmith's works are often made by his women, and though they may not be fully "liberated" they certainly work to be "at liberty" to choose their mates, as both Miss Richland and Kate Hardcastle eventually do. Their activity in a patriarchal age suggests an early "feminism" that is marked by subtle action in a time when feminism was usually embodied in pleas to set up women's academies or voiced in plaintive essays. Moreover, the marriages that take place aid Goldsmith in rejecting the Marriage Bill of 1753, a legislative act that Goldsmith saw as an attempt to impose a patriarchal law onto the law of nature.

In brief, the Marriage Act of 1753, introduced by Lord Hardwicke amidst a great deal of controversy, was a legislation open to much criticism and (mis)interpretation. Its main aim was to put a stop to "clandestine" and "fleet marriages" that occasionally saw heiresses elope, fortune-hunters seduce, and, most common of the abuses, sailors fall victim during drunken shore leaves to prostitutes or pension-hunting women who would marry such unprepared military men and then claim the benefits of being military spouses. The bill required parental or guardian consent for minors (under 21 years of age) and also imposed a three-week "calling of banns" period between the issuance of the licence and the actual marriage ceremony. It was designed to prevent "undesirable" marriages, but the visions of certain abuse and the feeling that here was yet another law to control the lower classes quickly emerged. Country ideologists and opposition party members perceived the bill as a subtle attempt to close the marriage market, especially to Primrose-type social climbers and those from the merchant class. Whether this was the intent is not at issue: Goldsmith and other conservatives believed it to be the case and responded loudly.

Although Goldsmith's major spokesman for marriage per se is the title character of *The Vicar of Wakefield*, it is Lien Chi Altangi, his "citizen of the world," who voices the dismay of the middle class about the state of marriage in England during the decade after Hardwicke's marriage act: "In order therefore to prevent the great from being contaminated by vulgar alliances, the obstacles to matrimony have been so contrived, that the rich only can marry among the rich" (II, 310).[1] One major middle class complaint about the Hardwicke act was that the Marriage Act turned women of virtue who had little or no fortunes into difficult cases, while at the same time it made wealth, not moral goodness or ability to love, the dominant reason for marriage. Other thinkers—often pamphleteers who sought safety through anonymity—also attacked the Marriage Act of 1753. One certain "Freeholder" writes,

In this country a law by which marriages are restrained, by which the propriety of them is preferred to their ease and frequency, can effect our nobility but in one light, in the benefit which arises to them from the fondness shown by men who have acquired fortunes in trade... and [through which] the marriages of heiresses might become a monopoly for peers. ("Considerations" 1753)

Goldsmith is more subtle than this, avoiding words such as "heiress" and "peer" and substituting for them the characters of the fully emerged and literate (and therefore meaningful) middle class: the family of a Vicar, the daughter of a rural gentleman, and the young woman overseen by a guardianship, among others. It is these women—all of the middle class—who so fully must observe the rules of "virtue." The Marriage Act, to Goldsmith, appeared to make mercantile aspects of marriage more important than aspects of the heart, and to make wealth more important than virtue. Hence, he sought to show otherwise, as did others.

John Shebbeare's *The Marriage Act* (1754) immediately assailed the controversial bill by depicting the numerous ways that the bill could be circumvented by villains and the many methods by which the bill could be abused by avaricious guardians and cruel parents. Shebbeare's lengthy work depicts tyrannical parents and guardians, lying lovers, and even an unfortunate priest who is deported for performing an illegal marriage that he believed was a genuine love match. But it was the power granted to parents and guardians that Shebbeare fronted in his political novel, showing the abuse that so often attended such arbitrary power. Goldsmith was quick to see the same woes but did not restrict his attack on the Marriage Act to the novel. As Felicity Nussbaum observes, "Restoration and... eighteenth-century plays, as well as eighteenth-century novels, dramatize increased conflicts between the romantic inclinations of young lovers and patriarchal fiat" (*Brink* 12). This "patriarchal fiat" is Goldsmith's concern in numerous genres. Throughout his varied canon, Goldsmith depicts the mercantile attitudes of not exclusively the patriarch but of patriarchal-oriented women as well as they suppress romance in order to gain "fortune." The young women of Goldsmith's works must also battle an older generation of women who think like the males around them; in this sense, these young women are doubly virtuous, defeating history as well as the socialization process that created money-oriented parents and guardians. In effect, then, Kate Hardcastle, Miss Richland, and Sophia Primrose (each who suffers from a deceitful suitor, a seducer, or an abductor) manage to avoid the fate of Richardson's Clarissa Harlowe, certainly the clearest example of what can happen when natural reasons for marriage are displaced by mercantile or reputational reasons.

Miss Richland of *The Good Natur'd Man* is the victim of a greedy guardian, as are both Tony Lumpkin and Constance Neville of *She Stoops to Conquer*. The bill, it was argued, allowed parents/guardians to replace love and virtue with monetary offers that they would control. Of course, actual cases were rare, although in 1755 William Dodwell assured his pamphlet readers that "the abuse of power of guardians is a frequent subject of complaint,... and every one could specify many instances of it" ("A Letter" 42). Croaker of *The Good Natur'd Man* and Mrs. Hardcastle of *She Stoops to Conquer* both fail to see the virtue in their charges because they, as legal guardians of the dowries involved, are blinded by greed. Croaker nearly loses his son, and Mrs. Hardcastle boldly lies to her son Tony about his age. The ensuing militancy of these children—in particular, the women—is noteworthy. Olivia Primrose elopes, and Constance Neville attempts to. As Bridget Hill proposes, "children were increasingly challenging their traditional role of submission to parental authority" (69). Hill's statement can be further honed as it applies to Goldsmith: *women* challenged their traditional role—that in which a woman's key virtue was docile chastity—and revised it into a role of active participation in the marrying process. Their comic successes represent, in a way, Goldsmith's rejection of the marriage act as a piece of patriarchal legislative nonsense.

Likewise, the fact that Olivia is proven to be Squire Thornhill's "lawful" wife after the Squire's numerous debauches and false ceremonies also suggests that Goldsmith saw the possibilities for repeated abuse of the act and so satirized the legislature's short-sighted attempt to govern morality.[2] To add to this, Sir William Thornhill uses privileges afforded to a man of his stature (he is an MP) to marry Sophia almost immediately—a complete circumvention of the Marriage Bill's waiting period and a point that Robert Hopkins considers significant in displaying Goldsmith's rejection of this bill. These are the extremes of the act, however, and not the woes that befall the typical female of Goldsmith's works.

The effect of the act can be seen in the plights of Goldsmith's major female characters. Should one be wealthy, she became an object of mercantile avarice; should she be poor, she found herself, as in the case of Sophia Primrose, seeing "the immense distance to which [Sir William Thornhill] was removed by fortune" (IV, 168). In short, the proper "status" for a woman seeking marriage was multi-faceted: she had to have some money, surely; but she had to have "virtue" as well, a term that goes beyond the puritan notion of "virginity" and embodies within its chimerical denotation a sense of power—moral, societal, political—and a sense of place. Indeed, "virtue" in its various vicissitudes underlies marriage and marital matters throughout this time period. A study of marriage, then, will serve not only as a sociological end in itself, but will serve to re-define the term "virtue" that so often provides the impetus to marry. It will also explain the "distance" (or "space") that a poor girl like Sophia Primrose saw separating her from a baronet like Thornhill—a distance often closed by virtue.

First, some background into the marital ethic of the day, complete with its economics, is essential. Bridget Hill writes, "The dowry that was offered with daughters naturally became of crucial importance. Contemporaries thought that more women were competing for fewer potential husbands than earlier, and that this accounted for the rise in the price that must be paid for a husband" (71). Roy Porter certainly concurs: "Fathers had to dangle handsome dowries as bait to catch well-connected, landed, titled husbands for their daughters.... Newspaper announcements made no attempt to hide the horse-trading" (40). This reflects another of Schnorrenberg's statements: "Few makers of marriages worried overmuch about the emotional content of the marital relationship" (in Kanner, 191). Of course, this is the case because the "makers of marriage" were often males who were concerned with money. The economics of marriage must have affected the young women of middle- and lower-class families: how could they compete? Goldsmith offers the only alternative that a fortune-less woman could employ: virtue, the key to marrying well.

Goldsmith contrives to display the power of "virtue —especially female "virtue"—in bringing men into the marital fold. Of course, his canon comes replete with single women whose marital status (available) is accented by either beauty or wealth, but complicated by the woes that typically plague the women of eighteenth-century literary works: too few or too many suitors. For example, Miss Richland of *The Good Natur'd Man* faces the same distressing situation that ruined Richardson's Clarissa Harlowe: a powerful mercantile suitor is trying to manipulate the marriage market in such a way that he will be the sole remaining candidate. This is Lofty, whose name reflects his ridiculous behavior. He is challenged by Croaker, who has nominated his son as the future husband to Miss Richland (or rather, to Miss Richland's *wealth*), despite the fact that his son, Leontine, has already declared his love for another woman. Croaker insists to his son, "Miss Richland's fortune must not go out of the family; one may find comfort in the money, whatever one does in the wife" (V, 31). He later adds, "You have your choice—to marry [Miss Richland], or pack out of doors without any fortune at all" (31). Miss Richland embodies the plight of many women in a patriarchal world. She is not consulted as a marital being but is treated singularly as the object of male mercantilism. As Nelly Furman writes, "In a world defined by man, the trouble with woman is that she is at once an object of desire and an object of exchange, valued on the one hand as a person in her own right, and on the other considered simply as a relational sign between men" (61). Miss Richland means "fortune" to the Croaker patriarch. This, and not her person, is her "sign."

Miss Richland's fortune, then, is her albatross: she cannot possibly discern between her genuine suitors (those who act out of love) and her mercantile pursuers. Then there is Honeywood, the true love interest who cannot manage his money. Miss Richland calls him "so bad an economist of his own" (V, 66) and his Uncle describes his gentle nephew as being confused in his "pursuit of splendid rather than useful virtues" (V, 51).[3] Miss Richland has what young Honeywood lacks: money, but more critical to this reading, "useful virtue" rather than "splendid" virtue. Indeed, *The Good Natur'd Man* is as much a play about the pre-marital troubles of a rich single woman of "virtue" (including a wicked guardian empowered by the Marriage Act to select her mates) as it is about the profuse generosity of the man she eventually takes as her husband.

The two most important single women of Goldsmith's dramas—Miss Richland and her counterpart in Goldsmith's more famous drama, Kate Hardcastle of *She Stoops to Conquer*—must gain their marital ends (since both DO want to marry, and have, unlike Clarissa Harlowe, some power in the matter) by comic and benevolent manipulation of their potential husbands. Honeywood's closing speech in *The Good Natur'd Man* reveals one such manipulation:

Honey. Yes, Sir, I now too plainly perceive my errors. My vanity, in attempting to please all, by fearing to offend any...Henceforth, therefore, it shall be my true study to reserve my pity for real distress; my friendship for true merit; and my love for her, who first taught me what it is to be happy. (V, 81).

The signifying words are "study" and "taught": Honeywood's teacher will be Miss Richland, who has, in an economic sense, reversed the Pygmalion myth and created an economic savant suitable to become her husband. "True merit" —in this case, a reference to Honeywood's ability to distribute economic charities wisely—is part of his plan of study, in which again he is subordinate to Miss Richland, whose own act of generosity has freed Honeywood from his financial (and self-made) distress. Women "make" men in Goldsmith, by teaching them, rebuilding them, or completing them, and therefore it can be said that women make the marriages that take place.

The women's rewards, nonetheless, should not be misunderstood or trivialized: the gaining of a wise, faithful, respectable husband in this period of time—considering the "competition for husbands" that Hill argues was so fierce—was the eighteenth-century version of a woman's heaven on earth. But the fact is that the women shape the men in order to claim the best husbands possible, doing so by displaying some form of "useful virtue," whether it is frugality, genuine charity, or moderation.

She Stoops to Conquer provides a particular example of the role of virtue, as one can see the fashion by which the male's libido is affected by the status of virtue in the woman. Marlow, the urban rake, has set his sights on Kate Hardcastle, who is at this time playing a "poor relation" and lower class member of the family. Marlow has no qualms about trying to seduce Kate because he believes that lower order women are worth debauching but not marrying due to an *assumed* lack of virtue. As Michael McKeon puts it, "female chastity is required far more insistently of gentlewomen than of those lower down the social scale, where the transmission of property is less at issue" (157). But before Marlow can debauch Kate, his friend Hastings protests, "I believe the girl has virtue," to which Marlow replies, "And if she has, I should be the last man in the world that would attempt to corrupt it" (V, 178). That is, the mere suggestion that Kate has "virtue" precludes the rake from attempting to debauch her. Marlow is later won over by this "poor" side of Kate and proposes to her: "What at first seem'd rustic plainness, now appears refin'd simplicity. What first seem'd forward assurance, now strikes me as the result of courageous innocence, and conscious virtue" (V, 210). "Conscious virtue"—even in a woman who the mercantile Marlow believes has no fortune—brings to Kate Hardcastle a reformed, loving, wealthy, attractive and "educated" husband. Moreover, by maintaining this "virtue," Kate has restored nature to the romance (by displacing money as the main goal), has defeated the mercantile efforts of her greedy step-mother, reconciled the match to her hostile father, and, in turn, freed her friend Constance Neville and her step-brother Tony

Lumpkin to pursue the "love matches" that they nearly lost because of parental pressure to marry into wealth.

It is my contention that Kate's willingness to take control of her situation—even though the situation is initiated by her father's announcement of a suitor that he hopes will be her future husband—amounts to a "feminist" rather than a "personal" action. Kate is, after all, a role player of great skill, dressing for her father for half of the day, for herself the other half, playing a fairly wealthy middle class woman for her father and yet appearing as a bar maid for Marlow. She controls her world by finding a way to "suit her own fashion" while acquiescing to her father's demands. In spite of Kate's feminine prowess, there is little scholarship that deals with *She Stoops to Conquer* as anything but a "laughing comedy"; there is virtually none, moreover, that acknowledges the possibility of a feminist reading of Kate. Tom Davis, in his introduction to the Norton edition of the play, observes that Kate "undergoes voluntarily (as no one else does) the reversal of class-roles, and does this in order to create a space for lovers to talk in that is independent of class and of the constrictions that reduce Marlow...to silence" (xxv). The terms "space" and "silence" are of particular interest here. What is it about Kate that can "create a space for lovers" but her virtue? Is this the same space—the "distance"—that separates Sophia Primrose from William Thornhill? Is it not Sophia's virtue that closes that same "distance" and creates her strength? And why is it Marlow who is silent instead of Kate?

Perhaps the answers to these questions lie in another "feminist" view. Kate has anticipated the thrust of Mary Wollstonecraft's *Vindication of the Rights of Woman*. Kate has, in a summation of Wollstonecraft made by Katherine Rogers, "carried on the feminist tradition that a woman should be strong and reasonable and not allow herself to be reduced to a mere sexual object" (Rogers 183). Kate withstands Marlow's attempt to "reduce" her because *she* controls her own "space." Kate is also able to elevate Marlow's mind to an appreciation of the woman rather than the object. Like Miss Richland and Sophia Primrose (to be shown), Kate's many virtues include her "reasonable" mind. In fact, all of Goldsmith's successful marriages involve a woman "of sense." This is Goldsmith's model for marriage: where wealth and beauty are present, they are coincidental to and usually dependent on virtue, which in turn is tied to "space" and "sense," terms that bear close scrutiny in this day of gender studies.

As virtue evolves from an external characteristic imposed by the patriarchy on the female of society into something "creative" to be nurtured by the woman, it gives way to the notion of created (and usually feminine) "space," much as Goldsmith assigns to his young women. In similar fashion, Ruth Salvaggio uses "displaced" to describe the plight of eighteenth-century women, and writes that "'Space' seems a particularly appropriate term, since the recent feminist critique of systems long dominated by men...is often described as an effort to seek out new spaces" (11). Luce Irigaray asserts of her own writing that she seeks "to (re)discover a possible space for the feminine imaginary" (in Salvaggio 11), and Claudine Herrmann affirms this when she observes, "Woman...has long since learned to respect...space for its own sake, *empty* space" (169). Kate Hardcastle cannot accomplish her aims in male space—the space of mercantile marriages—so she creates space. In the comic resolution, she becomes a stage manager, "spacing" her father and future father-in-law where she wants them on the stage so that they might witness the power of her virtue to bring strength to the stammering and often silent Marlow. Indeed, what a "reversal of class roles" (and gender roles!) this relationship represents, for feminism has long lamented the "silences" of female discourse,[4] yet here it is Kate who teaches the male how to speak in and of the world about him. The space that Mary Astell wished to create for women at the close of the seventeenth century in her woman's academy has become internalized by Kate Hardcastle, and she uses it to create a place in which virtue outweights wealth.[5]

Miss Richland must also deal with space, for Honeywood, worried about his "dissipated virtues" (80), seeks to flee England because he is afraid to approach Miss Richland about a "connection." The words "connection" and "attachment" describe the missing element of this would-be marriage; as usual, it will be up to Goldsmith's active woman, who must forfeit half of her fortune to marry her beloved rather than the man selected by her avaricious guardian, to create a place for lovers again. In her willingness to forego fortune so that she might marry for love, Miss Richland shows her awareness of—and eagerness to avoid—what Mary Astell describes as a verifiable hell for women—a hell created by a bad marriage: "to be denied one's most innocent desires, for no other cause but the Will and Pleasure of an absolute Lord and Master, whose Follies a Woman with all her Prudence cannot hide, and whose Commands she cannot but despise at the time she obeys them; is a misery none can have a just Idea of, but those who have felt it" (90). Rather than suffer this possibility, Miss Richland manipulates romantic space and sacrifices fortune to bring about the "connection" that she desires. In fact, like Kate, Miss Richland closes the *physical* space that separates her from happiness when she offers her hand "to detain" Honeywood from fleeing his bad economy. Such a gesture is important, for it is again the woman, in actuality, who must "stoop" to *conquer—* not be conquered by—her man.

Furthermore, Miss Richland also, like Kate Hardcastle, reverses roles, for Honeywood has, much like a passive eighteenth century woman, been "slave to all" (V, 80) until Miss Richland offers her hand and completes the connection. She frees him from the role of passive servant, from living according to the rules of others. Miss Richland's version of "conscious virtue," called by Sir William Honeywood the "useful virtues," convinces Sir William to support the connection that is shakily forming between his profligate nephew and a woman of "sense without pride, and beauty without affectation" (65). Hence, Miss Richland avoids becoming a sexual object and increases her value as a person by showing her willingness to sacrifice wealth for love—an act that certainly sets her above the mercantile men of the play. She is also regarded for her "sense" and natural behavior ("without affectation"), attributes of the great Restoration Comedy heroines: "caution and intelligence were women's only protection in the socially unequal battle of the sexes" (Smith 205). Honeywood, meanwhile, is a stammering idiot, much like Marlow: without an active woman of virtue, he would flee to America, the place of (in Goldsmith's own words from *The Deserted Village*) the "mad tornado" and the "American tiger," and suffer even more. Miss Richland's "useful virtues" serve to close the distance between a sensible woman and a badly misguided but good man.

Just as Kate Hardcastle and Miss Richland have had to teach their respective husbands how to perceive useful virtues, the women of Goldsmith's *The Vicar of Wakefield* must learn (or teach) lessons about "virtue" in order to improve their status into a marriageable one and to close the "distance" between themselves and those males that the mercantile patriarchy would proclaim as out of reach. In Sophia and Olivia Primrose especially, Goldsmith demonstrates the "price" of virtue.

Olivia's fate, best summed up by her song "When Lovely Woman Stoops to Folly," demonstrates the price a woman pays for virtue (that is, for losing her "virtue"). Identity is at stake as much as is dowry or eligibility, as will be demonstrated, but first a review of the sub-text of virtue within *The Vicar* may help to demonstrate the pervasiveness of "virtue" in Goldsmith's canon and its seemingly inevitable tie to marital potential.

Upon moving into their new neighborhood, the Primrose family is told of their new landlord, Squire Thornhill, "that no virtue was able to resist his arts and assiduity, and that scarce a farmer's daughter within ten miles round but what had found him successful and faithless" (27). Virtue, it seems, is singularly a woman's attribute, for nothing is said about the Squire's moral code. The Vicar admits his anxiety at this man's character, but not so his wife, who sees the challenge set for her ambitious daughters ("whose features seemed to brighten with the expectation of an approaching triumph"—27) and, as their mother, appears "pleased and confident of their allurements and virtue" (27). If only the Primrose parents would heed the insight of Thomas Holcroft's *Anna St. Ives*:

The reformation of man or woman by projects of marriage is a mistaken, a pernicious attempt. Instead of being an act of morality, I am persuaded it is an act of vice. Let us never cease our endeavors to reform the licentious and the depraved, but let us not marry them...(Quoted in Hill 87)

In effect, the plot of *The Vicar* becomes a contest of virtue: if the woman wins, she gains a huge dowry, a reformed rake (axiomatically proclaimed to be the best husband), and, in this case, a famous name. If she loses, however, her cost is more than humiliation and shame: in Olivia's case, the loss of her virtue will cost her her name.

The plot of virtue continues. Primrose, sensing the upcoming disaster perhaps, reduces the conflict to one of his famous axioms: "That virtue which requires ever to be guarded, is scarce worth the centinel" (38). In a time known for the adage "Virtue untested is no virtue at all," this is an odd stance for a clergyman and father of two marriageable daughters to take. Mrs. Primrose cites the fact that "some sensible girls...had skill enough to make converts of their spouses" (44) and trusts the passionate Olivia (who is the daughter who "wished for many lovers"—21) to convert the local rake into a monogamous husband. Thornhill then introduces his two prostitutes, posing as great ladies, into the Primrose clan, where they immediately begin "a very discreet and serious dialogue upon virtue" (55). By now, there is indeed no "centinel" for Olivia and the exchange has been set: the allurement of fine clothes, of money, and of regional power for the virtue of the Vicar's eldest daughter. But just as Ephraim Jenkinson gulls both Moses Primrose and his father, the scoundrel Thornhill will also gull the family out of Olivia's reputation.

The bait is dangled in this first conversation with the impostor-ladies concerning virtue. It is set in the second when Miss Skeggs complains, "I was obliged to send away the third [companion], because I suspected an intrigue with the chaplain. Virtue, my dear Lady Blarney, virtue is worth any price; but where is that to be found?" (63). To be brief, the Primrose daughters are immediately nominated for the posts of companions to the two ladies of the town, who ironically delay their approval; they cite the fact that although they do not "in the least suspect the young ladies' virtue" they must observe proper decorum and wait for a short time (64). Virtue is at the heart of the Primrose saga, taking on a broader meaning than chastity. It is increasingly probable that Olivia's "virtue" becomes emblematic of country morality, of middle order dignity, and of parental authority and education. But her pursuer is powerful. Unlike Richardson's Lovelace, Thornhill will not be destroyed along with his victim. As the prostitutes in his service symbolize, his is a mutating power, one able to covert virtue into vice, pride into shame, and identity into ignominy (in the true etymological sense of the word). The Primroses have but one friend in this battle to save the virtue of the eldest daughter, and he is Burchell.

Burchell is, of course, Sir William Thornhill, described early in the tale as a man whose "passions...were upon the side of virtue" (29). The convention of the wayward letter is employed by Goldsmith when Burchell's warning about the prostitutes (being sent to an unknown party) is opened and misapplied by the Primrose parents to their own daughters. As expected, the catchword in the letter is "virtue." Burchell's letter reads, in part, that "I would neither have simplicity imposed upon, nor virtue contaminated" (77). Unfortunately for the Primrose family, their misinterpretation drives Olivia into the Squire's arms, with the help of the fortune-hunting attitude of Mrs. Primrose. Trying to draw a declaration of love from the Squire, Deborah Primrose feigns a lament for the "girls that have [no fortune]. What signifies beauty, Mr. Thornhill? or what signifies all the virtue...in the world, in this age of self-interest?" (84). When Mrs. Primrose juxtaposes "virtue" to self-interest, she roughly parallels the "blazons" of the male and female, for a woman's virtue is, in fact, a form of marital "self-interest" and a public concern (and the cause, throughout history, of attacks on prostitution but not on the men who exploit it). Likewise, the "rake" male is an autocrat whose self-interest requires an immoral enhancement of his own reputational "virtue"—that is, his capturing of the woman's physical virtue. Thus, in drawing the Squire's attention continuously to Olivia, Deborah Primrose brings about the inevitable disaster: faced with a plain and graceless suitor that she *must* marry if the Squire does not propose (yet another example of parental pursuit of fortune through marital "barter"), Olivia elopes with the rake "outside" of marriage at the expense of her virtue because she cannot bear to see that precious virtue compromised for her parents' mercantile principles.

Certainly Olivia is a victim, much like the title character of Fielding's *History of the Countess of Dellwyn*. Rogers summarizes the Countess' fate in a statement appropriate to Olivia: "She is destroyed not by innate feminine worldliness, but by values corrupted by a father who preferred docility to virtue" (112). Olivia will not "docilely" marry a man whom she does not love to please her father. She rebels, as Hester Chapone, writing in 1750 of forced marriages, claims is her right: "[C]hildren have a right to resist, and to use every method their own prudence can suggest to get out of their parent's power; in short, to disclaim an authority which is made use of, not according to its true end" (quoted in Hill 74). Paradoxically, though, this is her true "folly," the cause of her apparent loss of "virtue," and the cause of great pain to the parents who manipulated her so mercantilely. In rejecting the role of the docile daughter, Olivia has no "place" left to go in the closed system of patriarchal England; that is, she has no place that this patriarchy would recognize as "virtuous." Her elopement leads her into infamy, not romantic bliss.

Chapter Eighteen, which immediately follows the elopement, is appropriately titled, "The pursuit of a father to reclaim a lost child to virtue." Primrose eventually finds Olivia at an inn and initiates a warm reunion, but when Olivia moans, "The rest of my wretched life must be infamy abroad and shame at home" (126), the Vicar perceives that her physical "virtue" is lost. The price Olivia pays is more than shame. Her father, aware of her loss of virginity, changes his warm tone to say, "Our wisdom, young woman—" (126). Olivia immediately senses the distance and reacts with, "Ah, why so cold a name, Papa?...This is the first time you ever called me by so cold a name" (126).[6] Primrose has denied his daughter her name because of her loss of physical "virtue." Her place in the family is also initially denied her by her mother: "Never...shall that vilest stain of our family again darken those harmless doors. I will never call her daughter more" (92). Olivia's status here suggests the accuracy of Felicity Nussbaum's observation about eighteenth-century women, for Olivia has suffered "the fall from chastity that transformed 'character' and all other experience" (*New*

151). The demotion from "Olivia" to "young woman" marks this transformation of character. Likewise, the cool reception given Olivia by her father also reflects the patriarchal view of physical virtue: "Chastity, narrowly defined, was the all-important factor in determining how a woman was valued, by others and by herself as well. It was equated with virtue or honor in women; and, once lost, it was assumed to be irrecoverable" (Rogers 9). Without virtue, Olivia is much more than a woman who has "stooped to folly": she is a nameless pariah, cast out of home and identity in the same fallen moment. Without an honorable marriage to replace the "natural" ties of the family, she seems doomed to follow Clarissa Harlowe into death.

But Goldsmith is writing comedy again in his saga of the Primrose family, and comedy is not the place for permanent infamy or lost virtue. Olivia, it turns out, is in fact "legally" married to the Squire through the intercession of a blackmailer who has substituted a genuine marriage license for the false document so that he might extort money from the Squire in the future. But the circumstances of this ceremony—one that restores Olivia's "virtue" in the eyes of her father—are significant in that Olivia was married by "a popish priest" in a ceremony that even she admits "was no way binding" (127). But Primrose, a strict monogamist of the Anglican church, exclaims, "you are now his wife to all intents and purposes; nor can all the laws of man...lessen the force of that sacred connection" (127). This depicts the strength of Goldsmith's religious convictions and those of the middle class as well: the "laws of man" cannot supersede the "sacred connection" of God's sacrament, even if the sacrament was administered by a rival (and hated) religion. Goldsmith could have employed any type of questionable clergyman—for instance, a defrocked Anglican minister—to cast doubt onto Olivia's marital status, but he chose to make a statement by using a Catholic priest. To the middle class, this suggests, marriage is a sacrament, not a legislation, and these two modes of directing behavior must be kept separate. Just as Marlowe's Doctor Faustus is told he cannot marry because marriage is sacred and he is damned, Goldsmith is saying that man's law cannot regulate a sacrament. What would become of the Toleration Act if Catholics, Jews, and non-jurors were required to place legal precepts above their faith? To Goldsmith, the "legitimacy" of marriage is determined by religion, not legislation. And, in judging by the size of the outcry against the Hardwicke Act, many others agreed with him.

In the meantime, Olivia, "restored to reputation" (179), is made the sole caretaker of one-third of the Squire's considerable fortune and is proven to be the only "lawful" wife that the rake has ever had. The power of marriage to legitimatize a woman's identity in the eyes of the patriarchy is clearly underlined by this "restoration." Thus, the vicar's "lost child" is not only "Olivia" once again, but is now a woman of fortune and a favorite of Sir William Thornhill, who is now her brother-in-law as well as her protector. Meanwhile, the Vicar's other daughter, Sophia, like her namesake from *Tom Jones*, personifies "wisdom" and patience and earns the great reward (within literature) for maintaining her virtue, the conventional tandem of fortune and reputation. She has matched "Burchell" virtue for virtue: chastity, restraint, wisdom. Sophia embodies the same attributes, though to a lesser and more comic degree, that Clarissa Harlowe possessed. As Katherine Rogers asserts about Clarissa, "Chastity, a virtue enforced by patriarchy and usually implying men's property right in women, becomes an assertion of feminine integrity" (125). But Sir William Thornhill, to his own credit, twice cites Sophia's "sense" and "sensible nature" as a key factor in Sophia's winning his heart. This is part of her "feminine integrity," part of the new context of virtue. Sophia's chaste virtue is not an object to be auctioned off by the patriarchy, but a statement of her own personal philosophy that closes the distances both between social ranks and the often embattled sexes.

It is no coincidence that Sophia appeared in the family portrait as a fair shepherdess, the emblem of Christian moral goodness, and that Burchell, in an equally bardic, rustic signification, carries a flute and recites pastoral ballads—again, a nod to rural virtue in the most traditional iconic form. The fact is that it has taken Sophia's love and virtue—after all, she was the daughter who "wished to secure one lover" (21)—to bring the polarized halves of this man of virtue, Burchell and Thornhill, into a single marital partner. Sophia's conduct echoes Mary Astell's idea of the proper behavior by a woman seeking a marriage offer from a male: "if she wou'd have him pursue, the strictest Vertue and Reserve [are] the only way to secure him" (125). It seems significant that Astell sees "vertue"—not fortune—as the way to "secure" a lover, although by Goldsmith's time "virtue" surely has taken on a meaning that goes beyond "chastity" and now includes "sense." It is also significant that Sophia is only eighteen years old and has, against the impulses of her parents and at an age at which the Marriage Act would preclude her from marrying, made the great conquest on her own. Sophia has taught Burchell that male virtue cannot be concealed in the guise of passivity. Paul C. Privateer writes that

Thornhill's marriage to Sophia, despite attempts to the contrary, legitimately reconciles two different and polarized classes. It also represents Goldsmith's opposition to the Marriage Act of 1753 which contributed to more social disunity because it discouraged intermarriage between the richer and poorer classes. (34)

Hence, Sophia's virtue not only secures her a rich and virtuous husband, but it also functions as a political emblem for the power of country ideology and a woman's innate "sense."

At this point, then, a re-definition of virtue becomes necessary and helpful. To J.G.A. Pocock, "To lose one's due share of authority...amounted to a loss of virtue, and since virtue consisted in a relation between equals its loss was not private but mutual" (87). In this sense, all of Goldsmith's women use their virtue as a type of "authority" that serves to maintain a mutual balance: between men and women as moral beings, yes, but also as representatives of country and city ideologies and as members of different but equally important economic classes in the delicate pyramid of English society. Their ultimate marriages always reaffirm the need for a balanced authority, making the virtue that leads to marriage a very important socio-economic factor indeed.

H.T. Dickinson argues that "The Country interest...maintained that civic virtue could not be achieved unless citizens possessed freehold land" (104). The marriages of Goldsmith's virtuous women (and those of such heroines as Sophia Western and Pamela Andrews) bring about the transfer of land or the marriage of virtue to property. Sophia Primrose, in particular, transforms her virtue into a great estate as well as into becoming the wife of an MP. Dickinson's statement systematizes virtue as an ethic embodied by "the Country interest." This too plays into Goldsmith's canonicity, for his women are almost exclusively rural women. Kate Hardcastle is a resident of Liberty Hall, set up by her father to escape "the follies of the town" (V, 106). Sophia and Olivia Primrose hope to gain the positions as companions referred to earlier because it will allow them to "go to town," an experience that these two rural maidens have yet to enjoy. The virtue that leads to Kate's and Sophia's mercantilely and romantically successful marriages is *rural* virtue—a virtue that sees the power of the country finally assert itself over the corruption of the city.

Michael McKeon is again useful. One of his statements about virtue is that it is "a quality that is not prescribed by status but demonstrated by achievement" (212). The active roles of Miss Richland (as economic savior and instructor of Honeywood) and of Kate Hardcastle (who, according to Tom Davis, "takes over Tony Lumpkin's satirical plot and makes it her own: an ameliorative, educational one"—xxv) are certainly signs of the achievement of virtue. Neither woman is destructive, but rather constructive. They re-create the male world of libidinous pursuit (both overcome mercantile suitors/rakes) and educate men to respect and value the creative and healing powers of female virtue. The happy endings of both plays, and indeed the ultimate success of their respective relationships, are to their credit and their credit alone. Throughout Goldsmith's gently satirical and comic canon, his women use their virtue not only to gain excellent marital partners, but also to fulfill the classical function of literature: to instruct and delight.

In summation, then, virtue is the means to an end—a marital end—that allows a woman to overcome differences in economic status, to maintain her identity even within a matrimonial state, and to bring about a symbolic balance of power between her own political landscape and those of her powerful (often urban) suitors. Virtue's many vicissitudes are present in Goldsmith's various works as he participates in the greatest of all eighteenth-century literary conventions, to show society the way to marry "well" and happily.

Notes

[1]The objection to the Marriage Act of 1753 is voiced elsewhere in Goldsmith's canon. In *The Vicar of Wakefield*, Primrose laments that "Again, the very laws...of this country may contribute to the accumulation of wealth; as when by their means the natural ties that bind the rich and poor together are broken, and it is ordained that the rich shall only marry with the rich..." (IV, 101). Letter CXIV of *Citizen of the World* is titled "Against the Marriage Act. A Fable" and depicts the "Genius of Love" in a search for true marital love. When this magical creature comes to England, however, he is so disgusted with the mercantile attitude of the women (whose wording includes "house in town," "settlement," and "pin money") that he flies away in disgust. Hence, Goldsmith sees the mercantile attitudes of prospective marital partners not only as "unnatural" but, as it drives away a deity of emotion, something sacrilegious as well. In countering this avarice, his matches, then, will mainly be "love matches" which depict that love can bring happiness while Olivia's marriage, as will be shown, demonstrates the initial unhappiness that grows out of a mercantile marriage.

[2]For an in-depth history of the tension leading to the Hardwicke Act of 1753, see Christopher Lasch's essay "The Suppression of Clandestine Marriage in England" in *Salmagundi* (no. 26, Spring 1974: 90-109). See also Robert Hopkins' essay "Matrimony in *The Vicar of Wakefield* and the Marriage Act of 1753" in *Studies in Philology* (no. 74; July 1977: 322-39) for a specialized and limited view of this topic. In the same vein, Goldsmith's contemporary opponents to the Marriage Act—many of whom were non-literary persons—included Charles Townshend, a liberal politician, who argued that "the highest bloom of a woman's beauty, is from sixteen to twenty-one: it is then that a young woman of little or no fortune has the best chance of disposing of herself to advantage in marriage" (in Cobbett's *Parliamentary History*, XV, 23). Note that Townshend allows the notion that a young woman may "dispose of herself" in matrimonial matters, an attitude not shared by the vast majority within England's patriarchal political system.

[3]An interesting motif emerges in studying the relationship between Honeywood and his well-to-do Uncle. They are, in effect, foil opposites to the Croaker-Leontine relationship that is so coldly based on money. The Croaker-Leontine father/son tandem approaches what Ann Rosalind Jones sees as the repressive aspect of a patriarchal society: "In a psycholinguistic world structured by father-son resemblance...and by the primacy of masculine logic, woman is a gap or silence, the invisible and unheard sex" (83). Croaker does not speak to Miss Richland honestly about his ambitions for his son, while Leontine is forced by his father's greed to lie about his romantic desires. On the other hand, Sir William Honeywood approaches Miss Richland anonymously and then openly about his misguided nephew. As in the relationship between Kate and Mr. Hardcastle, there is open communication about marriage (Kate's father assures her, "Depend upon it child, I'll never control your choice"—V, 112) between the open-minded patriarch and the maritally-inclined woman. But the relationships that produce loving marriages are *not* created at all by father-son tandems but rather by *uncle*-son (as recurs in *The Vicar of Wakefield*) and by father-daughter pairings. Goldsmith's use of non father-son relationships extends beyond *The Vicar* and the two plays to *The Citizen of the World* where the Man in Black sees his *niece* happily marry Lien Chi Altangi's son. In this sense, Goldsmith breaks the "father-son resemblance" and allows his female characters a chance to "speak."

[4]"Silence" is a pervasive theme among feminist ideologists. Adrienne Munich addresses the issue of the "silent woman" when she states "When women speak...they cannot help but enter male-dominated discourse; speaking woman are silent as women" (239). In the same essay, she asserts that "Agreement, echoing, and silence are forms of flattery, a rhetoric

of subordination" (256). Kate Hardcastle, however, is outspoken, while her male "counterpart" seems incapable of normal speech when in the presence of an assertive woman. Kate's success, in part, comes from her "breaking the silence" of conventional female discourse in shaping both the willing nature of her father to hear her out and in restoring male virtue—respect, confidence—to Marlow.

[5]Constance Neville, the other woman seeking marriage in *She Stoops to Conquer*, is not so fortunate in gaining a "space for lovers." Her plan to elope with Hastings discovered, Constance is almost immediately "sent off to [her] Aunt Pedigree's" by her guardian, the avaricious Mrs. Hardcastle. Not allowed to exercise her own marital choice, Constance symbolizes yet again the plight of a woman who is seen merely as a means to an economically profitable marital end. She is, in Sandra Gilbert's words, a "displaced person" who is victimized by "metaphysical alienation...symbolized by geographic dispossession" (xvi). Constance's expulsion is luckily curtailed by her appeal to her own greatest virtue, prudence, but this does not lessen the fact that she had no "place" in her guardian's mercantile world.

[6]The sub-text of naming in which a woman's identity is tied to her state of physical virtue is best demonstrated in other eighteenth-century novels, especially Richardson's *Pamela* and *Clarissa* and Fielding's comic response to the former, *Shamela*. In *Clarissa*, when the Harlowe family believes (wrongly at first) that Clarissa is no longer a virgin, their response is identical to that of the Primrose parents. Mr. Harlowe exclaims, "I have no child, I *will* have no child, but an obedient one" (17). He later tells Clarissa that she will not hear from him "till you have changed your name to my liking" (62). Mary Daly writes "[W]omen have had the power of naming stolen from us. We have not been free to use our own power to name ourselves" (8). This is exactly Clarissa's situation, for although she did not name herself she has "earned" her identity with her constant attendance to virtue. The Harlowe men will deny Clarissa her identity because she, they believe, has cost them a chance for a successful mercantile but loveless marriage. They punish Clarissa, a woman whose name is virtually everything to her, by taking that name from her. Like Olivia, the perceived loss of virtue has cost Clarissa her identity.

Works Cited

Goldsmith, Oliver. *The Collected Works of Oliver Goldsmith.* Ed. Arthur Friedman. 5 Vols. Oxford: Clarendon, 1966. (All citations from Goldsmith are from this edition and cited by volume and page.)

Anonymous. "Considerations on the Bill for Preventing Clandestine Marriages, By a Freeholder." London: W. Owen, 1753.

Astell, Mary. *Some Reflections upon Marriage.* In *The First English Feminist.* Ed. Bridget Hill. New York: St. Martin', 1986.

Chapone, Hester. *Posthumous Works.* 1807, Vol 2. 100-1. (Quoted in Bridget Hill's *Eighteenth-Century Women: An Anthology,* 74.)

Daly, Mary. *Beyond God the Father: Toward a Philosophy of Women's Liberation.* Boston: Beacon, 1973.

Davis, Tom. *Introduction. She Stoops to Conquer.* By Oliver Goldsmith. New York: Norton, 1979.

Dodwell, William. "A Letter to the Author of 'Some Considerations on the Act to Prevent Clandestine Marriages.' " London: G. Hawkins, 1755.

Dickinson, H.T. *Liberty and Property: Political Ideology in Eighteenth-Century Britain.* New York: Holmes and Meier, 1977.

Furman, Nelly. "The politics of language: beyond the gender principle? " In *Making a Difference: Feminist Literary Criticism.* Eds. Gayle Greene and Coppelia Kahn. New York: Methuen, 1986. 59-79.

Gilbert, Sandra M. "Introduction" to *The Newly Born Woman.* By Helene Cixous and Catherine Clement. Trans. Betsy Wing. Minneapolis: U of Minnesota Press, 1986.

Herrmann, Claudine. "Women in Space and Time." Trans. Marilyn R. Schuster. In *New French Feminisms: An Anthology.* Ed. Elaine Marks and Isabelle de Courtivron. Amherst: U of Massachusetts Press, 1980. 168-73.

Hill, Bridget. *Eighteenth-Century Women: An Anthology.* London: George Allen & Unwin, 1984.

Holcroft, Thomas. *Anna St. Ives.* 1792, Vol 4, 150. (Quoted in Bridget Hill's *Eighteenth-Century Women: An Anthology,* 87.)

Irigaray, Luce. *This Sex Which Is Not One.* Trans. Catherine Porter. Ithaca: Cornell UP, 1985.

Jones, Ann Rosalind. "Inscribing Femininity: French theories of the feminine." In *Making a Difference: Feminist Literary Criticism.* Ed. Gayle Greene and Coppelia Kahn. New York: Metheun, 1986. 80-112.

McKeon, Michael. *The Origins of the English Novel 1600-1740.* Baltimore: Johns Hopkins UP, 1977.

Munich, Adrienne. "Notorious signs, feminist criticism and literary tradition." In *Making a Difference: Feminist Literary Criticism.* Ed. Gayle Greene and Coppelia Kahn. New York: Metheun, 1986. 238-59.

Nussbaum, Felicity. *The Brink of All We Hate: English Satires on Women 1660-1750.* Lexington: UP of Kentucky, 1984.

—— "HETEROCLITES: The Gender of Character in the Scandalous Memoirs." In *The New Eighteenth Century: Theory, Politics, English Literature.* Ed. Felcity Nussbaum and Laura Brown. New York: Metheun, 1987. 144-67.

Pocock, J.G.A. *Virtue, Commerce, and History: Essays on Political Thought and History, Chiefly in the Eighteenth Century.* Cambridge: Cambridge UP, 1985.

Porter, Roy. *English Society in the Eighteenth Century.* New York: Penguin, 1983.

Privateer, Paul C. "Goldsmith's *Vicar of Wakefield*: The Reunion of the Alienated Artist." *Enlightenment Essays* 6, no. 1 (1975): 27-36.

Richardson, Samuel. *Clarissa: or The History of a Young Lady.* Ed. George Sherburn. Boston: Houghton Mifflin (Riverside), 1962.

Rogers, Katherine M. *Feminism in Eighteenth-Century England.* Urbana: U of Illinois P, 1982.

Salvaggio, Ruth. *Enlightened Absence: Neoclassical Configurations of the Feminine.* Urbana: U of Illinois P, 1988.

Schnorrenberg, Barbara B. "The Eighteenth-Century Englishwoman." In *The Women of England: From Anglo-Saxon Times to the Present.* Ed. Barbara Kanner. Hamden, Conn: Archon, 1979. 183-228.

Smith, Hilda L. *Reason's Disciples: Seventeenth-Century English Feminists.* Urbana: U of Illinois Press, 1982.

Townshend, Charles. Speech. In "The Suppression of Clandestine Marriage in England: The Marriage Act of 1753." By Christopher Lasch. *Salmagundi,* no. 26 (Spring 1974): 90-109.

The Symbol of the Androgyne in Blake's
The Four Zoas and Shelley's *Prometheus Unbound*:
Marital Status Among the Romantic Poets

Patrick Bizzaro

In the art of nineteenth-century England, as in the art of all ages, artists and writers have relied upon the symbol of the androgyne as a representation of the whole of humanity as an individual. On the one hand, even our earliest myths of the fall have relied upon the androgyne as the symbol of original perfection; before Adam relinquished his rib to form Eve, he was androgynous, potentially both male and female. The androgyne, in this sense, has come to symbolize our shared roots—the genesis of both women and men—as well as the unified and integrated individual who has fallen into sexes, disintegration, and time. But the androgyne has also come to represent the goal, the ultimate marriage or reunification of opposites, toward which humanity continues to evolve. This second use of the symbol of the androgyne is the one used by Blake in *The Four Zoas* and Shelley in *Prometheus Unbound.*

In considering marital status among the Romantic poets, one must inevitably consider "the marriage of minds" or "the reunification of opposites" most typically the goal of the internalized Romantic quest. While actual marriages do occur in poetry written by Blake and Shelley, each is interested in portraying marriage of a vaster, more socially beneficial kind. And that marriage is symbolized by the androgyne.

The myth of the androgyne as it occurs in literature is important, as are all such myths, not as a specific occurrence in a single poem, but in its use throughout all art as a manifestation of the social and economic realities to which people are subjected. When we isolate the myth in the writings of the Romantic poets, specifically here in Blake's *The Four Zoas* and Shelley's *Prometheus Unbound*, it reveals something of the unique character of each writer while reinforcing the fact that each writer was responding to the social conditions of his time and using the androgynous unification as the goal of his writing, symbolizing the freedom that cannot come about if the sexes remain polarized in a subject-object relationship.

In recent years, commentators have paid a great deal of attention to the androgyne as it occurs in literature. Since William Veeder has already provided an excellent overview of such commentary, I would like to begin here not with those specific studies Veeder highlights, but with the basic assumptions those studies, as a group, make about androgyny, since those assumptions are exemplified wholly, or in part, by the Romantic poets. First, these studies assume that we have fallen from the symbolic androgyne. In this use of the symbol, the androgyne represents not only the equality of man and woman, but social equality as well. When we fell from social equality, the divisions of the androgyne—which dispersed as did Blake's Albion into its many components—struggled to dominate each other. And this struggle is a political struggle but with universal significance. Second, the fall from androgynous oneness is into the world of time and space. As a result, we are imprisoned by our senses; symbolically, we have committed the crime of "original sin" and must be punished by imprisonment so as to restrict the disturbance of universal harmony. Thus, the androgyne is simultaneously the cause and the goal of human existence. Third, and a consequence of the second, there is hope for progress and change. The very fall into time suggests that an end to punishment is inevitable. The intensity of punishment diminishes with the passing of time until it disappears and the feminine and masculine principles reunite. As both the starting point and the goal of human history, the androgyne is an integrated, composed universal being. Yet, this progress, the recomposition and reintegration into the androgyne, takes place only after human will has been fully initiated in all its manifestations when it has completed its period of correction. Fourth, as in most of the poems by Blake and Shelley, even those which do not explicitly indicate the androgyne's influence, humanity is portrayed as moving toward perfection. In such poems, it seems to me, the poet demonstrates a belief that progress is inevitably linked with time. For Blake and Shelley, though, perfection can come about only through love. And therein lies the fifth assertion: love is the eternal link that, for the Romantic poets, will bring humanity to final fulfillment and all men and women to ultimate marriage. In this sense, when we speak of marital status in the work of the Romantic poets, we speak of the union symbolized by the androgyne, a union that is the goal of both the individual and of all of humanity, simultaneously. Blake and Shelley posit that love is at once a reconciling, creative, and imaginative symbol as well as the eternal link between the self with the world. As Carolyn Heilbrun insists, "our future salvation lies in a movement away from sexual polarization and the prison of gender toward a world in which individual roles and the modes of personal behavior can be freely chosen" (ix-x). I will contend here that, at their visionary best, Blake and Shelley knew this.

Some basic distinctions seem to be in order, however, before we explore *The Four Zoas* and *Prometheus Unbound*, for Blake and Shelley lived at different times and responded to slightly different social and economic environments. I agree, as a result, with Diane Long Hoeveler's important distinction between the androgyne in Blake and that same symbol in Shelley, a conclusion that creates a needed context within which we can begin to study the visionary work of each. Hoeveler concluded that though Blake and Shelley do rely heavily on the androgyne, Shelley's reliance in poems such as "Alastor" and "Epipsychidian" is inconsistent. Often, Shelley is unable to reconcile the masculine and feminine forces in his poems and suffers a kind of disillusion about the world and the possibility for redemption. He often attempts the necessary reunification not by means of love, but by means of revolution against and destruction of all religious and political systems, which ostensibly serve to fragment cosmic unity. But the Romantic poets know that such physical rebellion is ultimately destructive not only to society, but to the self as well unless that rebellion is the product of enraged love. Even then, as the poems discussed in this essay will demonstrate, rage must burn itself out before the androgyne can reunite. While rebellion born of rage is temporal, the love that results in androgynous reunification is transcendent and the poems that best portray such reunification are, indeed, visionary.

Blake makes a distinction between the revolution that destroys structures, on the one hand, and the heightened state of being that creates the androgyne, on the other, by distinguishing that which he describes as "hermaphroditic" from the mythic androgyne. "Hermaphroditic," in Blake's use, refers to Satan, who attempts to dominate reality rather than transcend it; yet, Blake's use of the hermaphrodite avoids traditional application of the term. In Night VIII of *The Four Zoas*, for example, Satan is introduced as

> a Shadowy hermaphrodite, black & opake;
> The soldiers named it Satan, but he was yet unform'd & vast.
> Hermaphroditic it at length became, hiding the Male
> Within as in a Tabernacle, Abominable, Deadly.
>
> (VIII, ll. 103-6)

Harold Bloom tells us that "Blake's Satan is a shadowy Hermaphrodite because he embodies the self-congratulatory state of Ulro, the chaotic condition in which a brooding subject endeavors to contemplate all reality as being drawn up into itself" (258). If we accept Bloom's view, the hermaphroditic Satan is only capable of absorbing and fusing the object-world into his consciousness in a type of solipsism and, as a result, remains "unform'd." The creative world vanishes for Satan, and he exists alone in a state of subject-object division, a state of hell, Ulro. In the traditional use of the symbol of the androgyne, by contrast, subject and object blend to create the object world and, in creating, encompass it. While Blake's Satan exists in Ulro, the traditional symbol of the androgyne exists in what Blake calls Eden; while Blake's Satan represents the uncreative fusion of male subject and female object, the traditional androgyne represents the all-creative unity of subject and object, the original undivided Albion, Oneness. Blake's description of Satan as "hermaphrodite" is a description of the attempted fusion of subject and object in a fallen world where the outer, passive, feminine

Spectre is dominant and the emanative aspect non-existent. While Satan's world is a world of illusion, Albion's world is real.

Blake presents us, then, with two types of beings: the androgynous Albion and the hermaphroditic Satan. Since Hoeveler argues this general distinction between the hermaphrodite's symbolic function in poetry as opposed to the androgyne's, let me here deal more specifically with what the use of the androgyne reveals about Blake and Shelley and their respective views of humanity and its progress toward perfection.

Albion, the universal being, is the perfect creative union of all opposites. Albion contains all of reality and is, therefore, human and divine, male and female, subject and object. In this form, the androgyne is characterized as a perfectly-integrated Adam, balancing Blake's two-fold faculties of male and female as well as the four-fold faculties of reason, passion, sense, and spirit. The Satanic hermaphrodite, however, is an anti-androgyne. Albion exists as the symbol of innumerable heavens, Satan as the symbol of innumerable hells. Mark Schorer writes that "The plurality of the heavens and hells results from the dogma that in his lifetime every man determines his own heaven or hell through his leading love" (101). In Blake's mythology, the androgyne and anti-androgyne must exist since, as Blake posits in *The Marriage of Heaven and Hell*, "Without Contraries is no progression." Though the two figures—Satan and Albion—reinforce Blake's dialectic, Albion is the mythic, archetypal androgyne with whom this paper is most concerned.

As an androgyne, Albion is the most important single figure in Blake's mythology since Albion encompasses all. Though existing in other of Blake's verse, the story of Albion's fall and regeneration and the relationship between the fall and the social condition of humanity are nowhere more apparent than in *The Four Zoas*, the work Bloom describes as "The Completed Myth." *The Four Zoas* is a transitional poem in which Blake developed and expanded his earlier ideas through an elaboration and a deepening of what Schorer calls "the psychology of revolution" with which he had been dealing almost from the first (266). The major emphasis in this work shifts from a desire to move away from social convention to a more anarchistic desire, that we can only be free if we free ourselves. In creating four component parts of Albion, Blake creates the four basic mental functions of the human psyche: reason, passion, body, and spirit. These four functions divide after Albion's "fall" into "four living creatures": Urizen, Luvah, Tharmas, and Urthona, the four "Zoas." Blake immediately clarifies the concept of the integrated, androgynous, Albion:

> Four Mighty Ones are in every Man; a Perfect Unity
> Cannot Exist but from the Universal Brotherhood of Eden,
> The Universal Man, To Whom be Glory Evermore, Amen!
>
> (Night I, l. 9-11)

Though the hero of "The Four Zoas" is Albion, the tale officially begins "with Tharmas, parent pow'er, dark'ning in the West" (I, 1. 24). Like Albion, Tharmas begins as an androgynous figure, soon to turn hermaphroditic: while Albion is asexual, Tharmas soon becomes bisexual. Prior to the fall, Tharmas was responsible for maintaining harmony among the zoas, promoting eternal unity, on the one hand, and social equality, on the other. But Tharmas does not remain the unified spiritual being. Because he is capable of unifying all other faculties of the mind, since his fall must inevitably bring about the fall of the three other zoas, a fact intrinsically important to the poem, the poem opens by focusing on Tharmas.

Tharmas becomes the victim of Urizen and Luvah in their self-conscious desire to usurp each other's power and destroy the universal harmony and social equality that prevailed before the fall. One product of the fall is the contraction of each faculty's powers until Tharmas and his feminine created self or emanation, Enion, are regarded as separate beings. Tharmas becomes a multiple world: with his duality discovered and established, his hermaphroditic bisexuality becomes sexuality. When Enion separates from Tharmas, a dual problem results: psychic disintegration, on the one hand, and the social inequality of destroyed patriarchy, on the other. The "sexual" ethics that result are not unlike the sexual confrontation of Adam and Eve in the post-diluvian world of *Paradise Lost*.

To overcome these problems, individual identity must first be established and then sacrificed for the greater good. This gradual extinction of identity, the theme of the *Zoas*, brings together Blake's purely personal and individual vision with the surrounding social conditions by means of the mythic androgyne. And these two levels of meaning are essential to the development of the poem.

The poem, itself, opens with confusion over this duality as represented by the separation of Tharmas and Enion. Enion laments over the fall:

> All Love is lost: Terror succeeds, & Hatred instead of Love,
> And stern demands of Right & Duty instead of Liberty.

(I, 36-7)

In this description, the fall has resulted in a loss of love and liberty. For Blake, this loss accounts for evil and sin, division into sexes and self-consciousness; but, it accounts for social inequity, as well: only by regaining both love and liberty can social equality be regained. Liberty, in Blake's mythology, as characterized by Jerusalem, Albion's emanation, can be regained only by the act of love that reunifies Albion and Jerusalem, producing equality and universal harmony as well. Indeed, since she is estranged by the fall, Jerusalem is free from all conventions and limitations. The final act of love that reunites all humanity into the "Brotherhood" and Albion into the androgyne is an act that ultimately transcends all conventions and limitations. But such reunification will not be easy, as we find out immediately in Night I, when we discover that loss of love and liberty has led to the creation of time and space and the conflict between Spectre and Emanation.

In his temporal state, Tharmas has been divided into Enion, his emanation, and his own Spectre, his doubt concerning the physical/sexual in both the universe and, analogously, in the temporal world. Blake tells us that " 'The Spectre is in every man insane & most/Deformed' " (I, 103-4). For Blake, then, the Spectre represents self-conscious rationalism, the restraining outer cloak of reason that, without a controlling act of imagination, is a force of oppression. The result of Enion's now-sexual and temporal union with the Spectre of Tharmas, symbolic of the "Eternal Death" of the androgyne, is Los and Enitharmon, Time and Space. The idea of existence has been reshaped to reflect the physical world. In this new and fallen world, Time and Space give new dimension and separation to subject and object. As the conception of Time and Space affect human life, love between subject and object diminishes and nature in the form of earth-mother Enion tends to become lifeless matter. Milton Percival points out that "She [Enion], who with Tharmas, made up the immortal body is now the body of death" (44). All that remains of Tharmas and Enion are Los and Enitharmon. And from the beginning they make destruction inevitable; Time and Space provide their own punishment, shame and fear:

> Alternate Love & Hate his breast; Hers Scorn & Jealousy
> In embryon passions; they kiss'd not nor embraced for shame & fear.
>
> (I, 237-8)

But Los as prophet is also capable of seeing the fallen state and of knowing its cause and the remedy:

> Refusing to behold the Divine Image which all behold
> And live thereby, he is sunk down into a deadly sleep.
> But we, immortal in our strength, survive by stern debate
> Till we have drawn the Lamb of God into a mortal form.
> And that he must be born is certain, for One must be All
> And comprehend within himself all things both small & great.
>
> (I, 290-8)

Los recognizes that the fall of Albion—simultaneously the fall of all humanity—is the result of a failure "to behold the Divine Image.../And live thereby." As the constituent faculties of Albion have conspired against each other, so we have attempted to impose systems and institutions on each other, thereby ignoring the deities, "the Divine Image," which exist within each of us. The result is "a deadly sleep," the temporality of existence in a subject-object world, the passive acceptance of another person's system, for as Blake has said, "I must Create a System or be enslav'd by another Man's." Only by means of a redeeming Lamb of God, a Christ, an Orc, can the original Oneness result—the reintegrated, androgynous Albion and the redeemed, free humanity. Night I ends with the introduction of a

Christlike being, a Divine imagination and saviour, in the figure of Orc, who must descend into the temporal world to reassemble our scattered and conflicting parts, spread love throughout the world, and act as catalyst to the revolution of consciousness.

Night II deals to a large degree with the triumph of reason over imagination in the fallen world. The dream opens with fallen humanity "Turning his eyes outward to Self, losing the Divine image" (II, 1). The Self discovered is not the unified self of body and spirit, subject and object, Spectre and Emanation. Rather, solipsistic self-consciousness results, dominating temporal life, the conquest of imagination by reason. Humanity has given its power to Urizen, the "God, the terrible destroyer, & not the Saviour" (II, 338), the oppressive ruler of humanity, who builds his world upon the ruins of what once was. The world of Urizen, like England at the turn of the nineteenth century, is associated with industry, science, and rationalism:

> Some fixed the anvil, some the loom erected, some the plow
> And barrow form'd & fram'd the harness of silver & ivory,
> The golden compass, the quadrant, & the rule & balance.
> They erected the furnaces, they form'd the anvils of gold beaten
>   in mills
> Where winter beats incessant, fixing them firm on their base.
>
> (II, 27-31)

The repressive system of Urizen (and English society) has bound man in "adamantine chains and hooks," and must be rebelled against. The system of Urizen is erected on a foundation of false rationalism, a system "fixed" in legal concepts void of love. In Night III, Urizen forsees the birth of Orc, whom Urizen realizes he must ultimately serve, though the poem continues to be concerned over who will rule the masses, reflecting temporal, universal and psychic considerations. All the faculties except Urthona attempt to dominate Albion and, as a result, the whole of mankind (Urizen, Luvah in Night III, Tharmas in Night IV). But Orc, human protest and rebellion against the condition of the world, must prevail if the androgyne is to be brought about a second time.

In Night V the setting is provided for the birth of Orc.

> The groans of Enitharmon shake the skies, the lab'ring Earth,
> Till from her heart mending his way, a terrible child sprang forth
> In thunder, smoke & sullen flames, & howlings & fury & blood.
>
> (V, 36-8)

From the union of Los (Time) and Enitharmon (Space), Orc is born. Orc is revolution; and the act of rebellion, itself, is of an oppressed spirit, from a sense of love, acting out its rage. Los, however, self-divided and insecure, chains his son to the repressive rock of law only to repent his act upon entering Golgonooza, the city of imagination. Los goes back to the rock to release Orc only to find that Orc's body and chains have already been moved. This is the first suppression of revolution, yet Urizen is not any happier as a result. Orc's protest has reached Urizen and has given him the desire to seek a remedy for the inequities he has promoted. In Night VI, however, Urizen falls again and continues to practice the rationalistic promulgation of law which, Schorer tells us, "means the proliferation of error. The net of religion springs up behind Urizen, and as he wanders, carrying his [law] books,...he comes even closer to the roaring of Orc, to his rising fires" (277). In Night VII, Orc rises to rebellion.

Two alternate versions of Night VII exist, both of which are equally applicable in the social context of the androgyne. In the earlier version, Blake incites Orc to action after attacking Malthus' *Essay on Population* (1798). In this version, Los reunites with his Spectre and rediscovers his creativeness by an act of love, repentance of his earlier bondage of Orc. In this earlier version, Los describes the way to salvation:

> To form a world of sacrifice of brothers & sons & daughters,
> To comfort Orc in his due sufferings.
>
> (VII, 444-5)

Through the "Brotherhood" of men and the unification that results, man's freedom will be regained. Orc, himself, is described as "a father to his brethren" (480), the force that will bring all beings to eternal unity.

The later version of Night VII is concerned with the repudiation of slavery and child labor that arose under Urizen's rule. These institutions are the root of social inequity; because of them "the Universal Empire groans" (1. 17). Urizen has divided the whiteness of moral pretense from the blackness of social horror:

> For he divided day & night in different order'd portions,
> The day for war, the night for secret religion in his temple.
>
> (VIIb, 38-9)

The world of Urizen is fragmented, degraded by the partial perceptions that the fall into Time and Space necessitate. Only an act of revolutionary dimension will renew the world and give a second life to the androgyne, Albion. Night VII ends with the "Promise Divine," that

> "If ye will believe, your Brother shall rise again"
> [written] In golden letters ornamented with sweet labours of love.
>
> (VIIb, 293-4)

Faith and love, then, are the content of the "Promise Divine." And Night VIII opens with Albion experiencing that "Promise."

In Night VIII, Blake elucidates how love and revolution are both functions of passion, the first eternal and the second temporal. Here, also, the difference between the eternal androgenous embodiment and the hermaphroditic Satan is explained, "The State nam'd Satan never can be redeemed in all eternity" (VIII, 301). In contrast to the condition of the repressive and enslaving Satan is that of Jesus, who is love. Revolution, then, must destroy itself since it exists in the state of Satan, in the fallen world; yet the motive of revolution is eternal and transcendent, since love is the route leading to social equality and androgeny.

Revolution must be motivated by love if it hopes ever to destroy those systems which restrain imagination. Still, partial freedom is possible—and is a stage in humanity's progress toward perfection—as in Night VIII, when the confining rationalism and self-confinement of the individual are overcome. The old forms of theological and political oppression are replaced temporarily by new forms; though the new forms are not better, they represent improved and more-nearly ideal states of political and economic freedom. Not until Night IX, however, is the ideal fully realized, and then only through the coming together of opposites, the merging of Albion and Jerusalem.

The final section of *The Four Zoas*, Night IX, begins with Los and Enitharmon struggling to resurrect Jerusalem, who is simultaneously Albion's emanation and the personification of liberty (called Vala in the fallen world). Final revolution takes place:

> The thrones of Kings are shaken, they have lost their robes & crowns,
> The poor smite their oppressors, they awake up to the harvest,
> The naked warriors rush together down to the sea shore
> Trembling before the multitudes of slaves not set at liberty.
>
> (IX, 18-21)

Because revolution in the fallen world is self-destructive, Orc must be consumed by the rebellious energies he generates. As a result, Orc's fires must rage throughout the temporal world until, at last, everything is cleansed, and the "zoas" undergo transmutation, reuniting in their original form as Albion. Social equality is restored in "the New born Man."

> Man subsists by Brotherhood & Universal Love,
> We fall on one another's necks, more closely we embrace,
> Not for ourselves, but for the Eternal family we live.
> Man liveth not by Self alone, but in his brother's face.
> Each shall behold the Eternal father & love & joy abound.
>
> (IX, 638-42)

The "New born Man" of Night IX is in the "image of the Eternal Father." And with the recreation of the androgyne, Blake writes:

> Let the slave, grinding at the mill, run out into the field;
> Let him look up into the heavens & Laugh in the bright air.
> Let the inchained soul, shut up in darkness & in sighing,
> Whose face has never seen a smile in thirty weary years,
> Rise & look out: his chains are loose, his dungeon doors are open;
> And let his wife & children return from the oppressor's scourge.

(IX, 670-5)

The progress of man, beginning with the androgyne, the symbol of social equality, has returned to its original, unified state, a return to innocence. And the unification of humanity in a state of innocence is most apparent when "All the slaves from every Earth...Sing a New Song...Composed by an African Black" (IX, 1. 682-3, 686). Blake allows Luvah to state the central message of *The Four Zoas*: "Attempting to be more than Man We become less" (IX, 1. 709). The androgynous state in Blake, then, becomes a symbol of freedom from the restraint of rationalistic dogma. Humanity is diminished by attempting to be more than it is because it is the victim of time and space and becomes the self-conscious Spectre of its original self.

The symbol of the androgyne is introduced almost immediately in Shelley's *Prometheus Unbound*. As in the fall of Blake's Albion, Prometheus' separation from Asia because of his concern for humankind has led to the disintegration of the androgyne into the world of time and space. Prometheus is subjected to the wrath of Jupiter but has reawakened to a love which allows Prometheus to forgive Jupiter. By his compassion, Prometheus destroys the evil which hatred and defiance could not destroy. The dramatic situation of the poem moves from Prometheus' discovery of compassion to Jupiter's final destruction and humanity's resulting freedom.

Shelley glorifies the human mind, personified by Prometheus, in its endurance of all the torture that Jupiter can heap upon it. But Prometheus has fallen from Asia, the "epipsyche" or what Shelley calls elsewhere "the soul out of my soul" and what Blake characterizes as emanation, into a world of time. Rather than give in to Jupiter, Prometheus defies him, prophesying that the hour will come, since the fallen world is a world of time, when he will drag Jupiter from his throne. Jupiter has power over all time and space, but that power was given him by Prometheus in the same way that man has given power to the oppressive rulers of the world. Jupiter is

> Monarch of Gods, and Daemons, and all Spirits
> But One.
>
> (I, 1-2)

And that "One" is the source of love, symbolized by Asia. Jupiter is capable of controlling all but divinity, which exists beyond time and space; love is the motivation for rebellion outside Jupiter's realm. Without Asia, Prometheus is but a part of the world of human agony, since without Asia he lacks the ideal and eternal truth of love. The will of Prometheus, as love allows will to become self-determined, is alone capable of resisting the scourge of Jupiter.

> Wilst me, who am thy foe eyeless in hate,
> Hast thou made reign & triumph, to thy scorn,

O'er mine own misery and thy vain revenge.

(I, 9-11)

Jupiter is not monarch over Prometheus since Prometheus' desire to forgive is a manifestation of his self-determinacy. Prometheus has discovered epipsyche and his goals are now otherworldly, outside Jupiter's jurisdiction. Prometheus recalls his mundane curse:

> I speak in grief
> Not exultation, for I hate no more.
> As then, ere misery made me wise. The curse
> Once breathed on thee I would recall.

(I, 56-9)

Prior to forgiving Jupiter, Prometheus symbolizes oppressed humanity. Forgiveness is critical to Shelley's view of human progress toward perfection, since it reflects an understanding that the end to suffering begins in the individual perception of the oppressor; Prometheus' grant of dominion to Jupiter is an act that only Prometheus, himself, can overcome.

Similarly, humanity creates the evil which it suffers and finally destroys that very evil, embodied in (though I think not symbolized by) the Jupiter/ tyrannical ruler of its creation, thereby regaining freedom and happiness. But, as Prometheus finds the means of Jupiter's destruction within himself, so Shelley tells us that only by becoming integrated into the "One Brotherhood" (II, ii, 95) can we eradicate evil in the temporal, fallen world. The fallen Prometheus, then, symbolizes fallen humanity, divorced from the force of love. Fulfillment for Shelley's hero can only result from the marriage by love of Prometheus and Asia. The community of Oneness that results is simultaneously Prometheus' conquest of evil through forgiveness and humanity's potential for the conquest of social inequity through love and the understanding of others. In ceasing to hate evil, evil is overcome; by living a life of love, one lives ideally and cannot be oppressed by forces of political oppression.

Though Shelley seems to be more apt than Blake to blame external institutions for oppressing humanity, Shelley is concerned in this poem with the condition of human consciousness that would permit such institutions to reign. Shelley identifies two institutions which most enslave us, the church and the state. Of the two, Shelley hates the church more, because it is the more insidious; in its subtle demoralization of the mind, the church is more evil. Prometheus summons Jupiter to

> regard this Earth
> Made multitudinous with thy slaves, whom thou
> Requitest for knee-worship, prayer, and praise,
> And toil, and hecatombs of broken hearts,
> With fear and self-contempt and barren hope.

(I, 5-9)

Shelley repeatedly attacks the fear, self-contempt, and barren hope—the states of consciousness—that religion fosters. Because Prometheus has allowed Jupiter to reign over the world of time and space, religion flourishes.

In religion, Shelley sees the oppressive force which is the foe of the natural life and the happiness of humanity; in the "Knee-worship, prayer, and praise" paid to religion, Shelley sees the surrender of the happiness and independence of the human mind. But this submission occurs when people live without ideal love, when Prometheus lives without Asia. The oppressive forces of religion and government must be rebelled against to be overcome; but, in Shelley's argument, rebellion—a revolution in consciousness—must be passive and result from love. Indeed, since the imprisonment of Prometheus signals his separation from the life-giving epipsyche, Asia, Prometheus tells us: "I feel/Most vain all hope but love; and thou art far,/Asia!" (I, 807-9). Prometheus sees Asia as his only hope for salvation. Without her, though the strength of his desire to love allows him to feel compassion, he must continue to suffer and observe the suffering of humanity under oppressive institutions. Until Asia arrives, Prometheus must be "the strength of suffering man" until, by virtue of his reunification with Asia, he can be "The saviour" (I, 817).

The evil embodied in Jupiter makes him a Urizenic figure. While some commentators continue to argue, as Grabo did twenty years ago, that Prometheus gave Jupiter dominion over "All but One" so that Shelley may account for evil in the world (16), we must acknowledge that because of his moral greatness, wisdom, and ability to love, Prometheus embodies the human potential for goodness, that faculty of the human mind that may function in the ideal world. Jupiter possesses what Prometheus lacks: power and control over time and space. While Jupiter controls the physical sphere of Prometheus' suffering, Prometheus, by finding love, controls his own will. The fallen Prometheus, however, must transcend the time and space limitations of the fallen world; but, the ability to transcend is denied to Prometheus because he is separated from Asia.

In the context of nineteenth-century politics, however, Jupiter is a tyrant, not because he is malevolently oppressive, but because the virtues he once possessed have become evils. Shelley sees clearly that we are victims of our pasts. And herein lies the Shelleyan symbol of all religious and political institutions: The evil in Jupiter, as a symbol of all religious and political institutions, is that he persists. Unlike the titanic Oceanus of Keats' *Hyperion* who had the clearness of vision to tell Hyperion before the Titan's fall "as thou wast not the first of powers,/So art thou not the last.../Thou art not the beginning nor the end" (II, 188-90), Jupiter refuses to give way to the virtues that are actually needed in nineteenth-century English society. Past victimizations must be forgiven, and all people must come together in a single cause into the "One," or what Shelley terms "The Brotherhood" that is fostered in eternity by the immutable essence of love.

The second act of the poetic drama is devoted entirely to the action of Asia; and that she actually does act is important to this reading of *Prometheus*. Asia goes to Prometheus in response to a summons—not to his summons, but to a summons conveyed to her in a dream-vision. She is impelled to go to the abode of Demogorgon where she discovers, as Frederick Pottle tells us, that "There is...an Evil more radical [than Jupiter]; Jupiter is only a front man" (139). She asks "Who is his master? Is he too a slave?" (II, iv, 109) probing at the mystery of the universe. Demogorgon answers finally that "All spirits are enslaved which serve things evil" (II, iv, 110). Man is enslaved only by his willingness to submit passively to "things evil." The means of alleviating this submission is found in that "deep truth" which "is imageless," the immutability of "eternal love" (II, iv, 120). As Pottle tells us,

> Prometheus's action was to repent of his curse, to stop hating the manifested evil he continued unyieldingly to resist. Asia's action is to give up her demand for an ultimate Personal Evil [Jupiter], to combine an unshakable faith that the universe is sound at the core with a realization that, as regards man, Time is radically and incurably evil. (141)

In this discovery, Asia realizes that evil exists in the time and space world void of love. If she is to eradicate evil, and, thereby, help to free Prometheus, she too must practice forgiveness and love since that "deep truth is imageless," beyond time and space perception. Because Prometheus' rational power has given new shape to his idea of existence, time and space as well as subject and object have been given the dimension of separation. True love, for Shelley, is that eternal Brotherhood, not just of humanity, but of all people and nature. But the objectification of nature is the root of evil; and man has given this type of evil all its strength and has then been confined and tortured by it. The intellect must find the wisdom of universal love before it can ever be free. And in this realization, Asia impels Demogorgon, the symbol of Necessity, to action.

In Act III, Jupiter plans the eternal conquest of his realm by inspiring Thetis, "That fatal child, the terror of the earth" (III, i, 19), to overtake Demogorgon's throne. But Demogorgon, Jupiter's son, is mightier than Jupiter.

> Two mighty spirits, mingling, made a third
> Mightier than either, which, embodied now,
> Between us floats, felt though unbeheld,
> Waiting the incarnation, which ascends
> ...from Demogorgon's throne.
>
> (III, i, 43-8)

Jupiter has begotten in the image of Eternity a spirit mightier than either Jupiter or eternity. That spirit becomes incarnate with the might of Demogorgon, the figure of Orc and rebellion. Jupiter believed in time and, therefore, in the possibility of eternity. But time is an unreality that must submit to the necessity of the Eternal One, now embodied by Demogorgon.

The "fall" of Jupiter is symbolized by the reunification of Prometheus and Asia. What Mary Wollstonecraft Shelley pointed out 150 years ago is still true today: Asia, "the same as Venus and Nature" is, when Prometheus is freed, "united to her husband, the emblem of the human race, in perfect and happy union" (272). Asia, the symbol of love, had left Prometheus and reunification was not possible until she returned. When she tells The Spirit of the Earth "never will we part" (III, iv, 86), she blends with Prometheus, the potential for freedom before death, precisely because by practicing Divine love now "All things had put their evil nature off" (III, iv, 78). And the third act verifies the freedom of humanity that is implicit in the reunion of Prometheus and Asia:

> The loathsome mask has fallen, the man remains
> Sceptreless, free, uncircumscribed, but man
> Equal from awe, worship, degree, the King
> Over himself; just gentle, wise: but man
> Passionless?—no, yet free from guilt or pain,
> Which were, for his will made or suffered them,
> Nor yet exempt, though ruling them like slaves,
> From chance, and death, and mutability
> The clogs of that which else might oversoar
> The loftiest star of unascended heaven,
> Pinnacled dim in the intense inane.
>
> (III, iv, 193-204)

Shelley's Prometheus, then, symbolizes hope for the total freedom of man from social inequality and oppression.

The androgyne in Blake's *The Four Zoas* and Shelley's *Prometheus Unbound* symbolizes the ultimate concern for marital status as reflected in the writings of Romantic poets. What's more, as a study of these two poems demonstrates, analysis of the symbol reveals the unique character of each writer while showing as well how each responds to the social conditions surrounding him.

Blake, who wrote roughly twenty years earlier than Shelley, at the turn of the century, wrote at a time when many continued to hold the belief that the revolution that took place in America and France would find its way to England as well. As a result, we should not be surprised to note that the characters of Blake's poetry, as they progress toward androgynous reunification, simultaneously act out the drama of earthly rebellion and the drama of consciousness. On the one hand, the characters represent faculties of the mind and are unbounded by time; on the other hand, these characters are Titanic beings in a combat so ladened with significance that the liberation of all humanity is at stake. For Blake, then, reunification of the androgyne—the coming together of male and female, subject and object, reason and imagination—must come about through physical rebellion, through the activity of the Christlike Orc, and reflect at the same time the growth of human consciousness. Blake blames the fall on the domination of reason over other components of the human psyche. But the dominating influence of reason is also reflected in the political and economic oppression of the masses. Ultimately, Blake lives in both worlds—the eternal and the temporal—for revolution and the hope it offers must ultimately, at least at the turn of the century, occur both in the world and in the mind that perceives it. For Blake, the coming together of the androgyne precedes destruction of existing institutions and rebellion against the state.

By contrast, the coming together of the androgyne in Shelley *is* the act of rebellion since Shelley is involved almost entirely with the revolution in consciousness. Clearly, this particular use of the androgyne fittingly reflects the time during which Shelley lived. Hope for a physical revolution in England had long since been subverted (we tend not to consider how long twenty years can be when we study works from various centuries). As a result, though Shelley blames institutions such as the church and state for humanity's demoralized status, he focuses in *Prometheus Unbound* almost entirely on the revolution against enslavement of the mind. Nowhere in *Prometheus Unbound* do we see the masses overthrowing the oppressive government as we do in *The Four Zoas, Night IX*. Shelley could not envision such liberation; even for Blake, physical rebellion follows the merging of opposites into the state of perfect equality. Unlike Blake, whose view was simultaneously a matter of physical exertion and mental expansion, Shelley espouses forgiveness and the raising of consciousness; liberation for Shelley is entirely internal and unbounded by time and space.

The androgyne as a symbol of human perfection has been used by writers throughout all times. What it reveals, however, are the critical conditions, both social and economic as well as physical and mental, under which people live. No matter the age, the androgyne exists as a constant reminder of how far we must travel as planet dwellers to achieve perfect equality, and how much work is left to be done.

Works Cited

Blake, William. *The Four Zoas. The Complete Writings of William Blake*. Geoffrey Keynes, ed. London: Oxford UP, 1966. All lines quoted from this poem are from this edition and appear in parenthesis in the text.

Bloom, Harold. *Blake's Apocalypse: A Study in Poetic Argument*. Ithaca, NY: Cornell UP, 1970.

———— *The Visionary Company: A Reading of English Romantic Poetry*. Ithaca, NY: Cornell UP, 1971.

Grabo, Carl. *Prometheus Unbound: An Interpretation*. Chapel Hill: U of North Carolina P, 1935.

Heilbrun, Carolyn G. *Toward a Recognition of Androgyny*. NY: Norton, 1982.

Hoeveler, Diane Long. "The Erotic Apocalypse: The Androgynous Ideal in Blake and Shelley." Dissertation, University of Illinois at Urbana-Champaign, 1976.

Keats, John. "The Eve of St. Agnes." *Keats: Poems and Selected Letters.* Carlos Baker, ed. New York: Scribner, 1962.

Percival, Milton O. *William Blake's Circle of Destiny.* New York: Octagon, 1970.

Pottle, Frederick A. "The Role of Asia in the Dramatic Action of Shelley's *Prometheus Unbound.*" *Shelley: A Collection of Critical Essays.* George Ridenour, ed. Englewood Cliffs, NJ: Prentice-Hall, 1965

Schorer, Mark. *William Blake: The Politics of Vision.* New York: Random House, 1959.

Shelley, Mary. "Note on *Prometheus Unbound.*" *Shelley: Poetical Works* Thomas Hutchinson, ed. NY: Oxford UP, 1967.

Shelley, Percy Bysshe. *Prometheus Unbound. Shelley: Poetical Works.* Thomas Hutchinson, ed. New York: Oxford UP, 1967.

Veeder, William. *Mary Shelley & Frankenstein: The Fate of Androgyny.* Chicago: U of Chicago P, 1986.

Real Lives:
Didactic Realism in
Antebellum Marital Fiction

Thomas H. Fick

Life, with pertinacious facts, is too apt to transcend custom and the usage of novel-writers; and though the one brings a woman's legal existence to an end when she merges her independence in that of a man, and the other curtails her historic existence at the same point, because the novelist's catechism hath for its preface this creed,—"The chief end of woman is to get married"; still, neither law nor novelists altogether displace this same persistent fact, and a woman lives, in all capacities of suffering and happiness, not only her wonted, but a double life, when legally and religiously she binds herself with bond and vow to another soul.

—Rose Terry Cooke, "The Ring Fetter"

Until recently, most critics and literary historians have written about antebellum American marital fiction as if it were almost uniformly sentimental and unrealistic. In his recent study of marriage in American literary realism, for example, Allen Stein repeats the critical wisdom of the past fifty years when he maintains that "American fiction writers of all levels of competency through the first three-quarters of the nineteenth century rarely looked at the actual dealings between husbands and wives any more closely than Emerson did when he declared marriage 'the perfection which love aimed at, ignorant of what it sought' and 'a relation of perfect understanding, aid, [and] contentment' " (5). Stein's remark continues the largely impressionistic work of critics such as Fred Lewis Pattee and Herbert Ross Brown who have boldly—and inaccurately—asserted that antebellum fiction by women is invariably sentimental, idealized, and fundamentally evasive fantasy. And indeed Rose Terry Cooke, in the quotation that introduces this essay, seems to offer a similar objection: in both law and fiction, marriage too often ends a woman's complex "historic" life "in all capacities of happiness and suffering" (42). Yet Cooke makes this complaint only to set the stage for her exploration of the "double life" that much popular writing of the period did indeed ignore—a life which is frequently portrayed as leading not to perfect understanding and contentment but, as the protagonist of "The Ring Fetter" (1859) finds out, to privation and death. In short, popular works of marital fiction were frequently romantic idealizations; but many authors also tried to write beyond these cliches, and to explore a woman's double life in marriage.

In this essay I would like to explore the interpretative and methodological problems posed by antebellum marital fiction, and to suggest its complexity and diversity. The 'realism' practiced by many antebellum writers, I maintain, owes much to didactic fiction; it is not the ostensibly neutral and objective realism of James and Howells, but an active 'social' realism (what one might call 'didactic realism') intended to produce effects in the reader's extratextual world. Finally, I will illustrate the realistic vision of marital fiction by looking at works by Catharine Sedgwick and Alice Cary. Sedgwick's "First Love" (1849) is a nicely executed and representative antiromance which cautions against confusing the romantic ideal with the needs of real life and argues for a common sense vision of happiness, while Cary's more complex novel *Married, Not Mated* (1856) deals with the opposite danger of approaching marriage as a near-commercial transaction. Together these stories mark out the limits of the large body of antebellum marital fiction concerned with promoting an attitude toward marriage that balanced idealism and skepticism in what Catharine Sedgwick termed the "beau actual" (83).

The formulaic romance appealed as little to many nineteenth-century authors as it does to academically trained critics today; indeed, popular fiction about marriage frequently targeted rather than promoted the attitudes of romance. But unlike twentieth-century·critics, antebellum authors objected to the romance for extratextual, even more than aesthetic or formalist, reasons: they knew that for women, at least, distinguishing dream from fact was an absolute necessity. The idealized suitor of the romance, these authors suggested, could in real life inflict a lifetime of suffering on a woman who mistook the illusion for reality—who either married a romantic poseur and suffered the consequences, or refused the more prosaic pleasures of common, everyday life while waiting for the knight who never appeared. The presence of these dangers accounts for the strong tradition of antiromance in antebellum fiction, and at least after about 1820 the antiromantic tendency becomes separate from the more generalized distrust of fiction that marks many earlier works.[1] Later works did not object to the epistemological and metaphysical basis of romance, but to the practical consequences of "unrealistic" attitudes and expectations. The quarrel was not really with fiction at all; in fact, fiction was an important way of promoting appropriate means of dealing with everyday life.

I want to argue that by emphasizing the representative facts and dilemmas of everyday life, antebellum marital literature promoted its own realistic vision, even though by virtue of its didactic element this vision is "unrealistic" in modern terms.[2] We can see the unfamiliar but consistent values of realism at work in contemporary reviews and literary criticism: even champions of thoroughly didactic literature saw that idealized portrayals were ineffective. In 1834, for example, one reviewer advised that authors of moral tales "permit fortune to remain as she is, and indiscriminately heap her favors on the good and bad" even if this means that "bad men prosper, as bad men really do prosper in society" ("Moral Novels" 368, 370). A few years later, L.A. Wilmer argued that a strictly moral work is ineffective: "If the *chief* design of [an author of moral fiction] were to afford moral instruction, he would, most probably, defeat his own object" because his work would go unread. And to be readable an author must avoid paragons of virtue, who are "intrinsically correct," but at the same time "unnatural" (13). The effect of idealized moral literature, these reviewers argue, is much like the effect of romances: readers "will become disgusted with human nature, as they find it in real life." (In fact, Wilmer offers the example of a young woman who expects Sir Charles Grandison, and refuses several reasonable offers of marriage.) In short, the most effective moral literature was also the most realistic—in intent if not in every aspect of execution. For Wilmer, as for Mark Twain, the one-dimensional figures of secular romance or romanticized moralism could do only harm.

The emphasis on natural portrayals of mixed human nature can help to account for some of our earliest realistic writing, which appeared long before James and Howells established the criteria of what we now consider realism. For example, Caroline Kirkland has rightly been discerned as one of the first American realists, yet like most other writers of the period she assumes that fiction is a moral instrument whose purpose is to instruct rather than simply to record: "If not written by an idiot, [fiction] must have some meaning, and all meaning has a moral" ("Reading" 14). It is not surprising, then, that for Kirkland, as for Wilmer, fiction is flawed if it is too unrealistic effectively to instruct: "We are called upon to admire conduct," she writes in one essay, "which would, in real life, subject the performer to the suspicion of incipient fatuity, if nothing worse; and conversation, which, if it did not put the hearers to sleep by its formal dulness, would certainly, in any company with which we are acquainted, be considered insufferably arrogant, egotistical, or impertinent" ("Reading" 30). Like Wilmer, Kirkland argues that by encouraging unrealistic expectations, such books defeat their purpose: readers "must inevitably draw unfavorable comparisons with regard to their own truer and more natural instructors" ("Reading" 30). Kirkland's realism, then, proceeds from the desire to instruct effectively, rather than objectively to record contemporary life; as such her fiction owes a good deal to the literature of marriage, which, in its various forms, dominated nineteenth-century periodical literature and includes a large number of now-unknown but intriguing works.[3]

Marital fiction is largely an exercise in *practical* realism, a kind of realism scorned by critics who have absorbed the Jamesian bias against didactic or moral realism.[4] In order to suggest the quality of this realism, I will focus on two categories of tales which lie at opposite ends of the wide thematic spectrum of marital fiction. The more common 'antiromances, ' as I have noted, target illusion and encourage reasonable expectations based on existing conditions. A substantial number of other works, however, caution against an overly utilitarian approach to marriage, one that reduces marriage to a transaction, and women to commodities. Both sorts of fiction propose that marriage should aspire to what Catharine Sedgwick terms the "beau actual": a moral contract based in the possible, rather than the ideal, but which does not sacrifice the spiritual for the utilitarian. To modern readers the vision of the 'beau actual' may seem a sort of capitulation to the cult of womanhood, but this notion is mistaken. Antebellum authors offered their primarily female readership a way of *dealing* with their present conditions and so of achieving reasonable marital happiness within the confines of Victorian gender expectations; their feminism resembles the now seemingly conservative stance of social activists like Lydia Maria Child and educators like Catharine Beecher.

To understand antebellum marital fiction, we first need a better sense of its diversity of execution (or mode) as well as theme (or meaning). In fact no fiction could be more diverse simply because almost all nineteenth-century fiction dealt with marital status. As the popular nineteenth-century journalist Fanny Fern pointed out to a critic who condescended to domestic fiction, even the most successful male writers like Dickens, Thackeray, and Bulwer focused on marriage, and she asks rhetorically "Would a novel be a novel if it did not treat of courtship and marriage?" (285). Of course idealized versions of marriage were common enough; every age produces its own fantasies, and for most women in the nineteenth century marriage was a subject worthy of concerted dreaming. But recent scholarship has shown that "domestic bitterness" was of as much concern to the authors of antebellum marital fiction as were relations of perfect understanding (Habegger 34-7). There is a considerable body of what David Reynolds terms "the literature of misery" (340)—works which focus on the dark side of women's experience both in and out marriage, and which frequently involve nightmarish and even savage fantasies of violence and revenge against conventional patriarchal society (352). Both realistic and fantastic literature thus went far beyond pastel visions of domestic paradise. This dark vision extended to the lot of daughters as well as wives (in Lydia Maria Child's novel *Hobomok* [1824], for example, or Susan Warner's *The Wide, Wide World* [1850]).

The literature of misery and domestic bitterness, however, marks only one end of a spectrum that also includes what Henry Lewes termed "detailism"—in contradistinction to the "realism" of his companion George Eliot. In fact, while twentieth-century critics have argued that antebellum treatments of marriage were too idealized, too little grounded in the facts of everyday life, many nineteenth-century critics argued that marriage literature paid excessive attention to details of physical setting. As Lewes observed, "there are other truths besides coats and waistcoats, pots and pans, drawing-rooms and suburban villas" (Colby 22-3). The same assessment prevailed on this side of the Atlantic, even among successful practitioners of domestic literature. One character in a story by the writer and editor Sarah J. Hale, for example, complains that " 'the matter of fact in which some of our popular writers detail unimportant particulars, and draw out a story by dwelling on trifling incidents, such as we all know are constantly happening in common life, is very tedious and ridiculous.' " (211) This character could be thinking (to take one example among many) of a story like Alice B. Neal's "The Tapestry Carpet, or, Mr. Pinkney's Shopping" (1856), a domestic comedy about a man's mishaps trying to purchase a suitable carpet for the house. Clearly, domestic and marital fiction was not all idealization and pious generalities; it just as often served up a stifling particularity.[5]

Antebellum domestic fiction, as we can see, encompasses much more than misty portrayals of perfect unions. Furthermore, most writers were not exclusively "idealists," "moralists," or "realists," not only because almost all wrote in several modes, but because individual works combine romantic, didactic, and realistic elements. The lack of consistency results partly from the exigencies of professional authorship, of course, which required writers to fit modes to audiences, but the result has been that academic critics are able to choose a preferred mode as representative of an author's entire work. To David Reynolds, for example, Alice Cary is "a pioneering author of the literature of misery" (398) while Judith Fetterley finds that a "predilection for the fragmentary commits Cary to the mode of realism" (8). Both are correct: Cary chronicles married life in prose that is sometimes Gothic, sometimes realistic, and usually a blend of the two.

To begin making sense out of the huge body of antebellum marital literature, I would like to look closely at two works by successful and popular writers: Catharine Sedgwick's "First Love" and Alice Cary's *Married, Not Mated*. Both emphasize the need for a realistic approach to marriage, an approach that is equally endangered by the purely romantic and the purely utilitarian. Each is concerned above all with survival—with getting on in the real world, and with conveying information in a way that counters destructive expectations. Cary and Sedgwick are practitioners of didactic realism (to coin a useful oxymoron)—a term that would have been readily appreciated by contemporary readers, however much it seems to contradict current definitions of literary realism.

For a number of reasons Catharine Sedgwick is a good choice to begin studying antebellum marital fiction. Throughout her career she showed remarkable awareness of literary modes and conventions. Her first novel— *A New England Tale* (1822)—established the major conventions of what Nina Baym terms "woman's fiction," but in addition she worked with preexisting conventions in fresh and original ways. As Michael Bell points out in his discussion of *Hope Leslie* (1827), Sedgwick uses romantic conventions "not as meaningless stereotypes, but as effective ways of communicating a message that literate contemporaries would understand" (213-4). This mastery of convention is implicitly acknowledged by two recent collections of women's fiction, both of which open with exemplary stories by Sedgwick.[6] Clearly, her fiction is attractive both for its graceful execution and for its articulation of formal and thematic concerns—the implicit (and sometimes explicit) commentary on operative conventions as well as subjects. This is especially true of "First Love," which tells us about both contemporary attitudes toward marriage and Sedgwick's conception of the "real."

On the most obvious level "First Love" is an ironic commentary on courtship and infatuation; it tells us that love does not last, that passionate lovers may become strangers, and that the heart's final goal may be peace rather than adventure and romance. The story opens with a paean to

that first love to which all the freshest visions of youth are ministering and subsidiary—which copies its idol in the pure heaven of its own breast without spot or blemish—which fears no change, nor shadow of change—the love, while hope has never been cheated, expectation disappointed, or faith broken—the love that glows in the fire of its own enthusiasm, and is pure as innocence itself, and radiant with "clouds of glory" from our elder home.

The rest of the story is taken up with an anecdote whose ironic and deflationary conclusion balances the self-consciously sentimental tone of the opening. Told by the narrator's unnamed friend, this tale describes the course of Lady Anne Harvey's "first love": passion, parental opposition, separation, marriage to the father's choice, and finally, years later, a profound indifference to her first suitor's death. "There was no writing [in her face]" comments the second narrator when Lady Anne hears of his fate, "not the movement of a muscle—not the change of a shade in her color. After one minute, she asked, 'A little more soup, Charles?' " (84). As another of Sedgwick's homely realists puts it, " 'I used to be a believer in *first love*, now I think 'second thoughts best' " ("Second Thoughts" 383).

The theme of romantic deflation is skillfully if not subtly executed, and serves as another reminder that women in the nineteenth-century did not uncritically accept romantic conventions—indeed such conventions were a primary target. The anecdote begins with a description of sixteen-year-old Lady Anne Harvey's education in sentiment and romance; like Tom Sawyer, Lady Anne imagines her world in terms of literary conventions, and when her "cavalier" appears it is therefore not surprising that she takes him as romantic fiction incarnate. As long as their relationship remains clandestine, the romance thrives. The second half of the story, however, details what happens when the lovers must leave the shadows of romance for the light of common day, represented by Lady Anne's father—the class-conscious British aristocrat Sir Guy. The conventions of romance collide with the conventions of society, and the contest is brief and final: Lady Anne is forced to give up her knight. The battle, however, is hardly brutal because when Lady Anne discovers that her suitor is not the aristocrat his features and her imagination suggested, she capitulates with little grace but—given her situation and character—with considerable common sense.

The structure of this short story can help us to understand the relationship between the opposing attitudes we call romantic and realistic. Each section is helpfully supplied with a suitor who embodies the attributes of each mode. On the one hand we have Basil Astley, impoverished but handsome artist-admirer, the cavalier who is largely the construction of Lady Anne's imagination. On the other hand we have Charles Wyndham (Sir Guy's candidate), whom we encounter briefly over a bowl of soup at the end of the story. Although Wyndham remains a sketchy presence, the narrator does summarize his qualities—both fictional and personal—with wit and concision: he is "well born, well educated, well principled, and amiable— the *beau ideal*, or rather the beau actual of discreet papas" (83). Neither prince nor pauper, within the Anglocentric values of Sedgwick's tale Wyndham personifies a comfortable middle ground, as the adjective "amiable" suggests.

"Beau actual" characterizes both Charles Wyndham and the emphasis of many antebellum works centering on marriage. "First Love" belongs squarely in the tradition of the "antiromance," which typically presents the adventures of a middle-class Anglo-Saxon heroine who learns through hard experience that the romantic ideals gleaned from her reading can not be found in the real world, and that disappointment (perhaps even death) comes from trying to realize the *beau ideal*.[7] Two denouements are possible: either the heroine is awakened from her folly in time, or she marries her ideal and suffers the consequences. These plots inform a large portion of antebellum periodical literature about marriage. In E.A. Dupuy's "The Wilful One," for example, the heroine Marie Hamilton rejects her familiar local suitor to marry a charming young stranger against the wishes of her father, who warns her "This is fantasy!" (259). And so it turns out to be: her husband is a tyrant incapable of supporting her; her young son dies; and when she returns to her father she finds her first suitor happily married. (The frequently coercive patriarchal presence in each of these stories is disconcerting; nevertheless, the authors are using the undeniable fact of sexual hierarchies to convey useful advice to women.) Another popular author presents a solution to the temptations of fantasy in a story titled "Practical Romance." In this instance, the romance-reading heroine is saved from Marie Hamilton's fate only because her upright, reliable, but unromantic cousin Frank woos her in the guise of a dashing but propertyless young man, and only after the marriage ceremony reveals himself as the incarnation of the real—a somewhat mundane but far safer prince than the one she first chose. Reversing the usual fairy-tale plot, the dashing prince reveals himself as a mere commoner. Examples could be multiplied almost indefinitely. The often poor execution and questionable sexual politics of these stories should not blind us to the issue they deal with: the pressing need to give *practical* consideration to an institution that could deprive women of their legal, emotional, and even physical existence.

While popular didactic realism most often focused on romantic illusions, throughout the nineteenth century a substantial body of fiction also addressed the danger of marriages contracted for exclusively practical (sometimes mercenary) purposes—marriages where the "actual" completely overrides the "beau." A powerful example of this fiction is Rose Terry Cooke's "Mrs. Flint's Married Experience" (1880), which portrays the mistreatment and death of a widow pressured to remarry by a man who covets her property and is tired of paying for domestic help. In *Life in Prairie Land* (1846) Eliza Farnham provides a moving non-fictional example of the same situation, a burly Hoosier woodsman who explains how he came to choose his young wife: " 'I reckon women are some like horses and oxen'," he says, " 'the biggest can do the most work, and that's what I want one for' " (38). Outraged, the narrator responds that " 'Marriage is a moral contract, not a mere bargain of business' " (39), but the woodsman is unmoved. Not unexpectedly, as these examples suggest, in antebellum marital fiction men more often take the utilitarian view of marriage, and women more often suffer for it, but some works do focus on why women initiate utilitarian marriages and what happens when they do. Alice Cary's "Why Molly Root Got Married" (1853), for example, describes Molly's painful decision to forget her "first love" when she finds that success has made him a snob, and to marry the well-meaning and prosperous but boorish Mr. Pell, who can provide for her material but not her emotional needs. "Marriages of convenience," the narrator comments, "are sad affairs, even among the humble" (104). The unhappy result of such utilitarian marriages is the subject of Alice Cary's two-part novel *Married, Not Mated*, whose title clearly indicates its focus. I will restrict myself here to "Woodside," the first half of the novel, since it is by far the more interesting for my purposes.[8]

"Woodside" centers on Annette Furniss, who quite reasonably decides to escape her restrictive and emotionally impoverished life, but whose calculated choice to do so by marrying a young farmer for whom she feels no real affection leads her into another form of captivity. At the end of the novel Annette lives sequestered in her disordered room, incapable of giving attention either to herself or to any one else: the apparent control she exhibited in executing her plan of escape turns out to be an illusion. As this brief synopsis suggests, the novel is interesting partly because Annette *chooses* her loveless marriage; she is not a predatory male's passive victim.[9] In keeping with this emphasis, the novel also reverses a central convention of the antiromance, for Henry Graham, Annette's chosen husband, is a kind man rather than a heartless rake. He is thoughtful and sensitive (if a bit morose), a man whose intuitive sympathy with beasts makes him an American Orpheus: "A pair of beautiful white oxen drew near and struck their horns against the stile; the cows gathered gently around, for they had been used to his caresses and feeding; and the dogs now laid their heads on his knees..." (126). But Annette does not value him for his virtues; she sees him as the best available solution to her problem. Unlike Lady Anne in Sedgwick's "First Love," that is, Annette makes the mistake of paying too much rather than too little attention to the utilitarian 'actual' at the expense of the spiritual 'beau.'

The reasons for this desperate practicality are central to the novel. Annette is a "heartless, disappointed, and embittered woman" (59) because her miserly father has made her a virtual captive. As she tells her sister Hetty, " 'I have slept in a garret so open that the snows and winds blew over me, and all the while worked like a bought slave. I have thirsted for knowledge, and education has been denied me; I have wished for society, and am shut out from it by my ignorance and ill-breeding' " (39). Under such conditions the search for freedom becomes imperative, because Annette cannot even pursue the only two respectable professions available to unmarried women: teaching and sewing. As she bitterly comments, " 'I have suffered, and struggled, and starved here, as long as I can, and if I can't free myself in one way I will in another: by marrying Henry Graham' " (41). The lack of options is part of Cary's message. Yet despite the sympathy that Annette's dead-end position evokes, Cary is careful to suggest that Annette's calculation makes her situation worse: by imagining matrimony in purely functional terms she re-invents herself and her husband as commodities, and marriage as an economic transaction, thus intensifying her difficulty. In her marriage she will find another form of that captivity and emotional starvation from which she wished to escape. In this way, Cary presents Annette as a victim, certainly, but one who increases even if she does not initiate her own victimization.

The novel begins with a significant variation on a familiar gothic convention. We are first introduced not to the protagonist, but to her house, which—"curiously-fashioned" and "half-hidden" (13) among the trees— seems to evoke one of Poe's decaying mansions. However, in *Married, Not Mated* the gothic conventions are heavily gender-determined; as in Charlotte Perkins Gilman's "The Yellow Wallpaper" (1892), which likewise begins with the narrator's brooding speculation about a 'haunted house' that will become her domestic prison, we must read the tale as a cultural drama, rather than a drama of the individual psyche.[10] And in both cases the cultural drama involves marriage: Annette's house, which remains unfinished upon the death of her mother, is an externalization of Mr. Furniss's grief. More importantly, it foreshadows the various houses that will serve as prisons for those who marry wrong. The two daughters are prisoners in their father's house; one will die there, the other will escape by marriage, only to become a mad recluse.

The Furniss house also serves to introduce two modes of viewing marriage: the 'speculative' or mercenary and the romantic. In the first pages we overhear the reactions of two passers-by, whose responses represent these two views. First are the musings of a nameless 'speculator' disgusted at the waste of capital he sees in the ill-tended property, and who in his imagination divides and subdivides the lots, multiplying the original value. Next a poet— " 'crazed with care' " and possibly " 'crossed in hopeless love' " (14)— pauses to appraise the house through his own haze of romantic sorrow. These two perspectives define equally destructive attitudes toward marriage: as an economic transaction and as the fulfillment of romantic expectations. With the romantic sensibility Cary has little to do in "Woodside" except to define Annette's sensibility by contrast. Like the speculator, who sees houses as property rather than homes, Annette sees marriage as a transaction rather than as a 'mating'—solely as a way of escaping her father's house. She asks her suitor the extent and value of his land, and when she first visits she tabulates the cows and the woodlands: everything has its price. In this half of the novel Cary is concerned with what the speculative attitude leaves out: the reasonable affection that constitutes the marital 'beau actual.' And Annette's bitter practicality eventually works to sabotage the escape she desires.

As part of her marital campaign (military metaphors occur frequently in nineteenth-century marital fiction), Annette spends several months at her suitor Henry Graham's farm. There she meets Henry's brother Stafford, who is attractive, selfish, and melodramatically cruel: when his crippled nephew dies in a fit he will not allow the tragedy to interrupt his card game, he ignores his mad mother, and his indifference contributes to Henry's suicide. Although Annette understands his character she is far more attracted to him than to his brother. It is here that Cary shows her genius for reworking traditional plot elements. In the typical antiromance, Annette would marry the attractive, cultivated, narcissistic Stafford rather than the kind but rather pedestrian Henry, and she would suffer for indulging her shallow romantic values. In *Married, Not Mated* she does just the opposite: she tries to resist her attraction and to follow the voice of calculated self-interest, which tells her that Henry will be easier to win, and that from a practical standpoint his virtues will make him a better husband. At the end of "Woodside" she does in fact agree to marry Henry after seeing his kindness to her dying sister: " 'you are very good,' " she says, " 'and I have been very blind and very bad...[H]ereafter I may thank you more as you deserve, for all your kindness to her and to me' " (145).

We might, after this touching scene, expect the two to live in comfort and happiness; after all, Annette has resisted the questionable attractions of Stafford, and has escaped her former captivity in the company of a kind and attentive husband. According to the conventions of the antiromance she has avoided a young woman's most significant temptations. Yet when Annette briefly appears again in "Throckmorton Hall," the second part of the novel, she has become a recluse who spends her days in a filthy room and ignores her husband, daughter, and infant son. The reason for her condition is, I believe, relatively simple, though possibly distasteful to critics suspicious of moral fiction and enamored of the dark and ambiguous: throughout *Married, Not Mated* Cary suggests that a sensible marriage contracted without affection can be as crippling as one that results from blind infatuation. Annette has chosen Henry over Stafford because, as she telegraphically remarks, " 'a bird in the hand!' " (92). Yet as I have argued, this mercenary attitude, which considers men a commodity, forces women to think of themselves as commodities as well; far from being an assertion of power, then, this form of marital calculation embroils women in further difficulties, even when the spouse is kind and gentle. The clear but paradoxical implication is that Annette would have been better off marrying the selfish Stafford: she would have in any case been "mated" instead of just married.

This reading is supported by the example of two other marriages that are portrayed as successful not because the partners are faultless—quite the contrary—but because they are "mated" rather than married. Perhaps the most surprising marriage is between Stafford and Rosalie, the sister of Orpha, who narrates the second part of *Married, Not Mated*. It is surprising because in "Woodside" Stafford has been portrayed as unredeemably selfish; there seems no chance of a reasonably happy marriage. But Cary astutely does not propose any mystical transformation of character. Rather, in keeping with her fundamentally clear-sighted if gloomy understanding of human nature, in Rosalie she presents a woman as shallow and self-interested as Stafford, though never as cruel—someone, for example, who immediately understands the pompous nature of her guardian and flatters him appropriately. The marriage of these two limited people comprises one form of the 'beau actual.' For Cary, a successful marriage is therefore not an ideal but a relative thing, which eschews both the extremes of romantic mist— the "relation of perfect understanding"—and calculating practicality.

Less surprising but of the same sort is the marriage between the Grahams' servant Rache and her country suitor, Martin Muggins. Of indeterminate age, brusque, cryptic, and sometimes cruel, Rache is in some ways a caricature—comic relief of the sort supplied by blacks and the lower classes in other novels of the period. Nevertheless, her situation comments on Annette's in significant ways. Like Annette, she has escaped from the *de facto* slavery of her childhood (an abusive stepfather), and like Annette she puts no faith in the promises of romance. Unlike Annette, however, as a brilliant housekeeper she has the skills to remain independent and the determination to marry not well, but according to her tastes and personality. When she meets her future husband during the local debating society's discussion of (significantly) women's suffrage, she pursues him aggressively and successfully. Throughout their courtship, the emphasis is on a comic conjunction of personalities—the way each playfully and joyously responds to the other. There is none of the coy and desperate maneuvering that marks Annette's relation with Henry. It is significant that Rache and Martin keep their wedding secret for a month, as if the real issue is compatibility rather than legality.

At the end of "Throckmorton Hall" Cary holds out some hope for Annette and her miserly father. Richard Furniss marries a self-reliant widow and leaves his 'haunted' house to live in the paradise of antebellum domestic fiction: a small rural cottage. His daughter Annette's recovery begins with the suicide of her virtuous and kind-hearted husband—not precisely a conventionally auspicious beginning for emotional regeneration. But the recovery makes perfect sense. Even though her husband could not be more different from the villain of melodramatic marital fiction, his death nevertheless frees her from a marriage of convenience (an institutional evil), and it is precisely against such marriages that the novel was written.

The circuitous and unconventional way that Cary resolves the characters' problems indicates that marital literature is not the uniform expanse of sentimental, romantic trash many critics have seen. But even the best is not always easy to accept. Whether it argues against the excessively romantic ("First Love") or the excessively utilitarian (*Married, Not Mated*), most marital fiction no doubt strikes modern readers as didactic and hence unrealistic. Yet I believe that this literature is best approached as a version of realism because its avowed purpose is to promote respect for the exigencies of the extratextual world among its readers.

What I am suggesting may be hard to stomach—that we accept authorial claims to represent the real at face value rather than dismiss them either as excuses for writing fiction or as some other narrative tic. One difficulty is that in the literary economy of marital fiction, 'reality' is indistinguishable from moral codes; antebellum marital realism is pre-Darwinian insofar as it looks to human constructs rather than to the "blind, impersonal force" (Becker 130) of later realists and naturalists. And by adhering to a moral notion of the real, didactic realism performs an essentially conservative cultural function that is upsetting both to liberal critics who look for an enlightened ideology (or literary practice), and to formalist critics who value intricate aesthetic shape. But despite our continuing distrust of moral fiction, and our pride in scientific objectivity, there is a good deal of sense in looking to the human rather than the natural for the source of what constitutes our reality. Antebellum marital fiction deserves careful attention for what it can tell us about the social construction of reality as well as for its sometimes considerable intrinsic interest.

Notes

Research for this paper was begun in an NEH seminar directed by Emory Elliott. I would like to thank Professor Elliott and the members of the seminar for their helpful comments.

[1]For a discussion of the eighteenth- and early nineteenth-century suspicion of fiction, see Martin. On antebellum responses to fiction see Baym, *Novels*, especially Chapter 2, "The Triumph of the Novel," in which Baym argues that the supposed hostility to fiction in nineteenth-century America has been greatly exaggerated.

[2]That these works can only with difficulty be viewed as the direct *ancestors* of postbellum American literary realism should not obviate their claims to our attention as one form of realism. The problem is that in working backwards from our canonized writers we overlook other versions of literary realism; literary history becomes teleological, a matter of genres and modes working inexorably toward predetermined ends. This unfortunately excludes the serious consideration of works that do not already fit predetermined definitions. We need to pluralize realism as we have pluralized romanticism.

[3]Her best work, *A New Home—Who'll Follow* (1839) is quite explicitly presented as an "Emigrant's Guide" (8). See also Annette Kolodny's discussion of *A New Home* and *Forest Life* in *The Land Before Her* (131-58). Kolodny remarks that while Kirkland did not aim at fiction but 'veracious' narrative, she used plot and character in order "to make the sobering counsels usually reserved for emigrants' manuals palatable to readers bred on sentimental novels." (134)

[4]After the Civil War, American reviewers became increasingly hostile to what George Levine calls the "continuing tradition of self-consciousness" (15) in British realistic fiction, and especially to narrative intervention and authorial editorializing. Definitions of American literary realism have traditionally excluded both the shaping narrative voice and the narrative overtly shaped by a moral or social purpose. The common definition of realism as the

objective portrayal of contemporary social reality, however, is problematic for women's fiction because, as a number of critics have argued, realism may be complicit in systems of repression and constraint (Gilmore 144; Rogin 22; Seltzer 50). But it is possible that works may accurately deal with contemporary conditions without at the same time being wholly objective. Like other forms of realism, for example, "didactic realism" explicitly sets itself against idealism and privileges the everyday, but (under the best conditions) avoids complicity with the systems it records by foregrounding the conflict that can be obscured by a stance of neutrality.

Robyn Warhol's recent work on narrative strategies in nineteenth-century women's fiction suggests one way of understanding antebellum realism. Warhol proposes to add the term "engaging narrator" to our critical lexicon; unlike the "distancing narrator" the engaging narrator addresses a narratee directly in order to stir her to sympathy and ultimately to action in the extratextual world.

[5]The *subject* of the story is not at issue; domestic tragedy—even the purchase of a carpet—may be as significant (or insignificant) as an Indian ambush. See Baym on the pronounced critical bias in favor of uncircumstantial "melodramas of beset manhood" (idealized adventures exemplifying some abstract cultural essence) at the expense of "detailed, circumstantial portrayals of some aspect of American life" (67).

[6]Judith Fetterley begins *Provisions: A Reader from 19th-Century American Women* with Sedgwick's "Cacoethes Scribendi" (1830) while Susan Koppelman chooses "Old Maids" (1834) to open *Old Maids: Short Stories by Nineteenth Century U.S. Women Writers.* Koppelman remarks that not only does the story set "the classic pattern for a story written in defense of old maids," it introduces "the major themes characteristic of women's short fiction" (9-10).

[7]In American literature Susanna Rowson's *Charlotte Temple* is perhaps the best known example of this plot; many other works, however, are only tangentially interested in conveying a lesson, and, as Reynolds has convincingly argued, much sensational literature ("immoral didacticism") merely assumes a moral pose in order to explore, in often pornographic detail, the dark side of human nature (54-91).

[8]"Throckmorton Hall," the second half of *Married, Not Mated*, centers on Sally Throckmorton and her selfish, hypochondriacal husband Samuel Peter Throckmorton. Sally submits herself entirely to her husband, in the process loosing first her autonomy and finally her life. While Samuel Peter searches for a cure for his imaginary illness, Sally slowly dies of a real disease.

[9]The moderate optimism of the 'beau actual' runs counter to the emphasis of much current criticism, which focuses on the woman as victim. Thus Sandra Gilbert and Susan Gubar's hugely influential *The Madwoman in the Attic*, for example, locates the madwoman as the paradigmatic image in nineteenth-century women's texts—the embodiment of rage and frustration. Yet as Fetterley (5) and Baym ("Madwoman," 47-8) point out, in concentrating on the "anxiety of authorship," Gilbert and Gubar ignore the substantial evidence that women wrote with pleasure and success, and without anxiety. Likewise, an exclusive focus on women as inevitable victims can easily become misogynistic, and for this reason women writers were careful to assign some responsibility for their characters' fates to the characters themselves. To present women as impotent victims might "reveal" patriarchal culture, but it could also help to validate it in the worst possible way: as a natural and inevitable fact.

[10]Annette Kolodny argues that interpretive strategies are "learned, historically determined, and thereby necessarily gender-inflected" ("Map" 452). This, she argues, accounts for the initial incomprehension and even hostility that greeted Charlotte Perkins Gilman's "The Yellow Wallpaper." Male readers were unable to interpret a story which

used familiar Gothic situations and devices to explore cultural and social entrapment, rather than the more egocentric captivity experienced in tales such as Poe's "The Pit and the Pendulum," which in many ways Gilman's tale resembles.

Works Cited

Baym, Nina. "The Madwoman and Her Languages: Why I Don't Do Feminist Criticism." *Feminist Issues in Literary Scholarship.* Ed. Shari Benstock. Indiana UP, 1987. 45-61.

—— "Melodramas of Beset Manhood: How Theories of American Fiction Exclude Women Authors." *The New Feminist Criticism: Essays on Women, Literature, and Theory.* Ed. Elaine Showalter. New York: Pantheon, 1986. 63-80.

—— *Novels, Readers, and Reviewers; Responses to Fiction in Antebellum America.* Ithaca: Cornell UP, 1984.

—— *Woman's Fiction: A Guide to Novels by and About Women in America, 1820-1870.* Ithaca: Cornell UP, 1978.

Becker, George, ed. *Documents of Modern Literary Realism.* Princeton: Princeton UP, 1963.

Bell, Michael D. "History and Romance Convention in Catharine Sedgwick's *Hope Leslie.*" *American Quarterly* 22 (1970): 213-21.

Brown, Herbert Ross. *The Sentimental Novel in America 1789-1860.* Durham, NC: Duke UP, 1940.

Cary, Alice. *Married, Not Mated; or. How They Lived at Woodside and Throckmorton Hall.* New York: Derby, & Jackson, 1856.

—— *Clovernook Sketches and Other Stories.* Ed. Judith Fetterley. New Brunswick: Rutgers UP, 1987.

Child, Lydia Maria. Hobomok *and Other Writing on Indians.* Ed. Carolyn L. Karcher. New Bruswick: Rutgers UP, 1986.

Colby, Vineta. *Yesterday's Woman: Domestic Realism in the English Novel.* Princeton: Princeton UP, 1974.

Cooke, Rose Terry. *How Celia Changed Her Mind and Selected Stories.* New Brunswick: Rutgers UP, 1986.

Dupuy, E.A. "The Wilful One; or Scenes from the Life of Marie Hamilton." *Godey's Lady's Book* 20 (1840): 259-64.

Farnham, Eliza W. *Life in Prairie Land.* New York: Harper, 1846.

Fern, Fanny. *Ruth Hall and Other Writings.* Ed. Joyce W. Warren. New Brunswick: Rutgers UP, 1986.

Fetterley, Judith. *Provisions: A Reader from 19th-Century American Women.* Bloomington: Indiana UP, 1985.

Gilbert, Sandra, and Susan Gubar. *The Madwoman in the Attic: The Woman Writer and the Nineteenth-Century Imagination.* New Haven: Yale UP, 1979.

Gilman, Charlotte Perkins. "The Yellow Wallpaper." *New England Magazine* 5 (1892): 647-59.

Gilmore, Michael. *American Romanticism and the Marketplace.* Chicago: The University of Chicago Press, 1985.

Habegger, Alfred. *Gender, Fantasy, and Realism in American Literature.* New York: Columbia UP, 1982.

Hale, Sarah J. "Evening Amusements at Home." *Godey's Lady's Book* 20 (1840): 211-14.

Kirkland, Caroline. *A New Home—Who'll Follow? Glimpses of Western Life.* Ed. William S. Osborne. New Haven: College and University Press, 1965.

———. "Reading for Amusement." *A Book for the Home Circle.* New York: Scribner, 1853. 13-34.

Kolodny, Annette. *The Land Before Her: Fantasy and Experience of the American Frontiers, 1630-1860.* Chapel Hill: The University of North Carolina Press, 1984.

———. "A Map for Rereading: Or, Gender and the Interpretation of Literary Texts." *New Literary History* 11 (1980): 451-67.

Koppelman, Susan. *Old Maids: Short Stories by Nineteenth Century U.S. Women Writers.* Boston: Pandora, 1984.

Levine, George. *The Realistic Imagination.* Chicago: The University of Chicago Press, 1981.

Martin, Terence. *The Instructed Vision: Scottish Common Sense Philosophy and the Origins of American Fiction.* Bloomington: Indiana UP, 1961.

"Moral Novels." *The New-England Magazine* 6 (1834): 365-74.

Neal, Alice B. "The Tapestry Carpet, or, Mr. Pinkney's Shopping." *Godey's Lady's Book and Magazine* 52 (1856): 15-19.

Noble, Mary Florence. "Lilias Granger, or Practical Romance." *The Columbian Lady's and Gentleman's Magazine* 3 (1845): 180-84.

Pattee, Fred Lewis. *The Feminine Fifties.* New York: Appleton-Century, 1940.

Reynolds, David S. *Beneath the American Renaissance: The Subversive Imagination in the Age of Emerson and Melville.* New York: Knopf, 1988.

Rogin, Michael Paul. *Subversive Genealogy: The Art and Politics of Herman Melville.* New York: Knopf, 1983.

Sedgwick, Catharine. "First Love." *Sartain's Union Magazine* 4 (February 1849): 81-4.

———. *A New-England Tale; or, Sketches of New England Character and Manners.* New York: E. Bliss, 1822.

———. "Second Thoughts Best." *The Token and Atlantic Souvenir.* Ed. S.G. Goodrich. Boston: 1840, 378-83.

Seltzer, Mark. *Henry James and the Art of Power.* Ithaca: Cornell UP, 1984.

Stein, Allen F. *After the Vows Were Spoken: Marriage in American Literary Realism.* Columbus: Ohio State UP, 1984.

Warner, Susan. *The Wide, Wide World.* New York: Putnam, 1850.

Warhol, Robyn. *Gendered Interventions: Narrative Discourse in the Victorian Novel.* New Brunswick: Rutgers UP, 1989.

Wilmer, L.A. "Some Thoughts on Works of Fiction." *Godey's Lady's Book* 21 (1840): 13-15.

Text and Context in Fanny Fern's *Ruth Hall*: From Widowhood to Independence

Joyce W. Warren

When Fanny Fern's novel *Ruth Hall* was published in 1855, it created a sensation. In this largely autobiographical novel, Sara Willis Parton (1811-1872), writing under the pseudonym of Fanny Fern, satirized her male relatives (her father, her father-in-law, her brother, and her brother-in-law), who had provided neither compassion nor adequate financial assistance when she was left a widow. Although her novel was published under her pseudonym, one of the Boston editors who did not like his own satirical portrait in the novel revealed her identity, and the novel became a *roman a clef*. Fern was condemned by the critics for her "unfeminine" and "unfilial" writing. As the reviewer for the *New York Times* commented, if the novel had been written by a man, it would be "a natural and excusable book," but, asked the reviewer, how could a *woman* write such a book? (12/20/1854).

It is precisely because Fern was able to write in defiance of the restrictions that conventional nineteenth-century American society imposed upon women writers that *Ruth Hall* possesses the value that it does. Fern does not hide her anger, nor romanticize the position of women and the role of men. It is this "unfeminine" frankness that makes *Ruth Hall* both a significant literary achievement and a valuable social document.

With respect to its literary significance, Nathaniel Hawthorne, after reading *Ruth Hall* in February 1855, qualified the statements that he had made in an earlier letter to his publisher criticizing the work of American women writers and castigating the authors as a "damned mob of scribbling women." *Ruth Hall*, he felt, was a superior book because the author had not been inhibited by the straitjacket of convention that constricted most women writers:

In my last, I recollect, I bestowed some vituperation on female authors. I have since been reading "Ruth Hall"; and I must say I enjoyed it a good deal. The woman writes as if the devil was in her; and that is the only condition under which a woman ever writes anything worth reading. Generally women write like emasculated men, and are only distinguished from male authors by greater feebleness and folly; but when they throw off the restraints of decency, and come before the public stark naked, as it were—then their books are sure to possess character and value. Can you tell me anything about this Fanny Fern? If you meet her, I wish you would let her know how much I admire her.

(*Letters to Ticknor*, 1:78)

As a social document, Fern's novel is valuable because the author frankly and critically portrays the situation of a widow at mid-century. Fern does not sentimentalize the experience of widowhood, either to glamorize or melodramaticize the experience. Using her characteristically sharp, crisp prose which *Harper's Monthly* in 1854 praised as evidence that "the day for stilted rhetoric" was declining (July 1854), Fern reveals in *Ruth Hall* the societal shortcomings and familial conflicts that characterized the widow's experience. Although the family experience of her protagonist is particular, Fern's portrayal of the social factors surrounding widowhood is significant as it reflects the position of the widow in mid-nineteenth-century America. It was through her experience as a widow in a patriarchal society that Fanny Fern was brought to a realization of the need for a change in the position of women. Widowhood radicalized her and led to her advocacy of women's rights, and to her revolutionary conclusion that women could not be truly independent until they were financially independent.

In this essay, I will examine the text or narrative of *Ruth Hall* against the context of the situation that propelled Fern to write the novel. Before we analyze the novel and its relation to the specific events in the life of the author, let us look briefly at the societal attitude toward independent women that was prevalent at the time.

Women in nineteenth-century America were led to believe that they were weak and dependent creatures whose best defense was to rely on man, whose strong right arm and knowledge of right would guide him in protecting weak womanhood. In 1855, the same year that *Ruth Hall* was published, Ralph Waldo Emerson told the women assembled at the women's rights convention in Boston that women should remain in their parlors and leave public affairs to men. If a woman wanted anything done, he said, her best resource, and the one best suited to her abilities, was to rely on a good man: "Woman should find in man her guardian.... Whatever the woman's heart is prompted to desire, the man's mind is simultaneously prompted to accomplish" (*Works*, 11:403-26).

Coupled with this assurance that man would help and protect dependent woman, was the societal stipulation that respectable middle-class women *must* be dependent and must never—even if in danger of starving—be guilty of self-assertion. The "cult of the lady" insisted that women were selfless and passive. It would be vulgar and unfeminine to be so self-assertive as to earn one's own living. In an 1861 newspaper article Fern bitterly described the situation of a dependent woman in a society that would not permit her to help herself:

There are few people who speak approbatively of a woman who has a smart business talent or capability. No matter how isolated or destitute her condition, the majority would consider it more "feminine" would she unobtrusively gather up her thimble, and, retiring into some out-of-the-way place, gradually scoop out her coffin with it, than to develop that smart turn for business which would lift her at once out of her troubles; and which, in a man so situated, would be applauded as exceedingly praiseworthy.

(New York Ledger, 6/8/1861)

Just how insistent mid-nineteenth-century Americans were on this aspect of woman's behavior—passive dependence—is apparent in James Fenimore Cooper's 1850 novel *The Ways of the Hour*. In this novel, Mary Monson (Mildred Millington) is an independent woman, the only one of Cooper's heroines who acts to *save herself* rather than relying on male protection. When she is falsely accused of murder and her male lawyers are unable to save her, she successfully conducts her own defense and is acquitted. Cooper's verdict, however, is that she is guilty of self-will and self-assertion; apparently, the more feminine thing for her to have done would have been to allow herself to be hanged. Women's real power, Cooper insists, comes by "keeping within the natural circle of their sex's feelings, instead of aping an independence and spirit more suited to men" (*Works*, 24:311). Cooper's purpose in this novel is to attack the new laws that would give a married woman control of her property. Such laws, Cooper maintains, are contrary to the law of God: "The Creator intended woman for a 'help-meet,' and not for the head of the family circles; and most fatally ill-judging are the laws that would fain disturb the order of a domestic government...derived from divine wisdom" (*Works*, 24:364, 431).

This is the social context in which Fanny Fern wrote *Ruth Hall*. In order to understand the way in which the novel is a response to these social factors, it is necessary to examine the real events in the life of Fanny Fern, her own widowhood and her successful efforts to extricate herself from poverty, without the help of and in spite of the hindrance of her male relatives. *Ruth Hall* is based closely on the author's own life.[1] When her husband died suddenly of typhoid fever in 1846, Sara Willis Eldredge was left a widow with two young children to support. Her husband's creditors having taken whatever assets he had left her, she was thrown upon the mercy and good will of her relatives. Her father, who had recently remarried, grudgingly provided a small pension for her, and her father-in-law contributed an equally small amount. Their assistance was accompanied by recriminations, her father berating her dead husband for having been such a poor businessman that he had left her destitute, and her in-laws maintaining that her poverty was due to her extravagance as a housewife. At the same time that this pension was so grudgingly provided, her relatives—particularly her father— urged her to remarry as the best means of supporting herself.

When Samuel Farrington, a widower with two children, asked her to marry him, she at first refused. But, with pressure from her father and other relatives, she finally capitulated, and, frankly telling Farrington that she did not love him, she married him in January 1849. The marriage was a terrible mistake. Farrington was violently jealous and suspicious, and the evidence of her second novel suggests that he was also sexually offensive. In *Rose Clark* (1856), Gertrude, whose character and situation are patterned after Fern's, had married a widower after her husband died, and like Fern found that the marriage was a terrible mistake. Not only was her husband jealous like Farrington, she also says that he was a "gross sensualist" and describes the "creeping horror" with which she listened for his approaching footsteps: "Whole days he passed without speaking to me, and yet no inmate of a harem was ever more slavishly subject to the gross appetite of her master" (pp. 231-5, 245). In January 1851, Fern took a step that scandalized her relatives: she hired a lawyer and, taking her children with her, she left her husband. Farrington spread malicious rumors about her and sought to blacken her reputation.

When Fern left Farrington, her father and father-in-law refused to resume her support, apparently hoping that she would be starved into submission and return to her husband. She refused, however, and determined to earn her own living. Job opportunities were few, and although she worked long hours as a seamstress, she was able to earn very little money. She took the teachers' examination to teach in the Boston public schools, but she lacked the influence to obtain an appointment. Her father, who was a well-known editor in Boston, and her brother-in-law, who was a member of the school committee, could have used their influence on her behalf if they had wanted to. But clearly, the family had decided to offer no assistance that would enable her to be financially independent. She tried writing newspaper articles and sold her first one for fifty cents. She sent several articles to her brother, N.P. Willis, who was a successful editor and writer in New York, and asked if he could help her place her articles. He wrote back that he could not help her, and urged her to find less obtrusive work. However, she succeeded as a writer without his help. Her articles were copied in newspapers all over the country, and in 1853 she published a collection of her articles in book form. The book was a best-seller, and she soon became independently wealthy. Several publishers urged her to write a novel, and in December 1854, *Ruth Hall* was published.

Of particular importance in Fern's portrayal of widowhood in *Ruth Hall* are three social factors: the widow's vulnerability, her poverty of opportunity, and her powerlessness. It was these factors in Fern's own experience as a widow that led to her recognition of society's shortcomings. In order to understand how widowhood radicalized Fern, let us look at the correspondences between the novel and the life of the author with respect to these factors.

The first and most important characteristic of the widow in Fern's view was her vulnerability. She was both personally and economically vulnerable. After the death of Ruth Hall's husband, Fern portrays several ways in which Ruth is vulnerable. First, her in-laws and her father argue about her future, each claiming that the other should support her, and they resolve that they will starve her into giving up her children (pp. 65-72). Not only is Ruth vulnerable to the machinations of her relatives, but, as a lone and impoverished woman, she is also vulnerable to sexual advances by men. In Chapter XXXVI two loungers in the low-rent boarding house where Ruth's poverty has forced her to live discuss their chances of obtaining sexual favors from the new widow. "I like widows," one of them comments. "I don't know any occupation more interesting than helping to dry up their tears; and then the little dears are so grateful for any little attention." As they assess Ruth's charms and accessibility, they express contempt at the thought of marriage and boast that any woman can be "bought with a yard of ribbon, or a breastpin" (pp. 73-4). The next chapter shows Ruth's vulnerability in other areas: business and the law. Mr. Develin, executor of her husband's estate, concludes that it would be to his advantage to give her husband's clothes to Ruth's father-in-law, who might be able to help him in business, rather than to Ruth, who, although she does not know it, is legally entitled to them (pp. 75-7).

All of these aspects of Ruth's vulnerability are derived from Fern's own experience as a widow. Her granddaughter, Ethel Parton, wrote in her manuscript biography of Fern, that when her husband died and she was left without resources, Fern's father and father-in-law argued over who would spend the least in her support (p. 101). She was forced to give up one of her children to her in-laws, who sought by monetary means to force her to give up all claim to her children. In his will written in 1851 her father-in-law specified that the money from his estate could be used to support Fern's two daughters only if she relinquished them entirely to his wife, or after her death, to the trustees of his estate. With respect to sexual vulnerability, Ethel Parton describes in her biography, how, when Fern was sewing for a living, male employers made sexual advances (Parton, p. 103). Her vulnerability in legal and business matters is also revealed in her early newspaper articles, where she describes how her ignorance and inexperience cause tradespeople and relatives to take advantage of her.

Not only was the widow vulnerable, she was almost wholly without opportunities to help herself. Ruth Hall finds that sewing is the only means of support open to her. This means long hours of work with minimal remuneration. She attempts to found a school or to obtain a teaching position, but she cannot succeed without people in high places to help her or at least to recommend her. Similarly, Fanny Fern also worked long hours as a seamstress. Her relatives refused to help her obtain a teaching position, and there were no other avenues open to her. Fortunately she was a talented writer, but not all impoverished widows are able to use their writing talents to support themselves. Throughout her career Fanny Fern wrote of the plight of the underpaid seamstresses, and urged that more job opportunities be opened to women. It is no wonder that young girls are driven into prostitution, she said, when the only alternative open to them is to work at starvation wages as seamstresses.[2] Women printers, waiters, doctors, lecturers, artists, women working in the mint: these are only a few of the occupations that Fern wrote about in her columns.[3] As she said in *The New York Ledger* in 1863, she was always glad to see "any new and honest avenue of interest or employment" open for women (5/23/1863).

Finally, Fanny Fern wrote of women's powerlessness. First of all, because of her vulnerability and poverty of opportunity, Ruth Hall is powerless to give her children a comfortable home. In Chapter XXXVIII, after she is widowed, she sits with her children in their dingy boarding house looking out at a row of brick walls. When her child asks, "Why don't we go home?" Ruth feels her own powerlessness. She is also powerless to protect her children from the cruelty of others—including her own relatives—who ill-use them because of their poverty, and she is powerless to help them when they are sick because she cannot afford to pay a doctor (p. 126). She is powerless to command more money for her sewing or for her newspaper articles. "Only fifty-cents for all this ruffling and hemming," Ruth notes with dismay after working constantly on a sewing assignment for two weeks (p. 96). And although her newspaper articles increase the profits of her editors, the editors continue to pay her substandard wages because they know she desperately needs the money and has no other recourse: "Ruth accepted the terms, poor as they were, because she could at present do no better, and because every pebble serves to swell the current" (pp. 125, 131-2). Ruth Hall's powerlessness reflects closely the feelings of powerlessness that Fern herself felt during this period of her widowhood and which are contained in the cynical and sarcastic early articles that chronicle Fern's experience with hypocrisy, exploitation, and "summer friends."

Just as important as what is contained in the text or narrative of her experience in *Ruth Hall* is the material that Fanny Fern left out of the narrative. There is no mention in the novel of Fanny Fern's remarriage to Samuel Farrington and subsequent desertion of him. Ruth Hall is widowed and her male relatives treat her as Fern was treated—but without the excuse of her disobedience in refusing to remain with her objectionable husband. Fern may have left out the Farrington episode partly because she did not wish to be associated with him. He divorced her in 1853, two years after she had left him, and she attempted to forget what was for her a very painful experience. She may also have left out the Farrington episode because artistically the book is less complicated without it.

However, the most important reason why she omitted the second marriage was probably because the morality and propriety of her heroine would have been made suspect to a mid-nineteenth-century American audience if the Farrington episode had been included. Fern did not want to draw criticism on her heroine such as she herself had experienced when she left her husband. She wanted her readers to admire and sympathize with her heroine. If Ruth Hall had remarried and then left her husband, the majority of readers would have agreed with Fanny Fern's male relatives who condemned her for leaving Farrington. First of all, they would have felt that remarriage was the best way for a widow to support herself. Even more important, once she was married, the majority of her readers would have regarded her desertion of her husband as a criminal act. Consequently, they would have felt that her male relatives were justified in not helping her financially after she left her husband because such behavior made a woman's morality suspect. As Fern says in *Rose Clark*, Gertrude's relatives want to believe her husband's slanders about her: "If they *defended* her, they would have no excuse for not helping her. It was the cash, you see, the cash" (p. 347). Ruth Hall does not remarry. Her male relatives provide grudging assistance and no compassion, but she is not guilty of anything except poverty.

The omission of the Farrington episode from *Ruth Hall*, which otherwise follows so closely the events of Fanny Fern's own life, tells us something very important about the reality of the widow's situation at the time. First of all, Fern's experience had shown her that the independent woman would be judged harshly, and that it would be impossible to have a heroine who had left her husband, whatever the reason. Moreover, she also discovered that after her husband died, the widow had no identity. Fern's relatives wanted her to remarry to support herself and her children; but they also wanted her to remarry so that she would have a settled status. In *Ruth Hall* Ruth's relatives do not want to be burdened with her after she is widowed. Her brother Hyacinth does not want to "lose caste" by associating with the poor widow (p. 82); her father insists she is the responsibility of her husband's parents (p. 71). The concept of an unattached widow was discomforting to the widow's male relatives. She was a financial burden and an embarrassment. Moreover, they found it disconcerting not to know what she was going to do. Remarriage was a way of settling her.

The pairing of two sub-plots in *Ruth Hall* provides an indication of Fern's solution to the widow's—or any woman's—dependence. Whereas Mrs. Skiddy earns her own independent living, Mrs. Leon, who, as she bitterly admits, is herself only one of the pretty "appendages" to her husband's establishment (p. 51), ends up dying alone in an insane asylum, where she had been confined by her husband after "her love had outlived his patience" (pp. 109-12). Earlier, Mrs. Leon had warned Ruth never to marry her daughter to a man she does not love simply to obtain the money (pp. 51-2). Her death in the insane asylum where she had been confined by her husband when he wanted to get rid of her underscores the warning. That Fern intended to apply the warning not only to Ruth's daughter but to Ruth herself is clear from what we know of Fern's own disastrous marriage of convenience, and from the evidence of her second novel, *Rose Clark*. In that novel Gertrude Dean, who entered into a similar marriage of convenience after she was widowed, comments when she looks around the house that she feels she has sold herself: "my bill of sale every where met my eye" (p. 238). The contrast between Mrs. Skiddy's comfortable independence, which comes from "a purse well filled with her own honest earnings" (p. 109), and Mrs. Leon's tragic dependency emphasizes Fern's message that economic independence is necessary to maintain autonomy as a human being. The woman who is economically independent will not be vulnerable and powerless: her relatives cannot take her children from her; she will not be prey to sexual abuse; businessmen will not want to offend her; and her male relatives cannot easily dispose of her by having her placed in an insane asylum.

Like the character she created in *Ruth Hall*, Fanny Fern felt her own powerlessness as an impoverished widow. Her newspaper articles written at the time reveal that it was this vulnerability and powerlessness as a mother and as a wage earner that drove home the realization that only by gaining financial independence could she hope to gain the autonomy necessary to protect herself and her children from exploitation and abuse. And it was Fern's anger at her powerlessness that impelled her to create the narrative of *Ruth Hall*.

Clearly the narrative of *Ruth Hall* does not conform to the narrative constructed by society regarding women. Living in a society that did not countenance female assertiveness and independence, a society that preached the simultaneous doctrine of male protection for female weakness, Fanny Fern as a widow learned that the myth of male protection for dependent women was just that—a myth—and concluded that women would be better off if they learned to rely on themselves. As a widow, she found that male help was not always forthcoming, and that when it was proffered, it was often grudging and came with strings attached. Ultimately she found that it was used as a lever to exact the behavior desired by the benefactor. This latter was what Fanny Fern's relatives did in their attempt to force her to return to her husband. By withholding financial support, they hoped to starve her into submission. Similarly, when Ruth refused to give up her children, her father and father-in-law resolved to withhold support to force her to comply with their wishes.

The principal reason why Fern's novel was so shocking to her contemporaries was because she revealed the reality behind the myth with respect to male protection and also with respect to the dependency of women. First of all, she revealed the cruelty and indifference of her male relatives. Reviewers castigated Fern for her "unfilial" behavior in writing the book. As one reviewer indignantly commented, the novel was reprehensible because no man wants to think that a female relative of his would say such things about him—even if they were true.[4] Fern broke the unwritten law in nineteenth-century American society that women should not criticize men, that they should bow their heads in silent suffering and acquiescence despite injury and abuse. As a story in *Godey's Lady's Book* stated in April 1850, when a young girl was physically and mentally abused by her father, she was right not to complain, but should continue to honor her father, however cruel and unkind he might be; she would find her reward in heaven, the author piously noted (pp. 269-73).

Secondly, Fern's novel revealed that a woman could succeed on her own—that she could obtain financial security and support herself and her children independent of marriage. *Ruth Hall* is almost unique among nineteenth-century American novels in that it portrays a woman who achieves the American Dream, a goal at the time reserved only for male Americans; she becomes rich and powerful wholly through her own efforts—and the novel does not even end with a wedding. Fanny Fern's conclusion was that a woman would never be independent until she was financially independent.

This, then, was how widowhood radicalized Fanny Fern. When she was left a widow with relatives who would not help her unless she agreed to their terms, she realized that as a dependent woman she was powerless, vulnerable to abuse and exploitation, and with little or no opportunity to improve her situation—short of remarriage. The experience of widowhood brought her first to a strong belief in women's rights. Not only did she support women's suffrage and educational and professional opportunities for women, she wrote warmly on such controversial subjects as birth control, divorce and the mother's right to custody of her children (which at the time was not the law), venereal disease, prostitution, and equal pay for equal work. Although—or probably because—she was immensely popular (she was the highest paid newspaper writer of her day), she was able to express controversial opinions which most writers of her day—even those who supported rights for women—shied away from.

The cornerstone of Fern's radicalism, however, was her revolutionary opinion that all women should be able to support themselves independent of marriage. Although some women writers advocated economic opportunities for single women and widows, it was generally conceded that once the woman married, she did not need to continue her profession. Thus many nineteenth-century novels by women describe a poor girl, usually an orphan, who is forced to work as a teacher or writer, for example, in some cases becoming wealthy and successful. But her profession is regarded only as a stop-gap measure. That marriage is her true vocation, is the opinion of the heroine, the author, and the readers of the novel. In these novels, once the heroine has married, she gives up her profession. Fanny Fern, however, concluded that all women should have the capacity to be financially independent, whether they were married or not. She herself remarried in January of 1856, but she continued her writing career until her death in 1872. As she wrote in *The New York Ledger* in 1869, "I want all women to render themselves independent of marriage as a mere means of support" (6/26/1869).

The middle-class white woman in mid-nineteenth-century America was supposed to be selfless, passive, and submissive. The widow without resources and without the help of her male relatives could only fit the image if she allowed herself and her children to starve. She could accept her relatives' help if she was prepared to give in to their wishes (give up her children or remarry, for example). But if she wanted to maintain her autonomy, she would have to become financially independent. And Fern concluded that this was a desirable goal for all women: "sweet is the bread of independence," she wrote in 1871, after having maintained her own independent career for twenty years (*New York Ledger*, 7/8/1871). For, as she wrote in *The New York Ledger* on June 8, 1861, her widowhood had taught her that there is "no crust so tough as the grudged crust of dependence."

Notes

[1]The facts about Fanny Fern's life have been obtained from a variety of sources, including her private papers in the Sophia Smith Collection at Smith College, her husband James Parton's papers in the Houghton Library, Harvard University, information at the Massachusetts Historical Society, and information contained in her newspaper columns in *The New York Ledger*, the Boston *Olive Branch* and *True Flag*, the Philadelphia *Saturday Evening Post*, and the New York *Musical World and Times*. See also, James Parton, *Fanny Fern, A Memorial Volume* (New York: G.W. Carlton, 1873); J.C. Derby, *Fifty Years Among Authors, Books and Publishers* (New York: G.W. Carlton, 1884); Ethel Parton, "Fanny Fern, An Informal Biography," unpublished manuscript in the Sophia Smith Collection, Smith College.

[2]See, e.g., *Olive Branch*, 6/18/1854; Philadelphia *Saturday Evening Post*, 1/7/1854.

[3]See, e.g., *New York Ledger*, 5/23/1853, 7/18/1854, 4/11/1857, 7/16/1870.

[4]Review of *Ruth Hall*, in the New Orleans *Crescent City*. Cited in the Boston *Olive Branch*, 1/13/1855.

Works Cited

Cooper, James Fenimore. *The Ways of the Hour* Vol. 24 of *Complete Works*. Leatherstocking Edition. 32 vols. New York: Putnam, 1893?

Derby, James C. *Fifty Years among Authors, Books and Publishers*. New York: G.W. Carlton, 1884.

Emerson, Ralph Waldo. *Complete Works*. Centenary Edition. Edited by Edward W. Emerson. 12 vols. Boston: Houghton Mifflin, 1903-1904.

Fern, Fanny. *Rose Clark*. New York: Mason Brothers, 1856.

———. *Ruth Hall*. New York: Mason Brothers, 1855.

Godey's Lady's Book. April 1850. pp. 269-73.

Harpers Monthly. July 1854.

Hawthorne, Nathaniel. *The Letters of Hawthorne to William Ticknor, 1851-1869*. 1910. Edited by C.E. Frazer Clark, Jr. 2 vols. Rpr. Newark, N.J.: Carteret Book Club, 1972.

Musical World and Times. New York. 1852-1853. New York Public Library.

The New York Ledger. 1855-1872. Watkinson Library, Hartford, Connecticut.

The New York Times. December 20, 1854.

Olive Branch. 1851-1855. American Antiquarian Society, Worcester, Massachusetts.

Parton, Ethel. "Fanny Fern, An Informal Biography." Unpublished manuscript in the Sophia Smith Collection at Smith College.

Parton, James. *Fanny Fern, A Memorial Volume*. New York: G.W. Carlton, 1873.

———. Papers of. Houghton Library, Harvard University.

Parton, Sara Willis. See Fern, Fanny.

Saturday Evening Post. 1853-1854. Philadelphia Public Library.

"To Be Wise Herself":
The Widowing of Dorothea Brooke
in George Eliot's *Middlemarch*

Richard D. McGhee

In her "Finale" for *Middlemarch*, George Eliot herself anticipated the questions which many critics have raised regarding the fate of Dorothea Brooke:

Many who knew her, thought it a pity that so substantive and rare a creature should have been absorbed into the life of another, and be only known in a certain circle as a wife and mother. But no one stated exactly what else that was in her power she ought rather to have done—not even Sir James Chettam, who went no further than the negative prescription that she ought not to have married Will Ladislaw. (576)[1]

Unlike Sir James, however, few critics have been willing to change their minds about the mistake of marrying Dorothea to Will Ladislaw. It has been the cause for a "lasting alienation" of sympathy and judgment for the novel, its heroine, and sometimes its author.

Although he considered George Eliot to be one of the exclusive company in his "Great Tradition," F.R. Leavis would not allow that she had made "a profound analysis" of Dorothea's character, which Leavis considered to be "the weakness of the book" (80, 93).[2] This weakness is the result of George Eliot's lapse into an indulgence of daydreaming at the expense of her usual intelligence and self-knowledge. Leavis quickly makes clear that his reason for this conclusion is based upon his discontent with the relationship of Dorothea and Will Ladislaw: "George Eliot's valuation of Will Ladislaw, in short, is Dorothea's, just as Will's of Dorothea is George Eliot's. Dorothea, to put it another way, is a product of George Eliot's own 'soul-hunger'." (96-7). Will is a fantasy of ideal-love, not a real product of real forces.

Leavis allows Eliot much credit for her genius in analyzing the characters of other persons in *Middlemarch*, especially of Casaubon. But Leavis will allow no room for the "independent status" of Will Ladislaw. Somehow Dorothea does not deserve to enjoy the reward of her ideal-lover. Henry James, who would have disagreed with Leavis on the success of Dorothea as a "genuine creation," nevertheless saw a serious weakness in the character of Will Ladislaw, who "is a beautiful attempt, with many finely-completed points; but on the whole it seems to us a failure" (961).[3] James surely, however, located with his customary precision the main interest of the story in the fortunes of Dorothea Brooke. The "mechanism" for producing this "effect" he slyly avoids to identify. James may be right that the question is "trivial" whether or not Dorothea will marry Will, but surely he would agree that it is a part of the "mechanism" for making Dorothea's character "the greatest achievement of the book" (960-1).

Leslie Stephen calls Will "a stick instead of a man" (660).[4] He inclines to read the story of the novel as a satire against "young ladies who aim at lofty ideals" in a world of hard realities. If "Dorothea was content with giving [Will] 'wifely help'," not thinking there was anything else she could do, then, Stephen concludes, "she had a dash of stupidity" in her character (661). Isobel Armstrong would have none of this. She insists that George Eliot's great artistic success is precisely the result of her ability to "invoke a general body of moral and psychological knowledge or, rather, *experience*" and bring it "to bear on the novel" without condemning the characters who undergo that experience of moral and psychological education (120; author's italics).[5] The reviewer of the novel for the *Saturday Review* in 1872 recognized the special attention Dorothea requires: "The more a woman has aims of her own, and a sense of power to carry them out, the less is she guided by the common motives and aspirations of her sex" (648).[6] Stephen would say that Dorothea submitted to "common motives" and so she failed in the end. This reviewer can understand, or "acquiesce" in, her "first choice" of Casaubon, "more readily than in her second" of Ladislaw, who was merely "happy by luck, not desert." At least this reviewer believed Dorothea used her "sense of power" to choose Will freely, even though he does not deserve her love.

The power to choose is in the process of what James called "the mechanism" of the novel's movement. Dorothea had to find a way to direct that power toward "aims of her own." Hers is a "struggling growth to moral maturity" which "culminates in her being able to *imagine . . .* and to *feel*," as Edwin J. Kenney, Jr., has described it (747; author's italics).[7] Kenney finely emphasizes the point in Eliot's "Finale" that "no one stated exactly what else that was in her power she ought rather to have done" than to be a "wife and mother." Kenney suggests that Eliot "herself did not imagine any other possibility" than to use Will Ladislaw as a "final compromise solution" in "a diagrammatic device of contrast." Yet Kenney keeps hold of the point that Dorothea possesses a certain "power" of self-achievement that cannot be denied, regardless of whether or not Ladislaw is an acceptable reward for her achievement. This "power," Kenney cautiously suggests, is one which "seems to manifest itself best in communicating that vision to others, in recreating itself" (749-50).

The power to recreate itself is a power of considerable value, and it is this achievement in Dorothea's struggles which raises her to heightened interest. The struggle of her career is to be the subject of this essay, particularly that part of her struggle which is symptomatic of mourning and melancholia. To unbind her psychic energies from their mischosen objects is the aim of her struggles in the novel. Arnold Kettle could not value this quality of the novel sufficiently, because he, like Leslie Stephen, looked for evidence of individual triumphs over local, social conventions and ideological constraints.[8] The relationship between Dorothea and Ladislaw merely puzzles Kettle as one of "unresolved emotionalism" which can do little to help characters escape captivity "within the bounds" of their community. But this "emotionalism" is an expression of the psychic energy which Dorothea translates into a power of individuation, that does free her from the provincial scene of Middlemarch.

Bert G. Hornback sees this happening.[9] He has noted how broadly Dorothea's vision expands from her early myopia and naive egotism into a largeness of vision and moral selflessness that earn her the reward of Will Ladislaw. Hornback recognizes the difficulty of seeing Will as a "reward," and so he argues for the importance of Will's character as a symbol of "history." The particular "historical association" Hornback has in mind is that of "Pre-Raphaelitism" with its "aesthetic ideal." Therefore the union of Will with Dorothea is an aesthetic union with moral power, in which each has to make a compromise that deprives both of triumph. This notion of a compromise is central to very sympathetic readings of the novel by Frederick R. Karl and U.C. Knoepflmacher.

Knoepflmacher examines the "story's theme—the 'natural' education of a spiritually minded heroine," Dorothea Brooke, who is "a 'foundress of nothing'," which "lies at the core of *Middlemarch*'s superstructure" (75).[10] Dorothea's marriage "to the mercurial Will Ladislaw, a Victorian 'second best,' is the *via media*, the 'middle march' between her soaring aspirations and the grounding force of a prosaic reality," so that Dorothea's education brings her merely a "Pyrrhic victory" (76, 115). Knoepflmacher's thesis requires an emptying out of Dorothea's power onto an undeserving "second best," because a "middle march" will *require* a compromise of some kind at the end. This is, however sympathetic a reading of the novel, a more damaging analysis even than Leavis's, though it is in a different critical tradition. Frederick R. Karl's reading of the novel is as sympathetic as Knoepflmacher's, and it is as respectful of George Eliot's creative powers as Leavis's. Karl has the additional insight, or tact, to recognize that Dorothea's decision to marry Will Ladislaw is a "momentous" decision, made "in the face of considerable opposition" and after her "ordeal" of sacrifice to Casaubon has made her able to "make intellectual truth agree with the truth of feeling" (280).[11] Karl focuses on the importance of Dorothea's development as a freeing of her creative powers, and he recognizes that it is possible for her marriage with Will to be a consequence of "freedom in a liberating match" (282, 285). Nevertheless, the use of Ladislaw is to be criticized, even by Karl, because Will is "more a savior of Dorothea than a lover" (288).

Barbara Hardy has shown convincingly how clear the issue of sexual love is to an appreciation of the novel.[12] She has dealt with the matter as one of "evasiveness and suggestiveness" on the part of George Eliot. Will

Ladislaw offers to Dorothea, in Hardy's analysis, a satisfying love object after the embarrassing failure of Casaubon to be the same. But, because Eliot refused to name or even to "suggest" the sexual "passions," she has left "an unrealistic element in an unusually realistic novel" (292). This, Hardy concludes, "is the psychological and structural flaw in *Middlemarch*" (302). But when Lee R. Edwards first read the novel as a student, she felt she had found in Dorothea "an endorsement...of energy and social commitment on the part of a woman in combination...with the promise that these qualities did not render the possessor either a social misfit or a danger to herself or others" (685).[13] That was, in Edwards' reconsidered view, a "misreading" of the book, of the character, and of the character's energy.

Edwards' new reading insists that Dorothea's "energy" is misspent, her values betrayed, and her integrity compromised, because Dorothea married the second time. Perhaps she should never have married at all. Certainly, in Edwards' re-view, "the objection is not that Dorothea should have married Will, but that she should have married anybody at all" (690). Edwards would join the camp of those who, like Leslie Stephen, Henry James, and Dorothea's sister Celia, deplore Dorothea's choice in Will Ladislaw, but Edwards contracts the circle of objection into a smaller, more exclusive group, who, like Edwin J. Kenney, Jr., and Sir James Chettam, believe Dorothea should have refused marriage with anybody at all. When Edwards suggests that Dorothea should have had what she is denied by George Eliot, "the opportunity to find her own paths and forge her energies into some new mold" (p. 690), Edwards is missing the point that George Eliot herself made in the "Finale," which is in fact that Dorothea *did* find her own paths and *did* forge her energies into some new mold.

Edward Casaubon is, in psychoanalyst Jessica Benjamin's terms, a "father liberator," who draws Dorothea Brooke from her narcissistic melancholia into an identification with a false ideal: his death is her liberation.[14] Will Ladislaw is her true ideal of a person who resolves her conflicts between separation and dependency, "salvaging her self-esteem and independent will and desire" (132). He must succeed in resolving his own conflicts of separation and dependency before he can present himself to Dorothea's vision as a true ideal of desire, as the "essence of male identity" which most appeals to her need for separateness without loss of security. Dorothea's experience of what J. Hillis Miller calls "intersubjectivity," first with her Uncle, then with Sir James, Casaubon, and finally Ladislaw, produces the unique consciousness which is her self.[15] Dorothea's subjectivity develops through difficulties of melancholia, mourning, and reality testing.

Her melancholy is a form of secondary narcissism, which could destroy her ego's integrity, but she finds a saving object in an ideal "father," Casaubon. This has, however, the unhappy consequence of alienating her desires and converting her melancholy into the masochism of submission. Freud's essay of 1917, "Mourning and Melancholia," and his longer study of *The Ego and The Id* in 1923, are useful to begin an analysis of Dorothea's melancholia, but Freud's theories alone cannot satisfactorily explain why Dorothea's marriage has the disastrous consequence of masochism. Benjamin's post-Freudian, feminist analysis of "Women's Masochism and Ideal Love" offers a way to understand more clearly why Dorothea must learn to mourn her husband's death. Her mourning unbinds affections long misplaced, frees her energies to accept Will Ladislaw as ideal love without alienation, without masochism.

It may be proposed, in terms developed by Freud in *The Ego and The Id*, that Dorothea's manic/depressive behavior of extremes derives from a special, unsuccessful sublimation of her sexual instincts (libido). What George Eliot represents in an adult character is what Freud proposed as occurring in infancy and childhood. That, however, is only the most sensational part of the Freudian theory, otherwise practical for explaining normal human behavior as a precarious triumph over psychoneurotic tendencies. Dorothea Brooke is an example of a young woman struggling to achieve such a triumph. She has, again in Freud's terms, to transform object-libido into narcissistic libido. This requires her (ego) to withdraw love from the objects of her parents, and then to turn it back onto herself as the most economical way of making that withdrawal. She must, in effect, learn to love herself as if she were her own parents. This withdrawal of love can be experienced as melancholy, and the love of self can be experienced as an exultation, a triumph of ego. It can also begin to attract the attention of super-ego, an agent (or agency) of unconscious self-observation. The critical agent of self-regard can be harsh and repressive to such an extent the ego suffers anxiety and guilt for loving itself, for betraying parents. The project of the ego is to accommodate the super-ego without capitulating to it: it must be used to master instincts of id without itself becoming master of the ego. One way to do that is for the ego to translate, through the agency of the super-ego, instincts into ideals.

Dorothea is introduced at a point when she has withdrawn love from parental objects (which may include her Uncle) to a love of self, a love which is driven out again to find new objects for satisfaction. Those are the objects of Dorothea's religious and social ideals and causes. They, however, do not satisfy her libidinal needs for objects with which she can identify herself, either as reflections of her self to love or as displacements for original objects of parental love. She is ready, then, to cast about for a new object, something or someone who can realize for her libido a satisfaction of sexual instincts and tender affections both at once. She must find a new ego-ideal which can at once free her from dependence on parent (or on herself as the parent), especially the mother, and liberate her to be her own unique self separate from the ideal of her parent. The healthy and ordinary way to achieve that liberation is to search for an ideal love of a man as a "father-liberator" (in Benjamin's term).

Dorothea's first object of an ideal love is Edward Casaubon, who seems to her to realize all her desires for intellectual and emotional freedom because, as even she consciously recognizes, Casaubon is to be her father-lover. What is unconscious to her, however, is very conscious to many of Dorothea's friends and acquaintances, that she is mistaken in her choice of an ideal-object. Dorothea will be unhappy, all realize, in her vicissitudes of love for Casaubon; she will also be punishing herself in a way that is more perplexing to observers in the novel. Dorothea needs to punish herself by submitting to Casaubon as a master, since he is little more to her ego than an embodiment of the father-ideal of the super-ego.

Dorothea's move toward Casaubon may be a move from narcissistic guilt, but it will involve new submissiveness which is equally painful and equally unhealthy. She alienates her desire in her effort to free it for self-expression. His death is to be her opportunity for liberation, but she will not be able to accept that liberation until she works through the mourning and melancholia which come upon her. Her mourning is the ordinary psychological process of adjusting to the loss of a love object. Since, in the case of Casaubon, this person was also an ideal-love, a father-liberator, his loss is especially threatening for Dorothea's psychic health. She must feel great guilt for wanting Casaubon's death, and so she has to suffer the intense kind of mourning that is really a self-punishment that could become the serious illness of melancholia. Her bereavement is very real, because it is very necessary to her emotional health. It is very deep and painful, because she has so much to punish herself for. Her rescue is in her further progression from self to other, from ego-ideal as father, to ego-ideal as liberator, in the person of Will Ladislaw.

Long before she undergoes the severe depression of her honeymoon visit to Rome in Chapter 20, Dorothea Brooke exhibits symptoms of melancholy alternating with intense excitement and happiness. This association of depression and exaltation is not uncommon, as Freud observed long ago, in the special kind of depression he called *melancholia*. Although George Eliot generally explains the association as a figure of religious attitudes in Dorothea, Eliot nevertheless sometimes makes a more penetrating, and judgmental, observation about the peculiarities of Dorothea's behavior and feelings. Eliot admits the religious dimension, but insists that it is only a part, perhaps a small part, of the complicated pattern of feelings in Dorothea's psyche: "the intensity of her religious disposition, the coercion it exercised over her life, was but one aspect of a nature altogether ardent, theoretic, and intellectually consequent" (17). In circumstances which seemed to hem in her theoretic nature, Dorothea is bound to struggle, and "strike others as at once [behaving with] exaggeration and inconsistency" (17).

Her exaggerations and inconsistencies are symptoms of her melancholy/mania. They are in her character before her unfortunate marriage to Casaubon. Indeed, they are the intensities of her character which make inevitable the misfortune of her marriage, the "martyrdom" which Eliot early explains as Dorothea's special fate. In the experience of melancholy, the subject is very self-critical, abases herself, and inclines to represent herself as worthless. It is a kind of sickness because there are no real reasons to form this severe self-judgment; at least there are none to observers, and they must seem unreal even to the suffering person (for whom the "reasons" are unconscious ones). Dorothea enjoys renouncing pleasure. This is a form of the self-criticism generally characteristic of her behavior, and it is a form of the masochism to be examined more closely later in this essay. She enjoyed riding horses, and she was good at it, but "she enjoyed it in a pagan sensuous way, and always looked forward to renouncing it" (3). When, in fact, Sir James proposes to lend her one of his fine horses for riding, she impulsively refuses, and says that she has decided to ride no more at all. Besides being one of her defenses against the appeal of Sir James as a lover (as an erotic object which might interfere with her search for an ideal love), this renunciation is symptomatic of Dorothea's general inclination to melancholy and masochism.

Sir James, ever trying to adjust to Dorothea's strange behavior, observes to Celia that "your sister is given to self-mortification, is she not?" Celia knows this trait all too well: "She likes giving up" (10). This "giving up" is not admirable in Dorothea because it is so obviously a form of self-punishment, not ascetic self-sacrifice. She makes others feel uncomfortable around her. Celia thinks Dorothea's "notions and scruples were like spilt needles, making one afraid of treading, or sitting down, or even eating" (12). When Dorothea begins to dream of a possible union with Casaubon, she characteristically pours all of her passion into a longing for it as if it were definitely to be true. She stops herself, however, not because it is so much a fantasy of wishful thinking, but rather because it gives her too much pleasure to contemplate. Dorothea is victimized by the flow of her uncontrolled passions. Celia thinks to herself, "How strangely Dodo goes from one extreme to the other" (30). Mrs. Cadwallader, although she is a cad, can see through Dorothea more clearly than most in the novel: she "now saw that her opinion of this girl had been infected with some of her husband's weak charitableness: those Methodistical whims, that air of being more religious than the rector and curate together, came from a deeper and more constitutional disease than she had been willing to believe" (40).

Dorothea's "disease" of melancholia/mania is not deeply probed for its causes in the novel. It seems simply to exist as a characteristic of the young woman, as a type of person whose virtues are trials of spirit for one who has so little opportunity to exercise them in her time and place. Dorothea's vicissitudes are, therefore, consequences of a radical ambivalence, either in her character or in her environment. The history of her struggles is to be the history of her search for a resolution of that ambivalence through whatever social and psychic means she can discover.

The origin of Dorothea's melancholy of troubled spirit may be hinted at very early in the novel, when she and Celia divide her mother's jewels. Celia hesitatingly suggests the division, suspecting that her sister will not be eager for it. Celia has been counting the days since their Uncle handed them over to the young women, but Dorothea seems to have put them entirely out of her mind since they were put away six months ago. Dorothea's first response to Celia's suggestion is to express amusement that Celia has been keeping such careful count of the time which has passed. Then Dorothea dashes some of Celia's enthusiasm by saying, rather too casually, "Well, dear, we should never wear them, you know" (5). Dorothea seems to give the matter only a small part of her attention, as she is engaged in one of her favorite projects, drawing up designs for improvements of workers' cottages.

Celia is mortified. Even though she is accustomed to Dorothea's strangeness of behavior, this response surprises and deeply disappoints her. She suggests that they "are wanting in respect to mamma's memory, to put them by and take no notice of them." Dorothea is, for her part, equally surprised at Celia's intensity of feeling. She agrees to take the jewels out, but she cannot remember what she has done with the keys to the cabinet. Finally, the jewels are removed for inspection. The young women are mutually delighted by the spectacle of color and shapes they discover in the small collection of jewels. Even Dorothea is moved by the spectacle. She refuses to accept the pleasure, however, She insists that Celia take all the jewels, until she notices a ring and bracelet of diamonds and emeralds. They look to her "like fragments of heaven."

Dorothea takes the two pieces of jewelry, but only after she rationalizes their beauty for herself: "gems are used as spiritual emblems in the Revelation of St. John." She also rebukes herself: "what miserable men find such things, and work at them, and sell them." Still, Dorothea keeps these two pieces, much to Celia's surprise. When Celia asks Dorothea if she will wear them in company, Dorothea sarcastically responds, "I cannot tell to what level I may sink." This plunges both Celia and Dorothea into moody unhappiness with one another, and so Dorothea succeeds again in turning beauty and happiness into sadness and melancholy. She thinks to herself in such a way as to question "the purity of her own feeling and speech in the scene which had ended with that little explosion" (7).

There is little occasion or opportunity to probe Dorothea's relationship with either of her parents, since they seem to have been long dead when the novel opens. This episode of their mother's jewels is, consequently, a special occasion in the long and richly textured novel, which seems to avoid mention of the parents much too deliberately for the reader who is curious about the psychological origins of the heroine. Dorothea's seeming to forget the key to the jewel casket, her seeming to have forgotten the jewels themselves, her resistance to accepting them, and her self-punishment for accepting a small portion with pleasure—all manifest the symptoms typical of a neurotic condition. They suggest, as well, that George Eliot deliberately presents Dorothea's response to her mother's jewels as an ambivalent attachment to her mother herself. In this is to be recognized an original motive for Dorothea's search for a love-ideal, a husband, who can help her more firmly to reach greater independence from primary identification with her mother.

That search for a love-ideal makes Dorothea blind to the courtship of Sir James, whose character and interests are so narrow and immediate that they offer no very strong powers to help her develop her character. At least, she is so bound up by her own narcissistic (spiritual, intellectual) pleasures, that she cannot respond to any man whose values and character are not greatly different than she has been used to in her immediate family life. Sir James is too much like Dorothea's own family to provide her with the "father liberator" she needs in a lover. Dorothea has much to learn, however, before she will find the true image of ideal love she needs to liberate her spirit.

Her tendency to self-punishment can be explained as a rebuke to herself for desiring to be independent, for wishing to separate from her family and from her mother especially. Even if that is not clear to herself (or to the reader), what is clear is that Dorothea can conceive of a husband only in terms to which she is emotionally accustomed: he must be someone who makes her feel punished at the same time he helps her to achieve some measure of independence. That continues the consequence of her constitutional ambivalence.

What Celia calls mere strangeness in her sister, Mrs. Cadwallader calls Dorothea's "disease," and Sir James more accurately describes as "melancholy illusion" (44), is that propensity in her character which the narrator has called her destiny for martyrdom. Dorothea herself knows what she is looking for in a husband, though she has made the mistake of taking a psychological metaphor as a literal guide: "the really delightful marriage must be that where your husband was a sort of father," a proposition which the narrator quite correctly calls "very childlike" (4). Dorothea identifies Casaubon as the very image of her ideal. She is attracted by his "mind," as a man with much to teach her, and so he satisfies her masochistic longing to denigrate herself even as he moves toward separation from family: " 'he thinks a whole world of which my thought is but a poor two penny mirror' " (15). Casaubon digs about among "the dead" where, as he himself says, "my mind is something like the ghost of an ancient, wandering about the world and trying mentally to construct it as it used to be" (9). This is very attractive to Dorothea, who mistakes it as a sign of intellectual strength in Casaubon when it is in fact a dangerous beckoning to her own desire for regression to childhood dependence in the past. Dorothea feels, perhaps even knows, that she needs a "guide who would take her along the grandest path," but she is doomed by her masochism to submit to a guide whose attractions are forms of punishment rather than satisfactions of pleasure. What Celia cannot understand, as perhaps Dorothea does not herself, is that Dorothea should be attracted to such an ugly man as Casaubon.

As long as Dorothea persists in looking for a "father-liberator" of the type embodied in Casaubon, she will continue to suffer from the self-punishments of her melancholy disposition. It is as if she wished to be punished by her father for desiring him (to put it in somewhat classical Freudian terms), or as if she wished to be liberated from her own self-love (or primary mother love) by a person who cannot threaten her basic identity—by someone, in other words, like Casaubon, who is impotent in all senses of the word. She wishes to submit to such a person, one who makes her feel small and like a little girl: " 'I should not wish to have a husband very near my own age'," she tells her Uncle. " 'I should wish to have a husband who was above me in judgment and in all knowledge.' " Mr. Brooke does not help matters by telling her that "a husband likes to be master." Dorothea finds that much more attractive than she should: "I know that I must expect trials, uncle. Marriage is a state of higher duties. I never thought of it as mere personal ease" (26) Dorothea must marry someone who makes her feel uneasy as the price she pays for achieving the intellectual independence she has conceived as her ideal of desire. The narrator sees what Dorothea is after, and what is going wrong with Dorothea's judgment: "She had not reached that point of renunciation at which she would have been satisfied with having a wise husband: she wished, poor child, to be wise herself. Miss Brooke was certainly very naive with all her alleged cleverness" (42).

The irony of this sympathetic judgment is in the fact that Dorothea should be wishing to be wise herself though her own character and her own environment have combined to depreciate the value of that wish. If, however, she can be drawn deeply enough into the misery of her mistakes, Dorothea has the wit and strength to learn from those mistakes. This is to be her salvation, as the later events of the novel will show. She will work her way through to wisdom, even though her way will be even more painful and self-punishing than she has any reason to understand when she chooses Edward Casaubon as her ideal love.

Dorothea wants too much and too often to submit to Casaubon and his guidance. When she examines his house, Lowick, which will soon be her home as his wife, Dorothea can find nothing wrong with it, except that it is perfect. This makes her feel "some disappointment, of which she was yet ashamed, that there was nothing for her to do in Lowick" (52). Casaubon himself notes that she is "a little sad." When she is introduced to Will Ladislaw, she typically abases herself and her judgment, so that Will makes up his mind that "she must be an unpleasant girl," not only because anyone who could have engaged herself to Casaubon must be "unpleasant," but also because "what she said of her stupidity about pictures would have confirmed the opinion even if he had believed her" (53).

About one picture, however, Dorothea is not stupid. This is the picture she notices in the "bow-windowed room" of Lowick. It is the room where Casaubon's mother lived as a young girl, and it is the room where her picture hangs alongside that of "her elder sister." Dorothy's curiosity is raised by the picture of the elder sister, though she does not question Casaubon about it after he says, "My aunt made an unfortunate marriage." The irony of his remark, in the light of what lies ahead for Dorothea, is striking, of course. However, the more important point is far from clear so early in the novel. The more important point is that in this picture of Casaubon's Aunt, who is Will Ladislaw's grandmother, is the image of an enormous liberating potential for Dorothea's suffering soul. When she is able to hold it in her hand, feel toward it what she wants to feel for a man, Dorothea will finally have realized the fulfillment of desire that dissolves her alienation of spirit.

Before that can happen, however, Dorothea suffers the disaster of her marriage with Casaubon. Her disappointment at discovering that she had nothing to do to "improve" Lowick should have been a signal to her that she was not to be happy in that place, though not to be happy would only feed her propensity for masochism. If there had been something for her to do at Lowick, she might truly have been lost indeed. She needs to be driven into herself, to confront the emptiness of her self-denial, and so she needs to be deprived of the distracting interests she wants in the tasks to improve the world around her. Casaubon tells her that he intends soon to "let Will Ladislaw be tried by the test of freedom" (55); that is, in fact, what is about to happen to Dorothea herself, who in submitting to her husband as an ideal love, is about to be abandoned to herself as a pure subject. This is a paradox of great irony, because Dorothea had wanted so much to submit herself to a strong and independent man of great intellectual power. Her emotional ambivalence and melancholy character has, instead, driven her to choose a man of opposite qualities, and that will prove to be her path of liberation in the end.

Dorothea's yearning to be filled is conceived as "something she yearned for by which her life might be filled with action at once rational and ardent" (58). When she and Casaubon plan their honeymoon in Rome, she experiences, for the first time, a very conscious "annoyance" with her fiancée. This occurs when Casaubon informs her he thinks she should take Celia with them, so as to give Dorothea some equal companionship in Rome, since he plans to spend much time continuing with his historical researches. Casaubon's way of putting it to Dorothea strikes her as painful: "I should feel more at liberty if you had a companion." Then Dorothea is "ashamed of being irritated from some cause she could not define even to herself," a cause which has uncovered a "real hurt within her" (59). She had wished to submit herself to her husband, to lean upon him, to abase herself before him, as when she wished to "throw herself, metaphorically speaking, at Mr. Casaubon's feet, and kiss his unfashionable shoe-ties as if he were a Protestant Pope" (33). Now she learns she is to be denied the pleasure of such complete submission. The key is to see, with her growing understanding, that Dorothea's desire for subjection to a man is what lies behind her masochism. Therefore, when Casaubon proves to be powerless to satisfy her yearning for subjectivity, he will paradoxically prove to be the instrument of her education and liberation for something better.

When Will Ladislaw and Adolf Naumann see Dorothea in Rome, they see her in purely aesthetic terms to begin with. She is herself undergoing some painful instruction in aesthetics, as she tries to cope with the magnitude of what Rome has to show, at the same time she is trying to deal with the conflict of emotions she experiences in her relationship with her new husband. Dorothea needs some beauty in her life, especially now, but she is so emotionally crippled that she cannot properly respond to the beauty that surrounds her in Rome. Instead, she is caught up in a great crisis of spirit, the crisis of her melancholy, when the pain of rejection has begun to exceed the pleasure of her desire for submission. In Rome Dorothea sobs bitterly with an oppressed heart. She begins to recognize that her "feeling of desolation was the fault of her own spiritual poverty" (133).

Her weeping has been occasioned by Casaubon's sharp rebuke to her for suggesting that he might now get on with the writing of his book (139). That was, however, only an occasion to open up for Dorothea the vast extent of her spiritual emptiness. She feels "a stifling depression" (136), even "a certain terror" that she was sliding into helpless anger and "forlorn weariness" (136). She had hoped Casaubon would be able to feed "her affection with those childlike caresses which are the bent of every sweet woman," but instead he has denied her and emotionally rejected her (137). Her despondency is felt as humiliation, and her rejection has made her see that she is "a mere victim of feeling" (138). Her liberator is nearby, in the person of Will Ladislaw, but she is not yet prepared to admit to herself that she needs a liberator more substantial than the one she mistakenly believed to be Casaubon.

During her honeymoon with Casaubon in Rome, Dorothea discovers just how far she has alienated her desire, just how far she has gone in separating her ego from its ideal of independence. She has submitted her desire to Casaubon as an ideal to liberate her, in her conscious experience, from a narrowly defined reality of life in a provincial society, and, in her unconscious experience, from a childish, infantile love of herself or her parent (mother) in herself. The price she has paid is a price of punishment for the separation, for the desire to be liberated. Her punishment is the masochism of submission, and this is what is coming with terrifying force into her consciousness during her Roman honeymoon.

In Chapters 20 and 21, George Eliot narrates the crisis of Dorothea's discovery. It is precipitated by Dorothea's suggestion to Casaubon that he might begin to write his book now that he has accumulated so much information. He, for his part, has something akin to an anxiety attack, as he rejects her and her suggestion. Dorothea wishes to be what she imagined Casaubon to be: intellectually free. He of course is not free in any meaningful way at all. She may become so, if she can free her emotions to provide the energy she needs for her liberation. Casaubon is helping to free Dorothea by his rejection, though she naturally interprets it as a painful kind of self-punishment. "She was," Dorothea felt, "humiliated to find herself a mere victim of feeling, as if she could know nothing except through that medium: all her strength was scattered in fits of agitation, of struggle, of despondency, and then again in visions of more complete renunciation, transforming all hard conditions into duty." George Eliot herself observes, "Poor Dorothea! she was certainly troublesome—to herself chiefly" (138). Eliot shows by this that she has a deeper understanding of Dorothea than Dorothea can have of herself, as is true throughout the novel. In addition, however, Eliot turns what is a painful personal tragedy and psychic trauma into a scene of pity and childish exaggeration—which it is, though hardly deserving the condescension implied by the narrator's way of describing it.

The entire episode of mutual terror in recognizing their basic incompatibility is an episode of stunning psychoanalytical insights by the author, as Casaubon's terror of narcissistic vulnerability is matched by Dorothea's terror of masochistic submission. There is high comedy in the terror, partly because George Eliot insists on taking a stance of understanding which makes clear her sympathy for both characters and her confidence that Dorothea will emerge with psychic integrity somehow. When, for example, the narrator (Eliot) observes, "To Dorothea's inexperienced sensitiveness, it seemed like a catastrophe," the reader may feel that the narrator has less apprehension about the eventual outcome than Dorothea can have. In her art of narration, too, Eliot has introduced the reader to this episode as at a distance, when Dorothea is first observed from the viewpoints of Ladislaw and Naumann, who cannot perceive her real state of mind any more than the reader can understand why Dorothea should be so unhappy in the midst of so much beauty.

Encountering Will Ladislaw at this moment of crisis is a part of the aesthetic design for the novel to provide for a new phase in the development of the heroine. The tact of the design is a function of the artist's sense of psychological subtlety in providing Dorothea with the true ideal lover just at the moment when she needs him to help her beyond this crisis of alienation, separation, and masochism. Will goes to visit the Casaubons in Rome. In her apartment, alone, Dorothea is sobbing in consequence of the day's emotional discoveries, though she is not completely conscious of the reasons behind her need to cry. Then Ladislaw visits, and Dorothea "was alive to anything that gave her an opportunity for active sympathy, and at this moment it seemed as if the visit had come to shake her out of her self-absorbed discontent" (141). Dorothea cannot, however, as Eliot goes on to make clear, allow this to be her way of explaining why she is glad to see Will; she rationalizes her happiness of relief by thinking to herself that "it reminds her of her husband's goodness, and makes her feel that she had now the right to be his helpmate in all kind deeds." She resists Will's criticisms of Casaubon's research methods, to the extent that she overreacts when Will suggests that the Germans have already done the work Casaubon has spent his life trying to do.

Dorothea is thrown into yet another panic: " 'I do not understand you,' said Dorothea, startled and anxious" (144). But it should be noticed that her panic is expressed to herself as a panic of uselessness: "In her saddest recitative," she says, " 'But now I can be of no use' " (144). It may feel painful to Dorothea in her conscious mind to be deprived of this sense of purpose in her marriage, but it is necessary at a deeper, unconscious level of her mental growth if she is going to pass beyond the false-ideal of Casaubon. When he dies, he merely confirms what has already happened intellectually and emotionally (and, as most critics have recognized, sexually) in the Roman Honeymoon episode. It is more difficult to recognize, on all accounts (by author, character, and reader as well), that Dorothea might even deeply wish for the death of Casaubon as she is gradually becoming conscious of his emptiness as a means of her self-fulfillment. The more she resists Ladislaw, the more she insists on submitting to Casaubon, even after the disastrous honeymoon, the more she may be displaying a repressive force at work in her character. If this is so, then her mourning will be a continuation of her self-punishment for having fulfilled what she had wished.

There are a few clues that Dorothea is feeling her way towards a wish to be rid of her husband, and her relationship with Ladislaw is only the most important source of those clues. Casaubon comes home to find Ladislaw with Dorothea in the Roman episode. Dorothea contrasts the two, in her vaguely unconscious way of looking at them together: "When [Ladislaw] turned his head quickly his hair seemed to shake out light, and some persons thought they saw decided genius in this coruscation. Mr. Casaubon, on the contrary, stood rayless" (145).[16] Eliot's way of narrating this does not allow for a certain clarity in Dorothea's feelings in this perception. In fact, Eliot goes on to suggest that Dorothea may immediately act to deny to herself the feelings raised by this perception: "As Dorothea's eyes were turned anxiously on her husband she was perhaps not insensible to the contrast, but it was only mingled with other causes in making her more conscious of that new alarm on his behalf." Eliot knows more than she pretends here about what is happening to Dorothea. For one thing, the "alarm on his behalf" is a signal that Dorothea wants to be rid of her husband so that she can have Will Ladislaw, but she cannot of course admit that to herself (however much George Eliot might try *not* to admit it to *her*self). Dorothea must, instead, conceal such a wish beneath an anxiety of concern for her husband's welfare, a concern which will be increased when Casaubon has his heart attack.

Back home in Lowick, Dorothea finds her life, if anything, more empty than before. She "shrinks with the furniture" of the place. She is uneasy and "alarmed with dim presentiment." Her marriage has not liberated her as she had expected, because she has submitted herself to an ideal incapable of liberation. The effect of it all is to empty the world of meaning for her: "every object was withering and shrinking away from her" (190). In the midst of this new kind of neurotic depression, Dorothea is saved from despair by her notice of the picture of Aunt Julia, whose own history of an unfortunate marriage now makes her more significant as a symbol for Dorothea, who "felt a new companionship with it." It is a symbol of importance for the entire novel, for its plot and for its themes. It is, however, a symbol for special importance for understanding how Dorothea will complete her healing growth from neurotic love to healthy and happy love. The miniature of Aunt Julia will serve to recall a female parent of affection, the mother, with whom Dorothea can newly identify when she needs to do so, and the miniature will also objectify for Dorothea's conscious understanding that the ideal love she has been searching for is to be found in Will Ladislaw himself, the grandson of Casaubon's Aunt Julia.

Among those who sense, perhaps deeply understand, that Dorothea has fallen in love with Ladislaw is Casaubon himself. He cannot, nevertheless, explain it with clarity unless he also disguises it in such a way that it is an acceptable notion to his conscious ego. His insulting and hateful codicil to prohibit Dorothea from holding onto his property should she marry Ladislaw is but a conscious gesture of his unconscious recognition that Ladislaw is the unacknowledged rival for Dorothea's love. The triangular relationship here is very close to Freud's description of the classic Oedipus project, in which a healthy resolution will be for the "son" to oust the "father" and take his place as the lover of his "mother." That George Eliot has a sense for understanding this may be inferred from the ages of the characters themselves, the kinship between Casaubon and Ladislaw, and, most importantly, the identification which Dorothea makes of herself with Aunt Julia in the miniature, which in turn is identified with the love Dorothea feels and finally acknowledges for Ladislaw.

Throughout the year or so of her life with Casaubon after the crisis in Rome, Dorothea has fought against the depression of her withering spirit and unsatisfied longing for a new ideal-love. When she and Will meet, as in Chapter 37, Dorothea feels renewed and her feelings are revealed: "Each looked at the other as if they had been two flowers which had opened then and there" (250). Will's visit gives her strength to acknowledge the truth of her relationship with Casaubon: "She was no longer struggling against the perception of fact" (252), but Dorothea continues consciously to deny in herself what is an unconscious fact, that she has fallen in love with Ladislaw and wishes to be free of her husband: "She looked steadily at her husband's failure," though she instantly interprets that to herself as evidence of her "tenderness" for him.

When she proposes Casaubon alter his will to provide for Ladislaw rather than for herself out of Casaubon's property, Dorothea *feels* enlightened and lightened by the thought, though she is, by Eliot's analysis, blind to her real motives: "she was blind, you see, to many things obvious to others" (257). Of course her proposal is rejected, and she is devastated: "Poor Dorothea, shrouded in the darkness, was in a tumult of conflicting emotions," says the narrator. In her emotional darkness, Dorothea is undergoing another panic of anxiety: "Hearing him breathe quickly after he had spoken, she sat listening, frightened, wretched—with a dumb inward cry for help to bear this nightmare of a life in which every energy was arrested by dread" (259). She needs help to escape, and in this feeling Dorothea is drawing closer to a consciousness of what she must eventually acknowledge—rescue from the monstrous Casaubon by the heroic liberator Ladislaw. "But," as Eliot goes on to say in her ironic way, "nothing else happened, except that they both remained a long while sleepless, without speaking again."

Dorothea's marriage turns into "a perpetual struggle of energy with fear" (269). She is "smitten with hopelessness" in her relationship with Casaubon (270), but it is a hopelessness drawn from deep ambivalence, because it has to do with her unsuccessful effort to persuade him on the subject of inheritance for Ladislaw. Dorothea grows more and more melancholy in a general climate of melancholy for an increasing number of characters in the story (270, 270-1, 288, 293-4, 295-6, 304). Eventually, as if dying from melancholy himself, Casaubon's condition is diagnosed by Lydgate as "fatty degeneration of the heart." Increasingly Dorothea feels that Casaubon is pushing her farther and farther away, though one might think she is only increasing her consciousness of their distance from one another.

As the crisis of his last illness approaches, Dorothea's strength of independence from Casaubon grows. She has a "reaction of rebellious anger" against him, until "pity was overthrown" (294-5). She has reached a point which George Eliot can describe thus: "In such a crisis as this, some women begin to hate" (295). She eventually feels the melancholy of self-punishment for this honesty of emotion (295-6), but Dorothea is able in the midst of her anger, and on the threshold of hate, to analyze her condition, perhaps for the first clear time in her marriage: "The energy that would animate a crime is not more than is wanted to inspire a resolved submission, when the noble habit of the soul reasserts itself." She works her way into a renewed posture of "submission," but she realizes as she does the possibility of a redirection of her energies. Her realization is in the form of a concept of "crime," which indicates that her anger and hate for Casaubon are beginning to focus in consciousness; at the same time she has to exert greater energy to the task of repressing her new honesty of feeling.

When Dorothea wants to know more about her husband's condition, the truth of his ill health, she is motivated by more than her regard for his happiness. She is motivated as well by her repressed hate for him, and therefore by her desire to see him dead at last. The difficulty and delicacy of dealing with such struggles of mind and soul are represented by the narrative of Chapter 48, in which Dorothea is put to a test of loyalty by her husband, who dies (as if) to punish her for her failure, and she is free at last to redirect her desires for self-realization. She cannot be free, however, until she works through the mourning which is necessary to punish herself for her liberation. As long as she bound herself to Casaubon, she was helpless and benumbed for lack of "objects who could be dear to her, and to whom she could be dear" (329). She feels as if she is standing in the doorway of a tomb, watching as Will Ladislaw recedes into "the distant world of warm activity." This is before the death of Casaubon, and so it is an ironic perspective on that wish for his death. Dorothea pictures herself as dead, because she wants her husband to be dead; she suffers from "spiritual emptiness and discontent" which she has to bear "as she would have borne a headache" (329).

Then Casaubon asks her the fateful question he had been preparing, if she will promise to carry out his wishes such as he might express them in his will to be read after his death, without telling her what it is to which she promises herself. She does not answer, but she does not refuse either. In her is "the need of freedom asserting itself" (331), but she does not refuse him nevertheless. Instead she asks for some time to consider. In her time of reflection, she is driven even more deeply into a conflict of duty and desire, wish and denial. She debates within herself, as consciously as she is capable, until she "felt ill and bewildered, unable to resolve, praying mutely. Helpless as a child which has sobbed and sought too long, she fell into a late morning sleep" (332). She decides to "say 'Yes' to her own doom," to "submit completely" (333). This is a "natural" conclusion for her to come to, since she long ago in her psychic history had moved in the direction of masochism which has brought her to recognize that her ideal has turned into "the real yoke of marriage" (333). In this state of mind, she goes to find Casaubon in the garden to give him her answer, even as she wishes she could "smite the stricken soul that entreated hers" (p. 334). In that same instant of wishing she had the strength to say no, fearful that to say no would be to kill him, she finds Casaubon dead.

Later, "Lydgate was seated by her bedside, and she was talking deliriously" as she desperately sought to justify herself to her dead husband. Then Dorothea regains enough sanity to recognize that Lydgate is beside her, that he is not her husband. She pleads with Lydgate to go to Casaubon, to tell her husband she will "go to him soon" with her promise. In her delirium she has said more than she knows, that she is willing to punish herself so deeply that she could go to him in death. Certainly she says what is more true than she can know in her condition of mourning: "It has made me ill." She is so ill, despite her thinking she will be better (for "his" sake), that Dorothea was still "not able to leave her room" the day after Mr. Casaubon was buried. She remains in this state of being for many days. Even after she leaves her room, to be with Celia and Celia's baby, Dorothea is subdued by sorrow and she shows all the trappings of mourning. When she hears the dreadful news of the fateful codicil, her mourning is in jeopardy: "She was undergoing a metamorphosis" (340). Casaubon's threat against her and Ladislaw will be her justification for his death, and so her self-punishment can be lifted to be borne by the codicil itself. What is intended, therefore, to maintain her submission, turns into the very instrument of her greater liberation, as Dorothea is able to lift her anger and indignation, perhaps even her hate, into her consciousness when she hears of the prohibition against her love for Ladislaw.

Will Ladislaw goes through his own vicissitudes of separation and individuation, as he withdraws from dependence upon Casaubon, from temptations by Bulstrode and by Rosamond, from obligations to Mr. Brooke, finally to achieve independence and identity of such a kind that he becomes worthy of Dorothea's love and admiration. As soon as Dorothea discovers the indignity of Casaubon's codicil to his will, she is able to complete her conscious, public display of mourning. More importantly, she is able to complete the unconscious process of self-punishment and masochistic desire for submission which her marriage to Casaubon had realized. The codicil is specifically aimed at her possible marriage with Ladislaw (which, even for Casaubon, was interpreted as a relationship of dependence and submission by Dorothea), and this is the novel's version of a *felix culpa*, since it objectifies the desire which Dorothea has for her independent fulfillment in the same person who can publicize her separation from Casaubon as a "father liberator."

Dorothea goes through several, sometimes painful, stages of transformation in the process of emerging from her public display of mourning. She is, at the same time, working through her unconscious processes of repression, guilt, and anxiety for beginning to enjoy her independence and anticipation of self-fulfillment. Her real pain is caused, then, by both conscious and unconscious forces at work in her period of public and private bereavement as the widow of Edward Casaubon. It begins with her paralysis of will at the news of her husband's death, though this is a phase in which the novelist is very little interested (knowing that Dorothea's real bereavement is not to be shown merely in a focus on this public display). Then Dorothea begins to brood, slowly emerging from a melancholy lethargy. Celia upbraids her for so much brooding (339), and she proceeds to inform Dorothea about the codicil to "correct" Dorothea's misplaced affections. The effect of this information on Dorothea is electric: "the blood rushed to Dorothea's face and neck painfully." She underwent "a metamorphosis," of "vague, alarmed consciousness" in which "one change terrified her as if it had been a sin; it was a violent shock of repulsion from her departed husband." This is felt in the same moment as a "sudden strange yearning of heart towards Will Ladislaw." When George Eliot says that "it had never before entered [Dorothea's] mind that [Will] could, under any circumstances, be her lover," Eliot is not understating the matter (339-40). Everyone, except perhaps Dorothea herself, has seen the direction of her emotions toward Ladislaw, and she has felt it, though she has repressed it until she can acknowledge it as the culmination of her (irrational) mourning and melancholia.

Dorothea's conscious longing for Will intensifies with the passage of time, with the distancing of his relationships in Middlemarch, and with the alienation of her desires from the false ideal of Casaubon. "Her soul thirsted to see" Ladislaw (372), as she feels more deeply the "chasm" that seems to divide them. The more she openly tells herself that it is best for them to separate, the more deeply she yearns for him. But articulation of the need for him to go away from Middlemarch is an expression of her own need to feel the separation that is necessary for her own psychic health, as well as it is an expression of her public stance of independence. In one of their affecting meetings to bid farewell, Dorothea offers to give Will the miniature of his grandmother. This carries on with her conscious desire that he should inherit property which is rightfully his, but it is more important than that. She tells Will, "It is wonderfully like you." In this she can consciously say what she had unconsciously felt when she turned to the miniature during her period of marital disappointment and emotional distress, when she saw in it "new breath and meaning" for her. Then it came alive to her as "the delicate woman's face which yet had a headstrong look, a peculiarity difficult to interpret" (190). It was "difficult" because it reflected a desire Dorothea could not acknowledge to her conscious self, though she could give her repressed desires some relief by seeing in the miniature an illumination ("sending out light") of a face which "was masculine and beamed on her." This is clear to all except Dorothea: she is seeing Will Ladislaw in the picture of his grandmother.

After Casaubon's death, after Dorothea has paid her price of conscious and unconscious mourning, she is free to be more conscious in her appreciation of that miniature. Now she can tell Will, "It is wonderfully like you." The reason Will's rejection of the miniature has a "peculiar sting" (377) for Dorothea is that she feels he is rejecting her in rejecting her gift. The fortunate thing about his rejection, however, is that Will is acknowledging the independent identity of the woman he loves. Dorothea has realized in this moment of ambivalent feeling what her soul had always yearned for: "to be wise herself." She has found in the symbolic use of the miniature a means of mixing her identity with "mother" and her ideal-love of "father" as lover. This completes her separation and liberates her for a free choice of someone to love without guilt.

The miniature performs what Jessica Benjamin looks for in "the multiple functions of the rapprochement complex," those being "the need to separate, the need to avoid ambivalence, and the need to find a subject who represents desire and excitement" (126). Dorothea later makes a gesture of great symbolic importance for resolving the ambivalences which remain in her feelings of independence and subjectivity of desire: "she took down the miniature from the wall and kept it before her, liking to blend the woman who had been too hardly judged with the grandson whom her own heart and judgment defended" (378). All that remains of importance to the *psychic* history of this character's growth is for Will himself to recognize what he means to Dorothea. When he does, the wisdom for which Dorothea has been searching, tested, and proved worthy, is finally hers to cherish. She throws off the trappings of mourning, and she blossoms in her joy. The light she saw in Will and in his grandmother's portrait is now her own light, shed on those around her with effects "incalculably diffusive" (578).

Notes

[1]*Middlemarch*. Edited by Bert G. Hornback. A Norton Critical Edition (New York: W.W. Norton & Company, Inc., 1977). All citations of the novel are from this text, identified by page numbers in parentheses in the essay.

[2]Leavis, F.R., *The Great Tradition*. Doubleday Anchor Books (Garden City, N.Y.: Doubleday & Company, Inc., 1954). The sections on George Eliot appeared first in *Scrutiny* in 1945 and 1946.

[3]James, Henry, Review of *Middlemarch*, in *Galaxy*, March 1873. Reprinted in *Henry James: Literary Criticism*, "English Writers," in The Library of America, edited by Leon Edel (New York: Literary Classics of the United States, 1984), pp. 958-66.

[4]Stephen, Leslie, "On *Middlemarch*," from *George Eliot* (London, 1902), pp. 174-84. Reprinted in the Norton Critical Edition of *Middlemarch*, pp. 657-63.

[5]Armstrong, Isobel, " 'Middlemarch': A Note on George Eliot's 'Wisdom'," in *Critical Essays on George Eliot*, edited by Barbara Hardy (London: Routledge & Kegan Paul, 1970), pp. 116-32.

[6]*"Middlemarch," Saturday Review*, 7 December 1872, pp. 733-4. Reprinted in the Norton Critical Edition of *Middlemarch*, pp. 645-8.

[7]Kenney, Edwin J., "George Eliot: Through the Looking-Glass," Norton Critical Edition of *Middlemarch* (1977), pp. 733-50.

[8]Kettle, Arnold, *An Introduction to The English Novel*. Volume One. *Defoe to George Eliot* (New York and Evanston: Harper and Row Publishers, 1960). Harper Torchbooks. First published in 1951 by the Hutchinson University Library.

[9]Hornback, Bert G., "The Moral Imagination of George Eliot," from *Papers On Language and Literature*, 8 (1972). Reprinted in the Norton Critical Edition of *Middlemarch*, pp. 670-83.

[10]Knoepflmacher, U.C., *Religious Humanism and The Victorian Novel: George Eliot, Walter Pater, and Samuel Butler* (Princeton, New Jersey: Princeton University Press, 1965). First Princeton Paperback Printing, 1970.

[11]Karl, Frederick R., *A Reader's Guide To The Nineteenth Century British Novel* (New York: The Noonday Press; Farrar, Strauss and Giroux, 1965). Originally published in 1964 as *An Age of Fiction: The Nineteenth Century British Novel*.

[12]Hardy, Barbara, "Implications and Incompleteness: George Eliot's *Middlemarch*," from *The Appropriate Form: An essay On The Novel* (London: Athlone Press, 1964), pp. 105-31. Reprinted in *The Victorian Novel: Modern Essays in Criticism*, edited by Ian Watt (London, Oxford, New York: Oxford University Press, 1971), pp. 289-310.

[13]Edwards, Lee R., "Women, Energy, and *Middlemarch*," from the *Massachusetts Review*, 13 (1972), 223-38. Reprinted in the Norton Critical Edition of *Middlemarch*, pp. 683-93.

[14]Benjamin, Jessica, "The Alienation of Desire: Women's Masochism and Ideal Love," in *Psychoanalysis and Women: Contemporary Reappraisals*, edited by Judith L. Alpert (Hillsdale, New Jersey: The Analytic Press, 1986), pp. 113-38.

[15]Miller, J. Hillis, *The Form of Victorian Fiction: Thackeray, Dickens, Trollope, George Eliot, Meredith, and Hardy* (Notre Dame and London: University of Notre Dame Press, 1968), p. 2.

[16]See the detailed analysis by Mark Schorer, "Fiction and the 'Matrix of Analogy'," from *The World We Imagine* (1948, 1968). Reprinted in the Norton Critical Edition of *Middlemarch*, pp. 706-14. Schorer shows how Eliot uses the word *light* to create "a kind of apocalyptic drama," p. 711.

Marriages of Partnership:
Elizabeth Gaskell and the
Victorian Androgynous Ideal

Laurie Buchanan

Marriage in Victorian society was generally understood to be a union of opposites. Men, with their logical thinking and aggressive temperament, were better suited for the competitive nature of the business world. Women were morally superior, it was believed, so their "proper sphere" was the home, where they provided a loving and peaceful haven for their husbands, instilled moral principles in their children, and created a stable and harmonious atmosphere for their families. Women's and men's personalities were naturally complementary, then: where women lacked the rationality needed for business, men had no instinctive tenderness to provide nurturance.

Critics have suggested that this maintenance of "separate spheres" was necessary for the Victorians because women's work in the home provided stability needed during a period of technological change and psychological turmoil. As Judith Newton has explained, women's ways in a sense were validated because women, with their moral tendencies, were able to influence men by "enlarging [their] capacity to feel, [thus facilitating] a sense of community and greater social concern" (128). Ruth Yeazell shows that the popular use of the marriage plot in Victorian novels served to allay fears of violence: "Social and political anxieties are contained—and eased—in the narrative of such a courtship" (127).[1]

The issue of gender roles and marriages for the Victorians is thus an extension of the changes occurring in society, and it preoccupies what is, on the surface, literature concerned with psychological, philosophical, and social conflicts. With this in mind, much feminist literary criticism has focused on the heroine in women's novels who must gain "masculine" confidence and rational thinking without losing her "feminine" sensitivity and perceptiveness. But feminist scholarship has failed to perceive that often in these works the heroine's education is paralleled by a male figure who "learns" tenderness and empathy. In George Eliot's *Middlemarch*, for example, the sensitive Will is Dorothea's reward for self-understanding; likewise, Jane Eyre's Mr. Rochester is not good enough for her until he can empathize with her loathing of forced dependence.

Elizabeth Gaskell's novels also generally contain a marriage plot in which the heroine must gain confidence and strength while the hero comes to accept his "feminine" side. But she is exceptional among her female peers. Male growth is usually secondary to the heroine's, and attempts to delineate a man in terms of his psychology are limited, but Gaskell's novels contain studies of men that not only reveal striking psychological perception but place Gaskell among the more aggressive Victorians in challenging patriarchal rule. Gaskell's view is that class struggles and individual psychological confusion result from a patriarchy that inhibits self-knowledge and prohibits feeling in men. Victorians were proud of their technological progress and personal wealth, but, at the same time, they were doubtful of the good of progress when gained at the expense of the individual's sense of importance and the feeling that life is meaningful in itself. Gaskell saw that it was male values of rational thought, detachment and competition that gained them this wealth *because* they prohibit caring and sympathy. Thus, she reveals in her studies of men that society's conflicts reflect the men's own inner polarities.

When Gaskell was working on *North and South*, for example, she wrote her friend, Emily Shaen, that the hero, John Thornton "should be developing himself... [He should remain consistently] large and strong and tender, and yet a master" (*Letters* 321). Consequently, Gaskell created a hero who comes to recognize his impulse for "feminine" empathy and humanitarian understanding, while never losing his masculine status. Thornton's growth is shaped around the *balancing* of "male" masterliness and "female" empathy, or androgyny. In Carolyn Heilbrun's definition, androgyny is "a spirit of reconciliation between the sexes; it suggests further, a full range of experience open to individuals who may, as women, be aggressive, as men, tender" (x-xi). Thornton's androgynous behavior suggests Gaskell's ideal of wholeness.

On the other hand, men in her novels who are shaped by masculine codes of conduct that prohibit integration of feminine feeling with masculine rationality are seen as failed individuals. They are either, like John Barton in *Mary Barton*, emotionally frustrated into violent anger, or, like Mr. Hamley in *North and South* and Lord Cumnor and Mr. Gibson in *Wives and Daughters*, frightened into limited and negligent individuals. In these portrayals, Gaskell makes androgyny a moral challenge to the Victorian patriarchal system, which she sees as denying sympathy and caring in men while encouraging in them competition, emotional isolation and rigidity. For Gaskell, androgyny works inseparably on personal and social levels. Striving toward an androgynous ideal, the individual's wholeness and autonomy will allow a marriage of partnership rather than one of dominance and passivity. In this way, marriage symbolizes society in Gaskell's novels, where the integration of the best of "masculine" and "feminine" traits allows a common sense of respect and community.

Gaskell's novella, *Cranford*, probably best dramatizes her feelings about the patriarchy and the limitations inherent for the individual within the Victorian "separate spheres" system. The novella sets up a society that "is in possession of the Amazons [where 'a] man'...'is so in the way in the house' " (39). Cranford is a world of "elegant economy, [in which] we blinded ourselves to the vulgar fact, that we were, all of us, people of very moderate means" (42), where "their dress is very independent of fashion" (40), and where the women are bound together by their "love for gentility and distaste for mankind" (45). In short, these women have rejected the "vulgar" male world of money, power, and competition, "subjects that savoured of commerce and trade" (41), in favor of a society where sharing, caring, and tenderness are the fundamental goals. More concerned with maintaining a community than striving for personal material gain, Cranford sustains itself through women's friendships and interdependence.

In terms of androgynous issues, the novel contrasts masculine and feminine values. Negative male values are defined through such symbols as the "obnoxious railroad," which connects Cranford to nearby Drumble, and which the Cranford ladies have "vehemently petitioned against" (42). To them, trains represent scientific progress and the speed and force with which technology is invading individual lives. It is ironic that Captain Brown, who has connections with the railroad, "is killed by them nasty cruel trains" (55). Saving a baby from the oncoming machine, Brown is killed by the very thing that personifies progress and financial gain in the male world. His violent death reinforces the Cranford women's fear of technological growth and personal gain at the expense of individual importance. The loss of the significance of the individual is the reason they have established Cranford.

It is not, however, Captain Brown who represents negative male values. On the contrary, he has been accepted by Cranford because of his "excellent masculine good sense" (43) as well as for his "feminine" empathy which allows him to respect women's ways and not try to control or change them. For the women of Cranford, he embodies the best of masculinity and femininity: while thinking rationally, he is also nurturing and patient, a friend to the women and a mother to his daughter. His violent death, then, suggests Gaskell's fear of ultimate annihilation of human kindness and true wholeness by a world where technological progress reigns.

Gaskell's other male figures in *Cranford* also not only show feminine compassion and understanding but are more explicitly androgynous figures. Like Captain Brown, Thomas Holbrook "despised every refinement which had not its roots deep down in humanity" (69). He is, therefore, according to Patricia A. Wolfe, "worthy of [Miss Matty's] love" (162).[2] Matty's brother, Peter, returning to Cranford, is accepted there because he, too, shows his feminine compassion in his gentle, loving ways. Like Captain Brown and Thomas Holbrook, Peter provides "masculine good sense," assistance and protection, but he does not try to control Cranford. Therefore, each of these men can be nurturing, but none loses his masculine status. Peter, for example, has a demeanor of "tender relaxation" (207), but because he was a prisoner of war, he has also led the life of a survivor and hero. These men, then, are assimilated into Cranford community life because they embody humanity at its best: they are strong, courageous and self-confident, as well as tender, flexible, and giving.

Gaskell's depiction of men in Cranford falls within a pattern of androgynous males that she had established in her earlier works. In *Mary Barton* (1848), Job Leigh is father and mother to Margaret, nurturing her as a parentless baby and caring for her and the household when she becomes blind. Furthermore, while Job initially wants no part of the workers' union because of its tendency to use violence rather than communication to achieve its ends, he eventually agrees to join in order to maintain harmony. While his willingness to compromise might suggest the negative female aspects of passivity and self-sacrifice, Gaskell instead sees his actions as reflecting clear thinking and flexibility. It is Job who provides and sustains the moral outlook of the novel; it is his faith in love and humanity, seen in his caring and self-sacrificing, that signifies Gaskell's hope for a supportive rather than a destructive community.

Likewise, Thurstan Benson, the minister in *Ruth* (1853), is no patriarch; rather it is his sympathy and compassion that provide the moral theme in the book. Thurstan and his sister compose a family in this novel, and their mutual respect and interdependence contrast with their neighbors, the Bradshaws, whose home is run by a Brontesque Mr. Brocklehurst-like figure. Dominant and rigid, Mr. Bradshaw, Gaskell says, "was a tall, large-boned, iron man; stern, powerful and authoritative... [while h]is wife was sweet and gentle-looking but as if she was thoroughly broken into submission" (152). Benson, however, is part of a brother and sister household, in which, because there is no domination, "their lives were pure and good, not merely from a lovely and beautiful nature, but from some law, the obedience to which was, of itself, harmonious peace" (141). As a result of their androgynous personalities and relationships, these characters uphold the human right of love, tolerance and sympathy. The "harmonious peace" of their lives allows them to take Ruth in and instill in her self-confidence and renewed faith and love after she has been abandoned by her lover and scorned and rejected by society. Her death from a fatal disease after voluntarily nursing her child's father underscores her victimization, and it is Gaskell's condemnation of the hypocrisy and brutality of a patriarchy that insists on women's sexual ignorance yet ostracizes them when they fall prey to careless men.

While Gaskell's early works establish male models of androgyny and suggest a motif of the ideal of non-patriarchal, non-sexist behavior and society, *North and South* (1855) offers the same possibilities with a more conscious emphasis on her hero and heroine's psychological growth and the social possibilities such growth promises. Here, she confronts class problems through the relationship between John Thornton and Margaret Hale, whose antagonism initially represents the contrasting attitudes of the urban north and agricultural south. Hero and heroine delineate, as Margaret Ganz says, "the particular merits of the masculine principles of severity, self-reliance and authority, and of the feminine instincts of tenderness, dependence, and conciliation" (81); their union encompasses the idea of reconciliation of classes through sympathy and understanding. Margaret, learning a "right judgment" (489), tempers her emotions with rational knowledge, and Thornton learns the destructiveness of seeing his workers and Margaret as his possessions and objects. Thus, the theme of reconciliation in *North and South* delineates the consequences possible for an androgynous individual and society.

Described initially as a self-made man who depends only on himself for his success, Thornton defends his "right" of dominance: "[E]very man has had to stand in an unchristian and isolated position, apart from and jealous of his brother-man: constantly afraid of his rights being trenched upon" (169). Unlike women, who, because of their traditional training as mothers, generally value communication and relationships, Thornton as male alienates himself from others by asserting his authority in "communicating" his place as "master" in society. This, Gaskell suggests, is a decided result of the competitive marketplace; it is individual against individual rather than communication and community, the dominance of masculine over feminine values in a patriarchy. Thus, as Dierdre David states, "by the very nature of his aggressiveness. . .[Thornton] seeks to isolate himself from [others], to leave them behind, in his climb to power" (24).

In the riot staged by the poor and starving workers in his mill, for example, Thornton sees only "wild beasts" instead of men. As "master," he silently asserts control by standing "with his arms folded; still as a statue" (233). Then, to reinforce his "right" of power over his workers, he uses physical force to break up the unruly mob. Margaret, however, standing beside Thornton, is emboldened by her "womanly" empathy. In the same circumstances, she "[forgets] herself, and [feels] only an intense sympathy. . . [for these] workmen as if they were human beings" (230-231). Thus, unlike Thornton, who alienates himself further from his men by shielding himself behind rigid silence and violence, Margaret speaks to the men, pleading with them to leave Thornton's house and use their more reasonable natures in this crisis. But Thornton, using violence to stop violence, represents for Gaskell the physical force typically used by men to solve conflicts, what Patsy Stoneman sees as "subhuman" male "bestiality explicitly related to the refusal or inability of both sides to engage in speech" (121). Gaskell's point is to emphasize the potential chaos and the disruption of the necessary social intercourse by male aggression and anger when untempered by female need for communication and understanding. While Margaret's plea for compassion does not serve to calm the workers any more than Thornton's defensive and rigid silence, by contrasting male selfishness and pride with female selflessness and empathy, Gaskell seeks to encourage communication that would generate sympathy and compromise and heal wounds caused by the domination of one human being over another. Gaskell avoids economic issues of class oppression[3] but her theme clearly suggests that androgynous behavior can work toward understanding between people and therefore between classes. While remaining a "master," Thornton gives up his need to control and comes to see the importance of respect and communication: "Such intercourse is the breath of life," he says (525).

Thornton learns this compassion through his friendship with his worker, Higgins, his own eventual bankruptcy, and his growing respect for Margaret. These three experiences demonstrate Gaskell's vision of a fully formed person. In his loathing of violence and his preference for communication and compromise, Higgins' character echoes Job Leigh in *Mary Barton*. Embodying feminine compassion combined with masculine dignity, both characters represent androgynous figures. Forced by poverty into a confrontation with Thornton to regain his former job, Higgins shows both determination and patience, virtues Thornton admires. Thus, after first reinforcing his position of authority by making Higgins wait six hours for a meeting, Thornton's hard indifference diminishes and he allows himself to listen to his employee. Higgins reveals to Thornton his needs and motivations, thus showing his own pride and need for work as a means of self-worth. Thornton, seeing their shared values, sheds his authoritative pride, talks with Higgins and thus acquires respect for him. As Gaskell describes it: "Once brought face to face, man to man, with an individual of the masses around him, and... *out* of the clear of master and workman...[Higgins and Thornton] had begun to recognize that 'we all of us have one human heart' " (511). Through Higgins' patience, determination and lack of antagonism, then, Thornton begins to see his workers as humans rather than as animals he must control with violence.

As Margaret begins to understand his rational attitudes about labor management, Thornton stops seeing her as "an extension of his life that may be transformed by his devotion into an image of worship" (Lansbury 112) and comes to recognize her as his peer. He watches her develop strength and assertiveness as she cares for her ill mother and supports her emotionally weak father. Thornton also sees her courage and compassion in facing the workers during the riot. These crises lead Margaret to acquire independence, self-confidence, and dignity, and his feelings for her change accordingly from sexual attraction to admiration.

While Margaret has shown her growth in understanding masculine rationality, part of Thornton's respect for her also emerges from the necessity of his being forced to admit weakness and need. His bankruptcy, perhaps like Rochester's physical crippling in *Jane Eyre*, puts him in a dependent position and thus on a more equal plane with women. His losses in the stock exchange force him to take money from her to redeem ownership of the mill. For both Rochester and Thornton, experiencing a (female's) sense of powerlessness encourages the necessary empathy that deems them worthy of marriage to the by now similarly androgynous heroine. This reward is acquired when both hero and heroine suffer and grow simultaneously. Margaret and Thornton gain self-knowledge and sympathy through experiencing each other's feelings. Thornton has shown his humanity by accepting Margaret as his peer and by opening up a soup kitchen for his workers (where he also eats), and Margaret has given up her idealized image of the country for the more rational and realistic life in the city. That Gaskell sees Thornton and Margaret now as equal is symbolized by their marriage at the end of *North and South*.

For Gaskell, as for many of her peers, need for communication reflects male/female relationships as exemplified within her personal life. Her marriage was a typical one in which the man dealt with the rational world and the woman was the emotional and moral guide for the family. But Gaskell felt the pressure of her husband's alienation: "Wm I dare say kindly won't allow me ever to talk to him about anxieties, while it would be SUCH A RELIEF often" (45), she says in a letter to her sister-in-law, Anne Robson. While regretting the burdens this placed on them, however, women writers recognized that their emotional strength was a means of acquiring the power of survival. They saw that female need for communication and moral action allowed them a superiority which in fact contrasts with male psychological weakness. Thus, like Eliot's Dorothea Brooke or Bronte's Jane Eyre, Gaskell's heroines possess the emotional strength that in fact carries *men* through *their* crises or makes up for *their* constitutional weakness. Margaret, like most of Gaskell's heroines, in this way is like Dorothea Brooke. Ellin Ringler says in *"Middlemarch*: A Feminist Perspective" that though she is socially inferior to men, Dorothea's "natural" ability to gather and assert emotional strength shows that her "psychological strength prevails, and she emerges more powerful than the men.... Dorothea... turns to men in *Middlemarch* for guidance and is...consistently disappointed" (58-9). She, in fact, "becomes a teacher herself...[because, Eliot infers, the] major male characters...display...'moral stupidity' " (59). Thus, it is, ironically, the men who need and are guided by Dorothea's strength and steadiness of character rather than she who receives their protection and advice.

Like Eliot's Dorothea, Gaskell's women project empathy and psychological strength, enabling them to endure what men cannot. In *Mary Barton*, when Jem Wilson is imprisoned for the murder of Harry Carson, Jr., Mary saves him and morally justifies refusing exposure of her father as Carson's murderer until she can prove Jem's innocence. It is Mary who generates a return to stability, while her father, unable to rationalize his frustration and growing feelings of impotence, murders the Carson boy to get revenge on the upper classes. Likewise, in *North and South*, Margaret must replace her emotionally weak father when Mr. Hale decides to leave the ministry because he cannot reconcile his religious doubt. Margaret takes over all the "father's" responsibilities, arranging everything, from household management to care of her ill mother, to relaying intimate information to her mother that her father fears disclosing, to clearing her brother from charges of mutiny. She provides the strength necessary to keep the family together during a long period of continual crises, strength her father cannot provide. Mr. Hale, in fact, becomes more and more dependent on Margaret for emotional strength as he becomes less capable of dealing with the world.

What is important to Gaskell in family relationships is that the family structure provide emotional stability. It is the parents' self-assurance as individuals and their ability then as a couple to demonstrate control and provide the necessary support. This is the basis, as Jenni Calder says, of Gaskell's families, for members to "tend to share in the work and responsibility, and to be united by a sense of love and common interest" (68). But typically in Gaskell's novels, it is men who lack a sense of their emotional side and who thus are limited in their ability to communicate love and support. Because of this lack, they fail as fathers, husbands, and ultimately, as human beings. Like Eliot, Gaskell saw men as needing to rely on women for psychological strength. In *Mary Barton*, when his wife dies, John Barton feels "[o]ne of the ties which bound him down to the gentle humanities of earth was loosened...[and h]is gloom and his sternness became habitual instead of occasional" (58). Unable to count on his wife's emotional strength to console and guide him, and lacking strength of his own, he turns his frustration into violent anger which leads him to drug addiction, murder, and finally his own death. John is contrasted with Job Leigh, who, because of his androgynous nature, is more emotionally stable than John. John shows his emotional weakness by letting his anger and fear control him. He even goes so far as to become physically violent towards his daughter, Mary.

In *North and South* and *Wives and Daughters* (1866), Gaskell provides a more thorough psychological study of fathers and daughters. Like Hale's psychological impotence in *North and South* which affects Margaret's emotional security, in *Wives and Daughters*, when the widower Gibson remarries, his daughter, Molly, feels "as if the piece of solid ground on which she stood had broken from the shore, and she was drifting out to the infinite sea alone" (63). Gibson remarries not to find a companion for himself but to provide a mother for Molly. When Molly expresses fear and anger about his marriage, Mr. Gibson's reaction is to quickly leave the room rather than talk with his daughter. Thus, Gaskell reinforces Gibson's emotional isolation by his physically alienating himself from Molly and therefore from involvement in her potentially emotional adolescence. Perhaps it is because he is aware of his fear of emotions that he disengages himself from his daughter. But his leaving shuts both him and Molly off from self-growth and intimacy, and it ultimately closes Gibson off from his more human side. His just reward is marrying the morally blind and egotistical Clare Kirkpatrick. Fortunately, Molly appears to be more self-assured than her father; like Margaret, she has the strength that a clear understanding of herself allows. She can thus take control of her own maturing process and avoid her shallow stepmother's influence, while Mr. Gibson merely retreats into his work.

In all of these cases, men appear to *decide* that they cannot cope with emotional stress. They choose escape into "masculine" violence or weakness. Barton's turning his frustration into murder, though necessary to Gaskell's social plea, is a choice as clearly as Gibson's leaving Molly alone or Hale's beseeching Margaret to discuss her parents' private matters with her mother. Neither man has the moral courage to confront himself; each shows fear rather than "manly wisdom." As A.O.J. Cockshut says of Gibson, "[T]here is...a moral barrier within himself...which is a decision of will, not a failure of intelligence..." (93-4). Ignoring their familial responsibilities, these men reveal their psychological limitations; their avoidance of emotional involvement and fear of intimacy is ultimately Gaskell's moral judgment of them as human beings.

If Gaskell so consistently presents strong women and weak men, and if male characters are often moral failures, one might suggest that Gaskell saw a separatist "female utopia" rather than androgyny as an ideal. Instead, however, she punishes "feminine" passiveness, fear of the world and psychological fragility in her characters who embody these qualities. Even in *Cranford*, where she appears to celebrate a feminine society, her emphasis, as has been shown, is on androgyny and not on an exemplification of women's superiority. It is clear that the men in *Cranford* must not lose their masculine status as they gain feminine insights and compassion. Similarly, women must combine their feminine strengths with masculine knowledge of the world. As Wolfe explains, in *Cranford*, Matty grows from "extreme femininity" to a competent town leader who rules not through the rigid codes established by her father and upheld by her sister, but out of her own inherent dignity and growth to self-knowledge and good sense. Through Matty's integration of feminine compassion and masculine rationality, Wolfe says, Cranford learns to "emphasize its humanity as well as its propriety" (162); thus the "temperament of the town" is changed from her father's and Miss Deborah's limiting and "perverted sense of feminism to a natural application of femininity" (162). While celebrating female need for interdependence in *Cranford*, Gaskell also criticizes the destructiveness of feminine passivity and lack of knowledge and logic when not tempered by male assertiveness and self-confidence.

Similarly, Gaskell portrays men who embody mostly feminine characteristics as weak, negligent, fearful and generally unfit for the world. She suggests that it is their husbands' lack of understanding and inability to provide emotional support that cause the illnesses of Mrs. Hamley in *Wives and Daughters* and Mrs. Hale in *North and South*. Of the Hamleys, Gaskell says, "[P]ossibly Mrs. Hamley would not have sunk into the condition of a chronic invalid, if her husband had cared a little more for her various tastes, or allowed her the companionship of those who did" (73). While this might suggest that Hamley is cold and controlling, Gaskell views him as passive: when Mrs. Hamley dies, the Squire is depicted as pathetically weak. He has been dependent on his wife, Gaskell writes, "just as a child is at ease when with someone who is both firm and gentle" (286). In *North and South*, Mrs. Hale is an invalid, and when she sees Mr. Hale turning over his responsibilities as a husband to Margaret, she becomes jealous and more fretful, hardly the antidote to illness. Gaskell describes Hale in all his psychological withering: "[E]very day he was more overpowered; the world became more bewildering.... [H]e shrank more and more" (49). Contrasted with Gaskell's ideal of the tender yet "masterful" man, Hale's sensitivity is portrayed as pathetic.

Another emotionally crippled man is Lord Cumnor, the aristocratic society leader in *Wives and Daughters*. His punishment for his inability to take control of his life is his wife's nearly scornful alienation from him. Lady Cumnor responds to her husband's incapacity by asserting more strength, thereby replacing him in his traditional male role as maintaining stability within the family. She emotionally isolates herself because she resents Lord Cumnor's inability to provide direction and psychological support. Delineating his emotional dependence rather than a shared respect, Gaskell says Lord Cumnor is "always full of admiration for all [his wife's] words and deeds, and used to boast of her wisdom, her benevolence, her power and dignity, in her absence, as if by this means he could buttress up his own more feeble nature" (127).

These men demonstrate "female" sensitivity but to the point of emotional incapacitation. They therefore embody the negative aspects of femininity. But more importantly in terms of criticizing the patriarchy, Gaskell shows these men as victims of Victorian masculine codes of conduct which require control and dominance. She suggests there are no role models for passive men; thus, in the same way that John Barton's anger is turned to violence, their feelings are translated into weakness and failure to cope with the world. For Gaskell, their psychological negligence is as destructive as Barton's violence. This is not to say that women's ways are "better" but that both male and female traits should be combined for individual strength, autonomy and integration of self. When this is accomplished, one can, as Nina Auerbach says of Miss Matty in *Cranford*, see oneself not as isolated from the world, a "victim of the masculine system...but as part of a whole" (282). As a result of the patriarchy's insistence on male suppression of feeling, Hamley, Hale, Cumnor and Gibson represent those men who fail to positively incorporate their essential feminine sides. Thus they stagnate, remaining empty and unhappy.

According to Judith Newton, the Victorians recognized that "[m]ale selfishness and lack of feeling...are identified as a primary cause of problems in class and gender relationships" (129). Like her peers, then, Gaskell saw that feminine empathy was necessary in healing class conflict and easing psychological confusion. But she is unique among Victorian writers in the depth of her studies of men in marriage and their own personal fears and inhibitions. She is sympathetic with these men, showing how they are conditioned and confined by society's male dominant orientation. Through these analyses, Gaskell takes marriage out of its idealized position as reward for feminine growth and instead shows it as a limiting and disappointing institution for the individual within a patriarchy. The loss of the ability for empathy ultimately cuts relational bonds that are fundamental to sustaining a growing society itself. Like Eliot, what Gaskell really wanted was "to assert the rightful balance between feminine and masculine components" (Knoepflmacher 133). Thus, in writing novels that overtly exposed social ills, Gaskell uses the social tract of the time to examine more thoroughly external causes of male inner polarity within an androcentric culture. Gaskell reveals through masculine emotional weakness and the destructiveness of a competitive nature the importance and validity of feminine feeling and communication. Although ingrained behaviors and traditional presumptions about sex roles might argue against the development of an androgynous model, Gaskell continually demonstrates the possibility, even the necessity, of change. The ideal Victorian marriage becomes, for her, not a balancing of sex roles between partners but a balancing of typical roles within each individual in the marriage.

Notes

[1] There are many interesting and valid analyses of the causes, utilization and consequences of women attaining "power." Nancy Armstrong shows how women's novels were a way of acting on their power and were an outgrowth of society's need for stability. But, not all women were unhappy in their traditional roles. Donald Stone says that "many Victorian men...helped popularize the feminine cause...in spite of female opposition" (67).

[2] Holbrook's and Peter's function within Gaskell's theme of wholeness and humanity, is also discussed in both Patricia A. Wolfe's and Margaret Tarratt's articles.

[3] David says, however, that Gaskell "never questions the economic structure of industrialized society.... This doctrine, of course, is as mythical as the belief in the mutual independence of master and worker, for as long as the economic relationship of employer and employee pertains between Thornton and his men, they can have no intercourse with each other which is not affected by it" (20-1).

Works Cited

Armstrong, Nancy. "The Rise of Feminine Authority in the Novel." *Novel* 15 (1982): 127-45.

Auerbach, Nina. "Elizabeth Gaskell's 'Sly Javelins': Governing Women in Cranford and Haworth." *Modern Language Quarterly* 38 (1977): 276-91.

Calder, Jenni. *Women and Marriage in Victorian Fiction.* New York: Oxford UP, 1976.

Cockshut, A.O.J. *Man and Woman.* London: Collins, 1977.

David, Dierdre. *Fictions of Resolution in Three Victorian Novels.* New York: Columbia UP, 1981.

Ganz, Margaret. *The Artist in Conflict.* New York: Twayne, 1969.

Gaskell, Elizabeth. *Cranford.* New York: Penguin, 1976.

———. "To Emily Shaen." 27 October 1854. *The Letters of Elizabeth Gaskell.* Eds. J.A.V. Chapple and Arthur Pollard. Manchester: Manchester UP, 1966.

———. *Mary Barton.* New York: Penguin, 1970.

———. *North and South*. New York: Penguin, 1970.

———. *Ruth*. London: J.M. Dent, 1982.

———. *Wives and Daughters*. New York: Penguin, 1981.

Heilbrun, Carolyn. *Toward a Recognition of Androgyny*. New York: Harper & Rowe, 1973.

Knoepflmacher, U.C. "Unveiling Men: Power and Masculinity in George Eliot's Fiction." *Men by Women*. Ed. Janet Todd. New York: Holmes & Meier, 1981: 130-46.

Lansbury, Coral. *Elizabeth Gaskell: The Novel of Social Change*. New York: Barnes & Noble, 1975.

Newton, Judith. "Making—and Remaking—History: Another Look at the 'Patriarchy'." *Feminist Issues in Literary Scholarship*. Ed. Shari Benstock. Bloomington: Indiana UP, 1987: 124-40.

Ringler, Ellin. "*Middlemarch*: A Feminist Perspective," *Studies in the Novel*. xv (1983): 55-61.

Stone, Donald. "Victorian Feminism and the Nineteenth Century Novel." *Women's Studies*. (1972): 65-91.

Stoneman, Patsy. *Elizabeth Gaskell*. Bloomington: Indiana UP, 1987.

Tarratt, Margaret. "*Cranford* and 'the Strict Code of Gentility'." *Studies in the Novel* 18 (1968): 152-63.

Wolfe, Patricia A. "Structure and Movement in *Cranford*." *Nineteenth Century Fiction* 23 (1968): 161-76.

Yeazell, Ruth Barnard. "Why Political Novels Have Heroines: *Sybil*, *Mary Barton* and *Felix Holt*." *Novel* 19 (1985): 126-44.

"The Web of Self-Strangulation"[1]
Mothers, Daughters and the Question of Marriage in the Short Stories of Mary Wilkins Freeman

Mary R. Reichardt

"The family is the first community we know, and it takes the shape of Mother," Nina Auerbach states in her study of women in fiction, *Communities of Women* (34). For Mary Wilkins Freeman, this truth was indisputable. Although her own mother died when Freeman was still a young woman, the spectre of 'mother' as an authority and power figure continued to haunt her adult life, manifesting itself time and again in a majority of her nearly 220 short stories and in several of her novels as well.[2] And the pictures she paints of mother and motherhood are scarcely rosy. Far from the warmth and comfort of Alcott's Marmee in *Little Women*, for example, a woman who guides and nourishes her loving, closely-knit family, Freeman's typical mother is physically and emotionally burdened, her family broken and bereft of intimacy. What strength or fortitude she evinces is born mostly of desperation or necessity, and rarely of inner security or confidence. Her relationship with her husband is strained; at best, the two staunchly fulfill the duties of their separate spheres, she in the kitchen and he on the farm, and make no pretense of conjugal intimacy.

But more likely, a mother in Freeman's world is raising a child or children alone; her husband has either died or deserted the family, many times to "go west." This scene indeed reflects the reality of New England village life as Freeman knew it: economic depression was widespread between 1870 and 1900, and men and teenagers left behind the elderly and women with small children in search of gainful employment.[3] The strain on such women becomes, at times, unbearable. Children growing up in such an atmosphere quickly learn to be "seen and not heard"; lonely and misunderstood, they regard their parent with a fear that often continues into their adult years. And by far the greatest tension between mother and daughter in Freeman's stories occurs over the question of that child's marriage when she comes of age. A mother often bitterly resents her child's choices, and the child resents her mother's interference.

Freeman has several stories of the relationship between fathers and daughters, as well as between mothers and sons, but her largest group of stories explores the emotional ties between mothers and daughters in the

109

family. Freeman's young women expect, for the most part, to become wives and mothers. Yet their own experience with and observation of a woman's role in the family show them it is one replete with trouble and frustration. They see little to emulate in their mothers' lives.

Furthermore, many of Freeman's mother and daughter stories concern problems with separation and differentiation of the self, both mother from daughter and daughter from mother. Our knowledge of Freeman's biography, sketchy as it is in details about her early family life, may throw some light on this recurring theme. Her mother Eleanor was a firm, practical, and ambitious woman, her father Warren a sensitive, "weak but lovable" man (Foster 170). Though he possessed considerable talent as a builder and architect, Warren Wilkins' business ventures failed repeatedly, reducing the family through most of Mary's childhood and teenage years to near-desperate straits. Half way through his life, Wilkins seemed to give up. "Though still witty on occasion and fully presentable in black suit on a Sunday morning, Warren Wilkins began to slip into the background," Foster writes. "The neighbors thought of him as a 'putterer' and as one who was always doing little services for others, partly perhaps to maintain his own dignity" (37). Eleanor Wilkins bore four children, three of whom died before reaching adulthood. Mary's younger sister Anna Wilkins, a talented, active, and popular young woman and clearly her parents' favorite, died suddenly of "disease of the mesenteric" in 1876 (Foster 40). Mary was the only remaining child. The following year necessity forced the family to move into the house of their minister-neighbor where Mrs. Wilkins assumed the job of housekeeper. Three years later, in 1880, she herself died unexpectedly while still in middle-age.

Evidence from both Foster's and Kendrick's biographies of Freeman show the young Mary as both a strong-willed yet clinging and dependent child, sensitive and moody like her father. A dreamer and a brooder, she must have sometimes felt her energetic mother's displeasure as she sat at the window doing nothing but looking out for hours on end (Foster 42). Certainly, she experienced her mother's shame and the tension mounting between her parents as their financial situation worsened daily. Moreover, after Eleanor Wilkins' death, both father and daughter were sorely pressed to manage themselves: Warren Wilkins died three years later, and Mary spent her adult life under the care of a succession of dominating, mother-like figures.[4]

Few if any of Freeman's letters refer directly to her childhood, but several reveal her belief that men were, in general, immature and insufficient, even superfluous in the family. Women, on the other hand, were the practical ones, those in charge. In 1912, for example, ten years after she married, Freeman wrote to a close woman friend,

So your husband is off in pursuit of bugs and things again. Well, mine goes up once a week to look after business, and the rest of the time, smokes and stays here like a real nice happy boy. It pleases me to see him having such a good time. He gets nervous, and used up if he does not have good times. I imagine most men do. Women have, on the whole...more back bone under difficulties. Why not? They have had harder training. They or their ancestors have borne and reared the men...Also, women have not...enough time to waste on such disgraceful affairs as the Chicago Convention, where all the little boys without their ma's handy to spank 'em, fought and rolled in the dust of politics for office. (Kendrick 340)

Freeman's hesitancy to marry may well have resulted both from her childhood experience of a dominating mother and a weak father, and from her continuing childlike need for a mother herself. What we *can* ascertain is that her life-long dependency on strong women, and the tension portrayed between mother and daughter in many of her stories, indicate unresolved conflict with her own mother from her formative years. Moreover, this conflict not only colored her adult relationships with both men and other women but influenced her views of womanhood in general. The looming spectre of 'mother' thus becomes all important in understanding Freeman's themes.

* * * * *

In 1898 at the age of forty-six and yet unmarried, Mary Wilkins Freeman published a tale in her collection of stories set in the Puritan past, *Silence and Other Stories* which, bordering as it does between fantasy and reality, brings us closer than perhaps any other of her stories to the problem of a young woman's relationship with her parents. In "The Buckley Lady," Persis Buckley grows up happily in a pious New England family, but at the age of twelve a dramatic event completely changes her life. As she is gathering wood in the forest one day, a splendid coach with a handsome young gentleman inside appears. Catching sight of the beautiful young girl and falling in love with her, the man strikes a pact with her father: he will return to marry Persis one day; the family meanwhile is to prepare her accordingly. Thereafter, relieved from her usual chores, she is made to dress daily in her finest gown and to sit in the best parlor, stitching daintily upon a sampler.

Though the novelty of the situation attracts her at first, Persis soon grows restless and bored; unable to comprehend her parents' orders, "her first conviction of the inconsistency of the human heart was upon [her], and she was dazed." The days and weeks roll on as Persis' entire family deny themselves for this one child who "represented all the faint ambition" of their lives. The finest materials are purchased for her stitching; she is given piano and dancing lessons, and allowed to read such formerly forbidden novels as *Clarissa Harlowe*, all in preparation for the great event to befall her. Their staunch Puritan neighbors soon begin to impose "a subtle spiritual bombardment of doubt and envy and disapproval" upon the Buckley family, the preacher even directing a sermon toward them on "the folly of worldly ambition and trust in the vain promises of princes." Persis, "living the life of a forlorn princess in a fairy tale...waited in her prison, cast about and bound, body and spirit, by the will and ambition of her parents, like steel cobwebs, for the prince who never came."

Like all good fairy tales, the story, however, ends happily. At the age of twenty-five, after nearly thirteen years in her "prison," Persis falls in love with a local boy she has seen from her window. He manages to steal her away from her parents one night, but only by renting a magnificent coach and disguising himself as the handsome prince. His hopes dashed once he learns the truth, Persis' father goes to his grave, carving on his own tombstone a verse condemning his daughter's "ingratitude."

In the story of Persis Buckley, Freeman expresses in fantasy what she explores again and again in her more realistic short stories. A young girl, reaching marriageable age, suddenly finds her relationship with her parents or parent dramatically changed. With mounting anxiety, she realizes she is now seen more as a commodity to be sold than as a child to be nurtured. Indeed, as Freeman herself experienced in her many years as a single adult at home, a woman's opportunities for contributing to the family finances were laughably pitiful in a small, impoverished town that scarcely needed a second piano teacher or bonnet maker. An adult daughter at home, therefore, was often a financial burden on the family.

However, Freeman shows us that this was not the primary source of tension between an adolescent and her parents. Rather, as a daughter reaches maturity, the complex and highly emotional bonds uniting her to her parents—and especially her mother—are profoundly disrupted. Chodorow well describes this changing mother/daughter relationship in the following passage:

Mothers feel ambivalent toward their daughters, and react to their daughters' ambivalence toward them. They desire both to keep daughters close and to push them into adulthood. This ambivalence in turn creates more anxiety in their daughters and provokes attempts by these daughters to break away. (135)

Although Freeman's letters reveal nothing about her own mother's desire to see her married, her stories frequently express much anxiety and tension on the part of both mother and daughter over the question of the daughter's marriage. Donovan's statement in *New England Local Color Literature* that in Freeman's world "mothers...are trying to keep their daughters 'home,' in a female world" (121) is, when one examines these stories, simply not true. Freeman's mothers for the most part are actively engaged in procuring well-made marriages for their daughters, but not always for the most laudable of reasons; that is, the daughters' happiness. Perhaps because they themselves had poor or unfulfilling marriages, mothers in Freeman's world often expect their daughters' marriages to confer on them the emotional or financial security or prestige they found lacking in their own lives. They therefore use every means to push their daughters toward marriages which fulfill their own ambitions.

If they realize their mothers' duplicity (and Freeman shows that they often do), daughters feel trapped: their moral upbringing has taught them to be obedient to their parents' wishes, yet as they experience their mothers' interference, they grow increasingly frustrated with and even hostile toward them. As Gardiner has pointed out in "On Female Identity and Writing by Women," such suppressed aggression and anger often contribute to forming the image of the "bad mother" in a daughter's mind. "This mother-villain is so frightening because she is what the daughter fears to become and what her infantile identifications predispose her to become," she states (Abel, *Writing* 186). The "bad" or "villain" mother appears frequently in Freeman stories about marriage, as do several other mother figures that could be characterized in more general, and perhaps archetypal terms: the vampire, the witch, the self-sacrificing mother.[5] Only by the daughter's marrying can the ambivalent guilt and hostility on the part of both mother and daughter perhaps be expiated. Strangely, the mother figure is then sometimes, often grossly, glorified. Although written of Jane Austen's endings, Nina Auerbach's statement that "in the end, the malevolent power of the mother is ennobled by being transferred to the hero, and the female community...is dispersed with relief in the solidity of marriage" may also thus apply to several Freeman stories (55).

A daughter in a Freeman story, therefore, who for one reason or another rejects marriage or her mother's choice of a suitor, finds that the mother grows bitter and petty; the mother, on the other hand, sees her child's ingratitude not only as a personal offense against her but as an offense against Providence itself. In Freeman's world, then, the daughter's awaiting of a "handsome Prince" is merely a dream perpetuated by a mother who often has little else to hope for in life. Usually, he fails to appear. Freeman's many stories on this subject, some of them painfully poignant, involve the aftermath of that dream as mother and child struggle to readjust their relationship in the light of their personal disappointment.

Two of Freeman's early stories can serve to illustrate an ambitious mother's desire for her daughter to marry a man who has money; such a marriage would allow that mother prestige among her women neighbors. Mrs. Joy in "Up Primrose Hill" (1891), seeing daughter Annie snub the attentions of wealthy Henry Simpson, confronts her in anger. When Annie confesses she loves poor Frank Rice instead, her mother mocks her, further instilling guilt by bidding her remember the result of such "love" in her own life:

'Oh! Well, I s'pose that's all that's necessary, then' [Mrs. Joy says]. 'I s'pose if you— *love* him, there ain't anything more to be said.' The manner with which her mother's voice lingered upon *love* made it seem at once shameful and ridiculous to the girl...

'I guess you'll find out that there's something besides *love*,' [her mother continues]. 'When you get settled down there in that little cooped-up house with his father and mother and crazy uncle, an' don't have enough money to buy you a calico dress, you'll find out it ain't all— *love*...You know how I've dug an' scrimped all my life, an' you know how we're situated now; it's jest all we can do to get along...If you marry Frank Rice you'll have to live jest as I've done...You'll have to work an' slave, an' never go anywhere

nor have anything...An' if you have Henry Simpson, you'll live over in Lennox, an'
have everything nice, an' people will look up to you.'

Before such ridicule Annie is silenced, yet she inwardly seethes with
hostility toward her mother and disdain for that mother's choice. In one
of Freeman's most popular stories, "Louisa" (1891), however, a daughter's
marriage is not merely a choice but a necessity for the family: without it
an invalid mother and senile grandfather face starvation. Yet Louisa refuses
to marry the only single young man in the county, Jonathan Nye. The
story opens with mother and daughter confronting each other bitterly. Louisa
will not answer her mother's petulant entreaties and instead returns to her
dogged labor in the potato field. When Jonathan comes to call, she likewise
refuses to speak, but sits dully nearby as her mother strives to entertain
the embarrassed young man with glowing reports of Louisa's successful
schoolteaching (Louisa has, in fact, recently lost her school). Jonathan soon
escapes; when the door closes behind him, Mrs. Britton falls to berating
her daughter: 'You'd ought to be ashamed of yourself—ashamed of yourself!
You've treated him like a—hog!...I guess he won't want to come again.'
Louisa, responding only that she "doesn't like him," creeps off to bed "her
mother's scolding voice pursuing her like a wrathful spirit." Poor all her
life, Freeman states, Mrs. Britton considers her daughter's marriage to well-
off Jonathan "like a royal alliance for the good of the state...There was
no more sense, to her mind, in Louisa's refusing him than there would
have been in a princess refusing the fairy prince and spoiling the story."
    Louisa remains adamant; she will not marry. She has no other lover
in mind, but "she had her dreams." When her mother hears through
neighborhood gossip that Jonathan has begun to court another girl, she
further humiliates Louisa by suggesting that she chase after *him*. "'Twouldn't
hurt you none to hang back a little after meetin', and kind of edge round
his way. 'Twouldn't take more'n a look...Men don't do all the courtin'—
not by a long shot.' Louisa is shocked. 'I wouldn't do such a thing as that
for a man I liked, and I certainly sha'n't for a man I don't like,' she retorts.
'Then me an' your grandfather'll starve,' her mother shoots back.
    In desperation, Louisa walks seven miles to beg food from a relative
who years before has cut the family off in anger over a petty argument.
Exhausted and hungry, she nearly faints from the effort, yet "it was like
a pilgrimage, and the Mecca at the end of the burning desert-like road was
her own maiden independence."
    Freeman's mothers, in their frustration over their daughters' lack of
obedience in the question of marriage, sometimes resort to deception, trickery,
or emotional cruelty to exact compliance. In two stories which reveal much
about the mother and daughter relationship, however, "Hyacinthus" (1904)
and "Mother-Wings" (1921), Freeman's daughters triumph through their
own moral rectitude: each see her mother brought to her knees because of
her falsehood. In the former story, Mrs. Lynn, angry that daughter Sarah
dislikes wealthy but insipid John Mangam and instead prefers the eccentric

artist Hyacinthus Ware, reveals her jealousy of Sarah in an emotional outburst:

'You are a good-for-nothin' girl. You ought to be ashamed of yourself...You talk about things you and [Hyacinthus] know that the rest of us can't talk about. You take advantage because your father and me sent you to school where you could learn more than we could...' Then her face upon her daughter's turned malevolent, triumphant, and cruel. 'I wa'n't goin' to tell you what I heard...but now I'm goin' to.'

Mrs. Lynn's "secret" is a deliberate lie. She tells Sarah that Hyacinthus is living with a woman. "Sarah turned ghastly pale...'You mean he is married?' she said. 'I dun'no whether he is married or not, but there is a woman livin' there,' " her mother replies. Despondent over this news, Sarah reluctantly decides to marry John Mangam, and "everybody agreed that it was a good match and that Sarah was a lucky girl." However, at the last minute the woman "living" with Hyacinthus appears; she reveals herself to be his half-sister in town for a visit. Guilty at being exposed for a liar, Sarah's mother breaks down before her daughter "with a sob." Sarah, accepting her mother's humility, forgives her—and she marries Hyacinthus.

Likewise, in the later story "Mother-Wings," Mrs. Bodley, who has "advanced ideas" and ridicules daughter Ann for not keeping up with the "modern" girls in town, indirectly lies by leading her busy-body neighbors to think that Ann plans to wed a wealthy widower. Ann cannot figure out why acquaintances are offering their congratulations, and why Frank, the young man she is interested in, has suddenly stopped visiting. Finally realizing the truth, she angrily confronts her mother:

...[Ann's] little, gentle countenance was fairly terrible. 'Mother,' she said, almost solemnly, 'You have—lied.'
Mrs. Bodley cowered before the look and tone. 'You tell your own mother—that?' she said, but her voice was a mere whisper.
'Yes, I do. You have been making everybody think I was going to be married. They congratulated me, and I didn't know why. You made a fool of me. You have tried and tried to push me into everything else, and I have submitted....But to try to push me into marriage! To tell people such a shameful lie when all the time he has never said one word about marrying me!...It was a lie you told, mother, and you a church member!'

Alone, Mrs. Bodley chastises herself for having caused disaster by getting "in the path of divine Providence," but "it did not occur to her to acknowledge her sense of her wrong-doing to Ann." Yet eventually, when Ann's lover Frank returns to her, she too breaks down, acknowledging Ann's honesty and her own guilt: 'She will never tell you her own mother as good as lied,' she confesses to him.

In several Freeman stories a mother sacrifices her very self in order to see her daughter married, and she becomes oddly ennobled in the process. This self-sacrificing mother, furthermore, takes the form of a "witch-mother." Ann Douglas Wood in "The Literature of Impoverishment" has written briefly but perceptively about the recurring image of witchcraft in women's local color writing. Wood attributes Freeman's portrayal of the witch to a manifestation of Freeman's feeling that she was not only different from others and an "outcast," but that she may also have been in some way responsible for "sapping" the life of those around her.[6] Wood thus concludes that "witches were popularly supposed to have the power to blight life, and this power, Freeman, who had lost a lover, a sister, a mother and a father within a short space of time in her young womanhood, must surely have felt was hers" (27).

Whether Freeman felt personal guilt at these losses or not cannot fully be substantiated. However, evidence from at least two short stories "The Witch's Daughter" (1910) and "A Modern Dragon" (1887) indicates that Freeman sometimes associated a daughter's failure to marry and lead a "normal" woman's life with a powerful witch-like mother, who, therefore, must first be annihilated before the daughter can be united with a man. Moreover, in the end the daughter's guilt over, perhaps, wishing her mother dead, is expiated by her deifying this mother-love, in a parody of Christian sacrifice, as a purer and nobler love than that between her and her lover.

Set in past New England, "The Witch's Daughter" concerns old Elma Franklin who is feared by and ostracized from the community largely because of her odd appearance. Because of her mother's reputation, Daphne, Elma's beautiful sixteen-year- old daughter, has no suitors. Elma knows she is to blame: "Young men sometimes cast eyes askance at Daphne, but turned away, and old Elma knew the reason why, and she hated them." Daphne falls in love with one young man, Harry Edgelake, who, once his relatives discover the situation, is hurriedly sent away to school. She becomes disconsolate, and Elma bitter: "[She] watched, and he came not, and old Elma watched the girl watch in vain, and her evil passions grew."

Finally Elma, despairing over her failing daughter, decides that "if she were indeed witch as they said, she would use witchcraft." 'Sweetheart, thy mother will compel love for thee,' she whispers to Daphne. The honest girl at first refuses. However Elma insists, 'There is but one way, sweet daughter of mine. Step thou over thy mother's body...and I swear to thee, by the Christ and the Cross and all that the meeting-folk hold sacred, that thou shalt have thy lover.' Elma sacrifices herself in order to conjure up Daphne's young lover, Harry. Only as she lies dying is her deed seen by her daughter as a glorious one: "[Elma] sank down slowly...and she lay still at the feet of her daughter and the youth, and they stooped over her and they knew that she had been no witch, but a great lover."

An early story, "A Modern Dragon" likewise portrays a self-sacrificing witch-mother who is ennobled finally as the "greatest lover" of all. Mrs. King is known in town for her eccentricity: a proud woman, she wears her hair and skirts too short, ploughs in the fields like a man, and is reputedly a "spiritualist." Mothers warn their sons to avoid her daughter Almira. Almira, however, falls in love with David Ayres, a naive young man who has dared to court her. When David's mother forbids him to see her again, and Almira begins to pine away, Mrs. King lowers her skirts and goes to meeting one Sunday in an attempt to appear "respectable." This failing to work, however, she, with "the demeanor of a hunted criminal," takes a drastic step: she goes to Mrs. Ayres to beg her to relent. But to her utter humiliation, the woman remains immovable. Knowing now that only by her own death can the two lovers be united, Mrs. King falls gravely ill. After securing David's promise to wed her daughter, she dies, at which Almira cries out, 'I never will love him as much as I did you!'

Freeman's petty and manipulative mothers, her cruel or deceptive mothers, and her self-sacrificing or witch-like mothers all point to profound ambivalence, tension, and perhaps guilt in Freeman's mind over her role as daughter in relation to the question of her own marrying. Many of the mothers she portrays see their daughters largely as extensions of themselves; in striving to influence their daughters' decision in marriage, mothers seek to fulfill, even vicariously, some aspect of life they themselves have been deprived of: financial security, prestige, or, in the case of the self-sacrificing mother, simply a "normal" woman's life in the community. A daughter who cannot or will not comply with a parent's wish, moreover, is made to feel morally culpable. Whether this was indeed Freeman's relationship with her mother; whether Eleanor Wilkins pushed her eldest daughter toward a marriage which would ensure the material security of the small, impoverished family or would raise the Wilkins' name to its once genteel status; whether Freeman felt guilty at her mother's death, is not known. However, in all of these stories of a mother's oppressive will and a daughter's often rebellious need to 'have her own dreams,' Freeman clearly shows the lingering power and fearful hold the mother-figure exerted over her adult life.

Judith Gardiner has postulated that "the woman writer uses her text, particularly one centering on a female hero, as part of a continuing process involving her own self-definition" (Abel 187). Freeman's concentration on the issue of marriage as an indicator of the emotional health of the mother and daughter relationship furthers our understanding of her evolving self-concept. A single woman for most of her life and a professional writer and skilled businesswoman, Freeman often felt the acute alienation of being, as she herself expressed it in her quasi-autobiographical novel *By the Light of the Soul*, "outside the pale" of normal womanhood. Clearly, these feelings must have been engendered by her early relationship with her mother.

But Freeman's stories concerning marital status and the relationship between mother and daughter are important in broader terms as well. Written around the turn of the century, Freeman's fiction, like much other women's local color writing, was produced in a period of transition from an older, stabler view of marriage and motherhood gladly accepted and emulated by daughters, to a conscious—and yet half-shameful—rejection on the daughter's part of mother and of mother's ideal for marriage. A fascinating study would be, therefore, one which considers the changing presentation of the mother-figure and marriage in women's writing from this era. Freeman's work is, finally, of particular interest to us today for she spent her long and prolific literary career discovering, exploring, and coming to terms with women's roles as defined by her generation and area of the country.

Notes

[1]I am indebted to Alice Glarden Brand for this phrase which so accurately describes the feeling of near suffocation many of Freeman's adult children experience while still living at home.

[2]I have limited this paper to Freeman's short stories. Some examples of mother and daughter relationships in her novels are as follows: *Jane Field* (1892) where a daughter elopes against her mother's will; *Pembroke* (1894) where a mother discovers her unwed daughter pregnant; *Doc Gordon* (1906) where a daughter feels a rivalry with her mother over suitors; and *By the Light of the Soul* (1906) where after her mother's death a young girl must learn to live with a "cold" stepmother.

[3]An excellent first-hand account of the personal tragedy resulting from the New England decline is Rollin Hartt's "A New England Hill Town" from the 1899 *Atlantic Monthly*. Hartt records the result of this impoverishment and isolation on the remaining villagers.

[4]One was Mary John Wales, the friend with whom she lived for much of her life. Kendrick states that she was also "babied, spoiled, and shielded by both her husband and Henry Mills Alden, editor of *Harper's*." Furthermore, he adds, she was cared for by her household maids, one of whom called her "Mrs. Baby" (12).

[5]Such characterizations of the mother-figure have been classified and studied in the works of other female writers. See, for example, Gilbert and Gubar's *Madwoman in the Attic* for discussions of the "monster mother" in Emily Dickinson, the "absent mother" in Jane Austen, and the "witch mother" in Charlotte Bronte. Davidson and Broner's *The Lost Tradition: Mothers and Daughters in Literature* is also an excellent source for considering how mothers have been portrayed in both male and female writing throughout history. Finally, Homans' *Women Writers and Poetic Identity* discusses the importance of the mother-figure in three 19th century poets: Dorothy Wordsworth, Emily Bronte, and Emily Dickinson.

[6]Freeman's ghost story "Luella Miller" (1902) portrays such a 'vampire' woman who somehow "saps" the life out of all who try to love her.

Works Cited

Primary

Freeman, Mary Wilkins. "The Buckley Lady." *Silence and Other Stories.* New York: Harper and Brothers, 1898. 65-129.

_____ *By the Light of the Soul.* New York: Harper and Brothers, 1906.

_____ *Doc Gordon.* New York: Grosset and Dunlap, 1906.

_____ "Hyacinthus." *Harper's Monthly* Aug. 1904: 447-58.

_____ *Jane Field.* New York: Harper and Brothers, 1893.

_____ "Louisa." *A New England Nun and Other Stories.* New York: Harper and Brothers, 1891. 384-406.

_____ "Luella Miller." *The Wind in the Rose-Bush and Other Stories of the Supernatural.* New York: Doubleday, Page and Company, 1903. 75-104.

_____ "A Modern Dragon." *A Humble Romance and Other Stories.* New York: Harper and Brothers, 1887. 60-77.

_____ "Mother-Wings." *Harper's Monthly* Dec. 1921: 90-103.

_____ *Pembroke.* New York: Harper and Brothers, 1894.

_____ "Up Primrose Hill." *A New England Nun and Other Stories.* New York: Harper and Brothers, 1891. 305-20.

_____ "The Witch's Daughter." *Harper's Weekly* 10 Dec. 1910: 17Œ.

Secondary

Abel, Elisabeth, ed. *Writing and Sexual Difference.* Chicago: U of Chicago Press, 1982.

Auerbach, Nina. *Communities of Women: An Idea in Fiction.* Cambridge, MA: Harvard University Press, 1978.

Brand, Alice Glarden. "Mary Wilkins Freeman: Misanthropy as Propaganda." *New England Quarterly* Mar. 1977: 83-100.

Chodorow, Nancy. *The Reproduction of Mothering: Psychoanalysis and the Sociology of Gender.* Berkeley: University of California Press, 1978.

Davidson, Cathy N. and E.M. Broner, eds. *The Lost Tradition: Mothers and Daughters in Literature.* New York: Frederick Ungar, 1980.

Donovan, Josephine. *New England Local Color Literature: A Women's Tradition.* New York: Frederick Ungar, 1983.

Foster, Edward. *Mary E. Wilkins Freeman.* New York: Hendricks House, 1956.

Gilbert, Sandra M. and Susan Gubar. *The Madwoman in the Attic: The Woman Writer and the Nineteenth-Century Literary Imagination.* New Haven: Yale University Press, 1979.

Hartt, Rollin. "A New England Hill Town." *Atlantic Monthly* Apr. 1899: 561-74; May 1899: 712-20.

Homans, Margaret. *Women Writers and Poetic Identity.* Princeton: Princeton University Press, 1980.

Kendrick, Brent L., ed. *The Infant Sphinx: Collected Letters of Mary E. Wilkins Freeman.* Metuchen, N.J.: Scarecrow Press, 1985.

Wood, Ann Douglas. "The Literature of Impoverishment: The Women Local Colorists in America, 1865-1914." *Women's Studies* 1 (1972): 3-40.

Peter Altenberg:
The "Radical Bachelor"

Pamela S. Saur

It seems inevitable that literary history should adopt certain authors, because of their particular life stories and personalities, to some extent as fictional characters themselves. One author of this type is Peter Altenberg (1859-1919), one of a dazzling number of creative members of the coffeehouse society of turn of the century Vienna. The force of Altenberg's identity as an interesting coffeehouse "character" is evidenced by the fact that a life-like statue of Altenberg sits to this day—over seventy years after his death—at a table in Vienna's Café Central in the Herrengasse! Altenberg represents many movements of his times, for he is called an impressionist and aestheticist, a bohemian and a decadent; his age is called variously "fin de siécle" Vienna, "Young Vienna," the "Belle époche," "the age of Schnitzler" or "the age of Freud," to name the most famous genius of Altenberg's milieu.

Altenberg was a journalist and writer who published thirteen scrapbook-like volumes of aphorisms, short stories, notes, poems, and scenes. Most of his brief works, none of which is more than a few pages long, can be called sketches. His writings belong to literature, but in a sense they are not really fiction, for his books are more like journals or collections of confessions: they provide a record of the data gathered by his own senses. True to the impressionist ideal of living the moments of life as an aesthetic experience, his writings are eminently personal. He does not create imaginary fictional characters, but makes himself and those around him into fictional personae.

If there had been no Peter Altenberg, we might have wanted to invent one, for his writings and his attitude toward life provide a textbook-perfect example of impressionism, a highly influential movement in modern painting, an important element in twentieth century literature, and a useful concept in exploring the differing possible definitions of "realism" in art, for this movement defines sensual experience as the primary reality. Impressionism can be defined as an approach to life and art that emphasizes the beauty and value of experiencing life moment by moment as a series of sensual, particularly visual impressions. It is frequently contrasted with other types of early twentieth century "realism" such as naturalism, emphasizing the often suppressed negative aspects of ordinary people's struggles, or expressionism, emphasizing basic, emotional truths and conflicts that underlie the surface of life. While impressionism can be viewed as a very positive approach to cherishing each moment of life, it can also signify disintegration and loss of meaning or understanding, an inability or refusal to conceptualize undifferentiated sensual data, such as the dots of color of impressionist painting. In literature, Hugo von Hofmannsthal's famous "Lord Chandos' Brief" (Lord Chandos' Letter) captured an extreme example of such disintegration, one version of modern literary alienation—his character thought that everything was falling into incomprehensible pieces; in addition, it can be argued that one aspect of Albert Camus' "L'Etranger" is that sensual impressions seem at times to be all he can understand.

Altenberg's approach to life was highly aesthetic; it was at one with his roles of creator and appreciator of art. He prized the freedom to be open to new experiences at all costs, and as a result he resisted any restrictions or commitments. Thus, Altenberg was a thorough-going bohemian and opponent of bourgeois values that choose responsibility and restraint over freedom, the good of the family or society over the enjoyment of the individual, long-term, practical benefits over the thrill of the moment. A striking irony emerging from a study of Altenberg, however, is that the apparently random impressions and thoughts gathered in his volumes are quite consistent; indeed, they can be organized into coherent, systematic theories; a second irony is that his writings are didactic, for they contain clear messages about how others should live.

The works of secondary literature on Altenberg have discussed his bohemianism and aestheticism, and frequently pointed out that his main theme is women, for much of his writing consists of praising or defending women, both particular individuals and women in general. Emil Schäffer, for example, writes in "Peter Altenberg: Eine Studie:"

> In der Welt, wie sie Peter Altenberg sieht,
> herrscht das Weib. Als strahlende Königin
> gebietet sie auf blinkendem Thron, mit hellem
> Purpur angetan, and Peter Altenberg ist ihr
> demüthiger Ritter und stolzer Troubadour.[1] (74)

Another view is given by Jost Hermand, who mentions Altenberg's claim that he, as a poet, can understand the feminine soul, unlike crass bourgeois husbands:

> Wenn Altenberg eine Zentralmotiv hat, dann ist es das heimliche Bündnis zwischen dem Dichter und der unverstandenen Frauenseele, das sich ganz eindeutig gegen die lauten, bourgeoisen Ehemänner richtet.[2] (444)

While most secondary pieces do not explore the full consequences of Altenberg's attitudes toward women and toward life, an article in 1987 by Barbara Z. Schoenberg brings out both the theoretical consistency and the social implications of Altenberg's writings. She mentions the "seemingly haphazard manner of his writing and the numerous superficial inconsistencies and contradictions in his work" but emphasizes an underlying unity, namely "the total and uncompromising commitment to the amelioration of his bourgeois society" (52). She advances the thesis that Altenberg "[focussed] on 'woman' as a primary vehicle for criticism of bourgeois mores and institutions" (51).[3] While this thesis captures much of Altenberg's message, it seems to place the right elements in the wrong configuration. Women were more than a vehicle of social criticism to Altenberg, for he was genuinely interested in interacting with and writing about women and their beauty. Secondly, Schoenberg's formulation does not do justice to the force of Altenberg's own personality—as expressed for example in his rather frequent extravagant praise of himself! Altenberg was first of all an artist and self-styled artist of life, and his social criticism is not a first principle, but a principle that grows from his other views.

Viewing Altenberg as a dominant character in his own texts, indeed as an ideal or model, and "women" as their dominant theme, it follows that his relationship toward women is central to understanding his views of life and society. His collection of attitudes toward women make up a role that can be called the "radical bachelor." Altenberg would have been quite pleased to be referred to by this term, a name suggested by his statement, "Wenn man ledig ist, muB man radikal ledig sein..."[4] ("Buchbesprechung" in *Prodromos* (152) Altenberg did not merely accept the state of bachelorhood, but made it an ideal role if carried out properly. While his prescriptions for bachelorhood are chiefly related to his beliefs about relationships between the sexes, his rejection of marriage as an institution also stems from his impressionistic individualism. Altenberg lived his life long in Viennese hotels and cafes; he was clearly more attracted to cultivating his own sensitivity and impressionistic experience than to acquiring wealth and property or to encumbering himself with a family or a demanding profession. His impressionistic aestheticism can be seen in the smallest details of his life —he collected postcards and photographs of entertainers, not valuable works of art; he supported himself by humble, ill-paid, and anti-bourgeois writings not destined to last past a few days, namely newspaper reviews of nightclub acts. Altenberg lived in the familiar bohemian pattern—wearing peculiar clothes, keeping odd hours, drinking heavily, socializing endlessly in public cafes, befriending outcasts, particularly prostitutes, living precariously on meager earnings and handouts from friends, spending the money in his pocket on luxurious meals with no thought for the morrow.

Certainly Altenberg's writings must reflect his personal preferences, and, some would say, his personal neuroses, inadequacies or disappointments. However, he recommended his own aesthetic approach to life to all. For men, he rejected both the role of bourgeois husband and the role of conquering Don Juan; instead he recommended cultivating a true appreciation of women's beauty as a sensitive radical bachelor like himself. While he acknowledged that a perfect, lasting love was an ideal to be longed for, he thought of such an ideal as a dream of gods that most men can achieve only in piecemeal fashion, by collecting a series of ideal moments and by finding and cherishing glimpses of ideal beauty in many women.

During Altenberg's time, the early years of the twentieth century, the "woman question" was very much alive in Europe. While political debate and action spurred by women's "emancipation" was more vigorous in Germany and England, Altenberg was one of a number of Viennese of his day to construct theories on the nature of women. Most famous and influential of these at present was of course the psychologist Sigmund Freud, but others were also well-known in their day. They included writers Karl Kraus, Arthur Schnitzler and Hugo von Hofmannsthal, cultural historian Egon Friedell, and Otto Weininger, whose extremely misogynistic book of 1903 *Geschlecht und Charakter* (Sex and Character) was quite popular up until World War I. Weininger wrote that man represents spirit and intellect, women formless matter without free will or a soul, completely dominated by sexual matters. While contemporary feminism can find fault with many of Altenberg's ideas, his view toward women was much more positive than many others of his times.

Much of Altenberg's attitude toward women can be summarized by the word "idealization." His books contain extravagant praise of the superiority of women, an attitude reminiscent of chivalry and now regarded suspiciously as "putting women on a pedestal," for we know from experience that men's praise of women's superiority may often stem from ideas about women's different nature that harm the cause of women seeking equality, growth, or an active role in society. Altenberg's primary concern was not women's position in the power structure, but rather the artistically ideal, aesthetically superior development of men and women and their relationships. As a man, Altenberg honored the beauty of women to the point of worship. He considered feminine beauty a major component of the beauty of the world, and thus closely related to the beauty of art and the beauty of nature. He considered himself, as a self-styled artist, particularly sensitive to women, and therefore qualified to speak for women and to offer advice to both sexes. He advised women on how to live up to their ideal nature, men, on how to appreciate women's beauty, specifically by avoiding the stultifying bourgeois role of husband and the insensitive role of Don Juan, or conqueror of women, to adopt the ideal role of the "radical bachelor." Contemporary women would generally resist Altenberg's definition of women's proper sphere as confined to the world of beauty, art and nature, but it is important to remember that his bohemian notions of what should be important to men were consistent: for both sexes, he rejected action of the career-building sort in favor of the passive role of spectator. Certainly, Altenberg's views are dated and simplistic—after all, an all-bohemian society wouldn't have much of an economy—but their simplistic consistency sharpens our understanding of several related dichotomies of life, including such polar opposites as the bohemian versus the bourgeois, originality versus conformism, individualism versus collectivism, or passive consumption versus active production.

Like a medieval troubadour, Altenberg often uses the vocabulary of religion to express his devotion to women. He uses extravagant language, for example, to sing the praises of a number of nightclub entertainers, saying that the only human being created in God's image is the performer "La Zarina!" In a sketch bearing her name, he wrote: "Es ist nicht wahr, dass Gott die Menschen nach seinem Ebenbild schuf! In dieser Weise schuf er einem einzigen Menschen... La Zarina!"[5] (*Tag* 218) Altenberg's intense adoration of beautiful women causes him to view objects associated with them as precious, almost holy. In sketches showing this tendency, his aesthetic impressionism borders on fetishism, and is reminiscent of the worship of relics of saints. In one sketch, "De Amore," for example, he proclaims love for a woman's socks and the smell of her room, (*Wie ich* 144) in another he (or someone called "a poet") asks a woman eating tangerines to breathe on him, then, to let him chew on the tangerine peelings blessed with her precious saliva ("Aus dem Tagebuch der edlen Miss Madrilene," *Tag* 21).

The sense of sight, so important to impressionism, is emphasized in the title of Altenberg's first book, *Wie ich es sehe* (The way I see it). Sight is central to Altenberg's attitude toward art and life, and to the didactic message that emerges from his books. He hopes to teach people to see the world around them, as a sensitive impressionist does. In "Die Frauen," in one of many admonitions to men, he urges men to learn to see women's beauty; if they do so they will recognize women as parts of God's "living artwork": "Eine vollkommen schöne Frau als ein 'lebendiges Kunstwerk Gottes' erfassen können, ist der Gipfelpunkt künstlicher Entwicklung im Manne"[6] (*Lebensabend* 144). Altenberg was able to exalt his praises of feminine beauty both poetically and theoretically by frequently invoking the connections between religion, nature and art. His works also contain references to women as subjects of visual art, including descriptions of women ideally portrayed in many Japanese paintings, in paintings by the English pre-Raphaelite artist Edward Burne-Jones and in the sensuous portraits by his contemporary Gustav Klimt, who scandalized Vienna in 1903 with his gloriously decorative nudes.

According to Altenberg, the superiority of woman over man lies not only her beauty, but in her sensitive perception. Woman is bound to nature both by belonging to the natural beauty of the world, and by her own deep appreciation of nature; of course, recent feminist analysis has traced a long cultural history of associating women with nature, and pointed out that the association, while not entirely negative, can be harmful and restrictive. Many of Altenberg's aphorisms illuminate various aspects of his didactic mission to bring about a harmony between man, woman, and nature. He urged women to develop appreciation for nature's beauty, scorning the banal idea that nature is useful for purposes of sport and hygiene. In some sketches, Altenberg also speaks of nature as a competitor with man for the love of woman. If a man fails to understand a woman, she may prefer nature's company to his.

The ideal woman, according to Altenberg, is superior not only because of her closeness to nature, but also because of her closeness to art and to the artist, and he mentions drama and music as well as visual arts in this connection. In some sketches, Altenberg praises women's superior sensitivity to artistic as well as natural beauty, and he points out that art, as well as nature, may compete with men for women's affection. However, it is important to remember his own prominent role in his theories: when he speaks of the connection between woman and the artist, poet or genius, he is no doubt often thinking of himself and his own superior sensitivity. He praises women's perceptions, but assumes that he can express these perceptions better than women can themselves. At times Altenberg pointed out that both women and artists are too sensitive to be bound by the humdrum details of life; both suffer because they are used, but not understood by the rest of humanity. Thus, Altenberg's self-appointed role of spokesman for sensitive women is a prominent aspect of his concept of the ideal radical bachelor. His feeling of kinship with women is expressed humorously in this wish: "Eine Frau, die ganz genau so wäre wie ich, nur ohne—Schnurrbart! Das wäre es!"[7] (Fechsung 270)

Peter Altenberg idealized women in general, but he particularly idealized certain groups of women, including maids, females whose beauty, even existence, was often overlooked by insensitive people, actresses and performers, whose artistic roles he admired, and young girls. Altenberg thought that most men's appreciation of feminine beauty was impure, motivated by the hope of sexual exploitation. Only the sensitive artist, capable of fully enjoying the mere sight of a woman, would take as great an interest in a beautiful child, whose beauty is ideal in its innocence and in its unfolding. Altenberg sometimes showered young girls with gifts and love letters, considering their mothers' objections vain bourgeois attempts to lay down rules about the emotional aesthetic realm of love. His sketches on young girls often contain melancholy or angry protests about their inevitable fate, sacrificing their innocence to undeserving men. Although Altenberg regretted the loss of innocence suffered by these girls, he also idealized a later stage of a woman's life, the creative role of motherhood, which he considered both natural and artistic. Motherhood bestows a new kind of innocence by means of the pure love between mother and child.

While Altenberg usually thought of women as passive, beautiful objects rather than active creators of beauty, he did praise motherhood as a creative role, both godlike and artistic, not only because of the mere act of giving birth, but because he thought mothers and children were often united by an ideal type of love. He also valued the active artistry of actresses and entertainers, and he spoke admiringly of a woman creating a pot of soup, (Prodromos 88) and an outfit ("Mode" in Märchen 71) using in both instances the verb "erdichten," meaning to create a poem (ein Gedicht). While he was perhaps writing a bit humorously here, it is quite consistent with Altenberg's impressionism to advocate savoring a taste of soup or the sight of a well-dressed woman in the same way as one savors a poem. In such sketches, he identifies creative possibilities in women's traditional domestic roles.

The institution of marriage, linked to the "woman question," was undergoing a great deal of re-examination by Altenberg's contemporary writers. While Hofmannsthal held marriage in high esteem, Arthur Schnitzler, a doctor and friend of Sigmund Freud, wrote plays reflecting a negative view of marriage and a conviction that fidelity is impossible. Altenberg's friend Karl Kraus, a prominent writer and journalist, penned the aphorism, "die Ehe ist eine Mesalliance"[8] (Qtd. in "Die Unterschiede" *Lebensband* 193). Because Altenberg considered women so superior to men, it is not surprising that he considered most marriages tragic mistakes. He expressed rage by women who "threw themselves away" on worthless men, and in various sketches he referred to marriage as a cage, trap, or bad bargain for women.

Of course, no true impressionist could approve of the ideal of faithfulness in love, since faithfulness must kill spontaneous reactions to the stimuli of future moments; indeed he called the idea of exclusive love "pathological." One key passage attacks bourgeois society for attempting to govern the emotions and even the senses by means of marriage. He writes in "Ein Nachtrag:"

Man kann niemanden auf die Dauer gleichmäBig gern haben!...Die bürgerliche Gesellschaft will etwas äuBerlich, a tout prix...erzwingen, was es in der Welt aber tatsächlich nicht gibt! Nämlich eine *anständige Stetigkeit* und *VerläBlichkeit der Gefühlswelt*, ja sogar der Sinnenwelt, was eine *noch entsetzlichere Stupidität* ist![9]

(*Semmering* 135)

Altenberg takes great pains to point out that he does not advocate a masculine role of "Don Juan" as an alternative to marriage. According to him, a Don Juan, who tries to conquer and possess many women, is originally an idealist, searching and waiting for his ideal woman to come along, until he gives up and tries to satisfy himself with finding partial reflections of the ideal woman in many women, an attempt that he considers doomed to failure. The Don Juan's interest in the mere possession of women causes him to ignore the individual differences in women, the details of their beauty; moreover, the Don Juan misses the gradual process of love unfolding. Altenberg advises men to learn to wait, to wait as long as they must for the ideal woman to come along. The man who cannot wait, but tries to enjoy women without love, is damaging his own soul.

Altenberg, along with other Viennese writers of his time, such as Egon Friedell and Otto Weininger, sometimes expressed a distaste for sexual intercourse, a distaste that was encouraged by the Victorian attitudes of Viennese society, the atmosphere of severe sexual repression effectively attacked by Sigmund Freud. Although Altenberg was hostile to bourgeois notions of propriety, his aestheticism caused him to accept the then common belief that sexual intercourse is a degrading victimization of women. He thought that women were superior in their supposed distaste for sex, which would be repelling to men as well if they could become more refined and sensitive. Altenberg's hypersensitivity (which we could label neo-romantic or even neo-chivalrous) caused him to endorse a more spiritual, more "feminine" sexuality, to capture the intoxicating sexuality in the apparently most innocent interactions between men and women. He wrote in "Splitter:"

> Denn sexuell ist...der zärtliche Blick, die
> zärtliche Handberührung, das Spenden einer Rose,
> das Fragen nach dem Befinden, das Aufheben eines
> Schirmes, einer Serviette, das Hineinhelfen in
> einen Mantel. Oft ist *das* sogar echte *sexueller*
> als das Sexuellste.[10] (*Nachfechsung*, 196)

Altenberg scorned the vulgar men who regarded such precious moments (impressions) as mere preludes to physical intimacy. He did not go so far as to advocate celibacy, but he obviously thought sex was frequently ugly.

In defining his own ideal role of the "radical bachelor," Altenberg advocated a kind of individualism, defined as fidelity to one's own integrity rather than a fidelity to any one woman. In "Fidelite," he instructs men to conform to his impressionist ideals by being true to their ever-changing selves and to the beauty of the world:

> Treue! Mann, sei treu! Dem eigenen Wachsen,
> dem eigenen Werden und der Weltenschönheit!
> Sei treulos dem Stillstand deines Geistes,
> deiner Seele und Allem, was müd und häßlich
> wird![11] (*Wie ich* 141)

Here, Altenberg reveals an obvious possible drawback to marriage, as indeed to any commitment—our inability to predict the future, including the future of our own growth and development. Defenders of marriage would be likely to concede this potential drawback, which could be thought of in existential terms, as one of those inevitable problems that arise from human interactions.

Interestingly, Altenberg carries this notion of fidelity to all women further, so that the idea takes on a social or even religious dimension, for some of his passages advocate fidelity to all humanity. In a movement from the individual to the social realm, Altenberg's open-eyed sensitivity leads him to see beauty in maids, and from that to protest the fact that maids are invisible or mistreated by insensitive people. Protesting against bourgeois narrowness in "Humanitas," he points out that many conventional relationships are based upon mere chance:

> Mein Kind, mein Geliebter, meine Schwester,
> meine Tante, mein Hund! Aber nie: Meine
> *Menschheit*! Meine 1000 Brüder und Schwestern,
> die *unbekannten* und dennoch *so gut* bekannten,
> wie die, deren Familiennamen man zufällig
> kennt![12] (*Prodromos* 227)

One technique that Altenberg recommends to find one's ideal woman in the real world is to seek ideal features in many women. The idea of concentrating one's senses upon a part rather than a whole is clearly reminiscent of impressionism in the visual arts. Many of Altenberg's descriptive sketches do not focus on a whole woman, but on a part of her, such as a hand, or a garment or sleeve. Just as the radical bachelor treasures moments of small contact, such as a brief touch, he treasures the vision of a part of a woman; seeking fulfillment or ecstasy from brief encounters or sights can, as mentioned, lead to the fetishistic tendencies exhibited in some of Altenberg's sketches. The idea that the ideal object of love can only be found part by part in the ideal features of many is expressed in "Die Dichterin":

> Dich habe ich nie geliebt, aber Du brachtest mir
> in einem Nichts ein Bruchstück jenes Ideales,
> das nicht ist und das nicht kommen wird!...
> Ein Teilchen des *Unerfüllbaren* warst du mir.[13]
> (*Märchen* 24)

Not surprisingly, Altenberg, like many romantic poets, idealized unrequited love. He often claims that yearning, hoping, and waiting are precious states experienced by the unhappy lover, but unknown to the less sensitive "happy" lover whose love is returned and rewarded. The so-called unhappy lover, like the sensitive impressionist, learns to appreciate the smallest favors. In "Die 'Unglückliche' Liebe," ("The 'Unhappy' Love") Altenberg reveals the ecstasy that a casual touch can bring:

> Aber wenn ich deine Hand beim Abschiede im
> Restaurant berühre oder auf der StraBe?!?
> Feiere ich da nicht meine Hochzeitsnacht mit
> dir, fast *physiologisch*?!?[14] (*Bilderbögen* 75-7)

Although impressionism values fleeting experience and change above commitment or consistency, Altenberg's thoughts nevertheless contain, paradoxically, a definite structure of theoretical consistency—it might be called the consistency of inconsistency, just as he defended the fidelity of infidelity and the happiness of the unhappy lover. Sifting through his collected volumes, one can gather thoughts that do form a system. Clearly, he opposed bourgeois marriage and presented reasons for doing so; he rejected not only the role of bourgeois husband, but also that of conquering "Don Juan," in favor of his collection of attitudes that make up his definition of the radical bachelor.

While he might have stopped here, his writings also contain a few concessions that there might—very rarely—be an ideal interaction or union between a man and a woman; presumably the possibility is needed for the radical bachelor to long for. Some of Altenberg's sketches explore qualities of an ideal love, which he parallels to a mother's love for her children: it should be the opposite of blind, for it should be based on truly knowing another person. We should imitate the mother, he thought, for she is the idealist of the real: she idealizes her children even though she knows them and all their imperfections. Furthermore, an ideal love should radically change an individual. As Egon Friedell says of Altenberg's concept of love: "Sie ist die innerste Umwandlung des Menschen."[15] (100) Once again, Altenberg's thoughts are reminiscent of chivalry, for he thought an ideal love would inspire, improve and develop both lovers.

Significantly, Altenberg refers to a model of marriage of which he seems to approve, and it is outside his own bourgeois society. In "L'homme mediocre," he describes a view of marriage he claims to have learned about from a group of African entertainers visiting Vienna. Here he displays a romantic idealization of "primitive" society. In their tribe, a man purchases a bride if he loves her, and they remain together as long as their love lasts. If they part, the woman is considered a virgin again and can remarry, for " *Aus Liebe* gibt es nur eine *unbefleckte* Empfängnis!"[16] (*Aschantee* 53)

A passage from "Buchesbesprechung" shows Altenberg's recognition that ideal love could exist, but it also reflects his doubt, for he describes an ideal, lasting love as God's dream:

> Zwei, die, im Weltenraume einzig für einander
> bestimmt—sich fanden! Dies, dies allein ist
> das Wesen der Ehe, wie Gott es sich erträumt
> hat in seinen romantischen Weltenplänen! Da
> allein entsteht dieses unbeschreibliche und
> mysteriöse Erblühen der rastlosen Selbstlos-
> igkeiten! *Die Dauer-Romantik!*[17] (*Prodromos* 152)

While Altenberg's impressionistic, aesthetic approach to life was shaped by his particular social environment, Viennese coffeehouse society of the "decadent" fin-de-siecle years, many of the problems he illuminated in his writings are still problems in different form today, over seventy years after his death. Marriage is still the cornerstone of bourgeois conformity, still an institution that inevitably restricts individual development and represses the wild and sometimes noble or creative impulses of youth. In recent years, one source of criticism of marriage has been the conflict many women experience between marriage and career ambitions. The bohemian Altenberg would have had difficulty identifying with this problem, but other aspects of his critique of marriage are still as valid as ever. While much of Altenberg's thinking was aesthetic and idealistic, he was not without a realistic social conscience, for he did protest against domestic abuse of wives, children, and maids. In our day, too, marriage is too often the cradle of violence rather than an ideal haven.

In a larger sense, however, Altenberg's concept of the "radical bachelor" goes well beyond his critique of marriage to define a general type of individualism, and in this sense, marriage represents all the restrictions society imposes on us. His idea of bachelorhood is based on his belief in fidelity to one's own integrity, a concept that anticipated by several decades the quest for an authentic existence promoted by the later existentialist movement. While Altenberg's books bring out the negative consequences marriage can have, they also present many positive and inspiring aspects of life that we often take for granted. His bachelorhood represents a never-ending and uncompromising search for the ideal, marvelous, and beautiful, in nature, art, human interactions, and sensory experience, and a determination to savor life, to "smell the roses," as fast-paced Americans frequently need to be reminded. Awe and appreciation of the small blessings of life are ideal characteristics of childhood: to a great extent the "radical bachelor" is a kind of Peter Pan, a "radical child" from whom we can all learn. Altenberg embodied the attitudes of the child, the adolescent, and the bohemian bachelor—all of these attitudes are most fittingly commemorated—whimsically and playfully—by Altenberg's statue that sits today amid the customers at a marble table in Vienna's Café Central. This statue, realistic enough to fool people at first glance, is the type of immortality the "radical bachelor" would surely have enjoyed.

Notes

[1]"In the world, as seen by Peter Altenberg, the woman reigns. As a radiant queen she rules on a gleaming throne, clad in royal purple, and Peter Altenberg is her humble knight and her proud troubadour." This translation is by the author, as will be those following.

[2]"If Altenberg has a central motif, it is the secret bond between the poet and the misunderstood feminine soul, a message that is unambiguously directed against loud, bourgeois husbands."

[3]Schoenberg's article contains a helpful bibliography of secondary literature on Altenberg, including useful comments on what these studies contain.

[4]"If one is single, one must be radically single..."

[5]"It isn't true that God created humankind in His own image! Only one single creature did He create thus:...'La Zarina.' "

[6]"The ability to perceive the perfect beauty of a woman as an artistic work of God is the summit of artistic development in a man."

[7]"A woman who was exactly like me, but without—a moustache—that would be perfect!"

[8]"Marriage is a misalliance."

[9]" *No one can love someone else the same amount forever!*...Bourgeois society forces maintaining the appearance of something, at all costs, that in reality does not exist! Namely a *respectable constancy* and *reliability of emotions*, and even the senses, which is an *even more outrageous stupidity!*"

[10]"For sexual is...the tender glance, the tender touch of the hand, the giving of a rose, the question 'How are you?', the lifting of an umbrella or napkin, the help with a coat. Often *these* interactions are actually *more sexual* than the most sexual of relations."

[11]"Faithful! Man, be faithful! To your own growth, your own becoming and to the beauty of the world! Be unfaithful to the standing still of your own spirit or soul and to everything that becomes tired or ugly!"

[12]"My child, my lover, my sister, my aunt, my dog! But never: my *human race*! My thousand brothers and sisters, *unknown* but *as well* known, as those, whose family names one knows by chance!"

[13]"I never loved you, but you brought me in a moment a fragment of that ideal that does not exist and never will come!...To me, you were a small piece of the *unfulfillable*!"

[14]"But when I touch your hand taking your leave in a restaurant or on the street?!? Do I not then celebrate my wedding night with you, almost *physiologically*?!?"

[15]"It is the innermost transformation of an individual."

[16]"When love is present, every conception is immaculate!"

[17]"Two people—out of the entire universe, suited just for each other—found each other! This, this alone is the essence of marriage as God envisioned it in His romantic plans for the world. Here alone originates the indescribable and mysterious blossoming of selflessness—in a *lasting romantic love*."

Works Cited

Altenberg, Peter. *Aschantee*. Berlin: S. Fischer, 1897.

_____ *Bilderbögen des Kleinen Lebens*. Berlin: Erich Reiss, 1909.

_____ *Fechsung*. Berlin: S. Fischer, 1915.

_____ *Märchen des Lebens*. 5th and 6th ed. Berlin: S. Fischer, 1919.

_____ *Mein Lebensabend*. Berlin: S. Fischer, 1919.

_____ *Nachfechsung*. Berlin: S. Fischer, 1919.

_____ *Prodromos*. Berlin: S. Fischer, 1906.

_____ *Semmering 1912*. Berlin: S. Fischer, 1919.

_____ *Was der Tag mir zuträgt: Fünfundsechzig neue Studien*. Berlin: S. Fischer, 1921.

_____ *Wie ich es sehe*. Berlin: S. Fischer, 1915.

Friedell, Egon. *Ecce Poeta*. Berlin: S. Fischer, 1912.

Herman, Jost. "Peter Spinell." *Modern Language Notes* 79 (1964), 439-47.

Schäffer, Emil. "Peter Altenberg: Eine Studie." *Wiener Rundschau* 1 (1897), 73-7.

Schönberg, Barbara Z. " 'Woman-Defender' and 'Woman-Offender,' Peter Altenberg and Otto Weininger: Two Literary Stances vis-a-vis Bourgeois Culture in the Viennese 'Belle Epoque.' " *Modern Austrian Literature* 20.2 (1987), 51-69.

Proving One's Worth:
The Importance of Marriage
in the World of Barbara Pym

Katherine Anne Ackley

Although many of Barbara Pym's characters want to be married, her portrayal of marriages makes one wonder why they bother. Marriages are often slightly antagonistic arrangements whereby each spouse has learned to tolerate the other's idiosyncrasies. In Pym's fictional world, men are ineffectual, childish creatures who want women to be little more than domestic servants and clerical help, believing such services are their due and taking for granted that women should devote themselves exclusively to their needs. Women are defined almost entirely in relationship to men, most having accepted the prevailing social belief that a woman is not fulfilled until she has married. Indeed, according to a widely held notion, it is, as Mildred Lathbury of *Excellent Women* reflects, the wedding ring on the left hand that proves one's worth as a human being, no matter how dull the man one manages to marry. Pym underscores the absurdity of this narrow view with wit and humor by creating unmarried central characters who, despite their reduced social status, are strong, self-sufficient women; by portraying married women as disappointed and disillusioned; and by intimating that widows enjoy the best position of all.

There are two kinds of women in Barbara Pym's novels, both of whom are defined by their connection to men: the married—including widowed—and the unmarried. As Prudence Bates's friend Eleanor Hitchens puts it in *Jane and Prudence*, one has to eventually settle down to being either "the comfortable spinster or the bored or contented wife" (200). Both married and unmarried women alike are portrayed as irritatingly preoccupied with deferring to men, serving them, and inflating their already healthy egos, but the unmarried woman is Pym's special province. Of Pym's thirteen novels, ten feature unmarried women. Only *Civil to Strangers, A Glass of Blessings*, and *An Academic Question* have married central characters. In *Jane and Prudence*, there are two central characters, one married and the other unmarried.

Most of the novels published in Pym's lifetime were written during the 1950s, before the contemporary women's movement, and her female characters belong firmly to preliberation days. When she first began writing novels as a young woman, "spinster" was viewed by many as an almost dirty word, despite the fact that during the period in which Pym was growing up and attending Oxford University, there was a large imbalance in the sex ratio in England. According to a study by Jane Lewis of women in England between 1870 and 1950, English women who were not married in their late twenties would very likely never marry. Lewis discovered that "of those women who were single and in their late twenties in 1921, 50 per cent were unmarried a decade later,"[1] a figure that is particularly striking "when compared with that for men, of whom only 30 percent failed to marry."[2] According to Lewis, because of the keen competition for husbands, spinsterhood was often called a " 'failure in business' in middle class households."[3] Pym's novels proclaim this imbalance quite clearly: there are close to twice as many women as there are men. Furthermore, unmarried and widowed women outnumber married women by about five to one. Pym comically reflects this unequal distribution of men and women in her very early novel *Civil to Strangers*, when the English people Cassandra Marsh-Gibbon joins for safe-keeping from Stefan Tilos form a tour group composed of three clergymen, three clergymen's wives, three widows, and eight spinsters. When Flora points out to her mother in *Jane and Prudence* that, at Prudence's age, the supply of available men is not what it was when she was an undergraduate at Oxford, she is stating a reality of Pym's own life. Despite this imbalance in the numbers of women and men, the general assumption of the society Pym wrote about was that women ought to marry and were not complete human beings if they did not.

Pym had begun early in life to half-seriously identify with the slightly odd excellent women she wrote about. In 1939, at age twenty-five, she referred to herself in a letter to Elsie Harvey as an old spinster "already rather queer in the head" (*Very Private Eye* 88), and she continued to make such references thereafter. The prevailing image of spinsters for centuries in both British and American literature had been to denigrate them. Usually they were pitied, ridiculed, or despised, seldom admired and even less frequently emulated.[4] Perhaps because of her strong identification with spinsters, Pym does not follow that tradition but rather explores in detail the effects of the social attitudes of the 1950s about unmarried women on their lives, particularly on their sense of self. What she reveals is a complex, at times ambiguous and conflicting, set of emotions. If they appear ridiculous occasionally, it is only because everyone in her novels is seen to be just slightly dotty at times. The sensible, steadfast characters are, for the most part, Pym's unmarried central characters, while not one of the men they love is equal to them in strength of character, in intelligence, or in compassion for others. Given this inequity, Pym's spinsters feel ambivalent about entering relationships. Indeed, several of them actually turn down marriage proposals, indicating that they are not desperate to marry. At the same time, they are keenly aware of the stigma attached to a woman's being unmarried. Their ambivalency results in large measure from the expectation that women must marry in order to truly fulfill themselves and the negative view of those who do not.[5]

Because marriage is valued highly for women, men's needs are regarded as being superior to or more pressing than the needs of women. This belief is reiterated with bemusement throughout the novels. We see this attitude expressed in Belinda's devotion to Henry Hoccleve and Harriet's to young curates in *Some Tame Gazelle* and in Mildred's falling under Rocky's spell and then acting as drudge for him and Julian, not to mention Everard, in *Excellent Women*. Countless women perform domestic tasks and menial clerical labor for men. Men are fussed over at meals, given larger portions, and granted special treatment. Mrs. Crampton automatically gives Nicholas in *Jane and Prudence* two eggs and Jane one and then serves a roast chicken with full accompaniments to Mr. Oliver. Jane thinks, sarcastically, "Man needs bird...Just the very best, that is what man needs" (52). Jane, comfortably married and enjoying perhaps the best relationship of any of the married couples in all the novels, repeatedly makes wry observations about the things women will do for men. When she meets Dr. Grampion, with whom Prudence is for the moment in love, she thinks with something like wonder of the splendid things women do for men: "Making them feel...they were loved and admired and desired when they were worthy of none of these things—enabling them to preen themselves and puff out their plumage like birds and bask in the sunshine of love, real or imagined, it didn't matter which" (75). Judging by the way women fawn over men, this statement is only too accurate.

Accompanying this elevated view of men is the idea that men somehow validate by their very attachment to them. This notion is reinforced in all the novels, often to ridiculous lengths, as illustrated by the comment in *The Sweet Dove Died* that "to be involved with a man's furniture, especially to have some of it in one's possession, even if only temporarily, adds considerably to one's prestige" (83). Even ex-wives have the distinction of having once married and hence proved themselves, as in the case of Lady Selvedge in *An Unsuitable Attachment*. Lady Selvedge is the ex-wife of Sir Humphrey Selvedge, whose infidelities forced her to divorce him. She is "usually known as Lady (Muriel) Selvedge. The parentheses gave a sense of not existing, unbeing perhaps was not too strong a word" (57). Still, because of her connection with Sir Humphrey, she has retained the title "Lady" and thus has the requisite prestige for performing opening ceremonies at social events.

Unmarried men are objects of great interest to women. Sophia Ainger states it bluntly in *An Unsuitable Attachment* when she tells Rupert Stonebird: " 'A single man probably inspires wider and wilder speculation than a single woman...His unmarried state is in itself more interesting than a woman's unmarriedness, if you see what I mean' " (248). Some men have purposely avoided getting married, some just have not had the time nor opportunity, and others are widowers or divorced. Men in this last group have had less-than-fulfilling relationships with their wives, who seem not to have made much of an impression on them. Tom Dagnall can scarcely remember his dead wife, hardly thinks of her now, and is not even sure what color her eyes had been. Edwin Braithwaite, looking at the naked breasts of women displayed on magazine covers, "suppose[s] that his wife Phyllis had once had breasts" (*Quartet in Autumn* 45). In *No Fond Return of Love*, Aylwin Forbes' wife divorces him because of his interest in other women, and in *An Unsuitable Attachment*, Edwin Pettigrew's wife had left him years before because he could not give as much attention to his marriage as he wanted to give to his animals. Fabian Driver woefully mistreated his poor dead wife and thinks only of himself. It is Fabian's photograph which adorns her grave, and Jessie Morrow's sardonic comment that " 'her death came as a great shock to him—he had almost forgotten her existence' " (*Jane and Prudence* 28) indicates the degree of his self-absorption.

When men and women do marry in the course of the novels, it is often as arrangements of convenience for the men. The wedding of Edgar Donne and Olivia Berridge ends *Some Tame Gazelle*, while Bishop Grote and Connie Aspinall are making plans for theirs. Belinda Bede's assessment of Olivia is that she seems perfectly equipped to be a clergyman's wife, taking care of him, protecting him, and perhaps even helping write his sermons for him: "A helpmeet indeed" (235). This thought is a reference to the scene in which Theodore Grote had proposed to her, assuring her that she is quite equal to being his helpmeet. Belinda more realistically puts it: "A man needs a woman to help him into his grave" (224). Belinda is not surprised when Connie tells her that Theodore has assured her that she is equal to being a bishop's wife, for Belinda knows exactly what he means. In *Jane and Prudence*, when Jessie Morrow and Fabian Driver become engaged, he tells Jane that Prudence would have wanted too much, something that the shrewd Jessie has realized all along and used to her advantage; and when Marius Lovejoy discusses his impending marriage to Mary Beamish with Wilmet in *A Glass of Blessings*, he tells her that Mary will be able to do so much for him.

Another reason men marry is identified by the rector Mr. Wilmot when he says in *Civil to Strangers*, that every man ought to have a wife if for no other reason than for safety. Stefan Tilos marries the woman his parents have selected for him not only because he needs a housekeeper but because she will be protection against Angela Gay. Stephen Latimer proposes to Jessie Morrow in *Crampton Hodnet* because he believes he could do worse, and marriage to her would protect him from the scourge of unmarried women who will not leave him alone. Mark Penfold's description of what he assumes is the arrangement between Catherine and Tom, though said when he is slightly tipsy and perhaps meant to be tongue-in-cheek, is probably the most accurate account of what many men desire: " 'It would be a reciprocal relationship—the woman giving the food and shelter and doing some typing for him and the man giving the priceless gift of himself...It is commoner in our society than many people would suppose' " (*Less Than Angels* 76).

Part of the explanation why men like Rocky Napier, Tom Mallow, and Fabian Driver, who expect much more of women than they are willing to give, are so attractive to women is that they are good looking and charming.

But there is more to it than that: women have been conditioned to see themselves as secondary to men, to believe that they must have husbands to give validity to their own existence. Within Pym's memory and the collective memory of all the women in her novels, this is the way women have always behaved toward men. Watching her daughter Flora look adoringly at her young man Paul, Jane thinks: "Oh the strange and wonderful things that men could make women do!...She remembered how once, long ago, she herself had started to learn Swedish...and when she had first met Nicholas, she had tried Greek. And now here was her own daughter caught up in the higher flights of Geography! He seemed a nice young man, but that was only the least one could say. Was it also the most?" (*Jane and Prudence* 158). Men are almost always valued more highly than women. In *Less Than Angels*, for instance, Minnie Foresight, attempting to listen politely to Miss Lydgate's description of her anthropological article, has an expression "of rather strained interest" on her face: "Women must so often listen to men with just this expression on their faces, but Mrs. Foresight was feminine enough to feel that it was a little hard that so much concentration should be called for when talking to a member of her own sex. It seemed, somehow, a waste of effort" (16). This is a brilliant summary of the way women are expected to view men, to appreciate this difference in their relative worth, and to respond accordingly.

Marriage is valued highly even by those who regard it as a nuisance, with married women generally viewed as more advantaged than unmarried women. Beatrix Howick in *A Few Green Leaves*, despite her own very satisfactory career as a don, feels that women ought to marry or have some sort of relationship with a man. Widowed for decades, she had early in life fulfilled her womanly role by having married and borne a child. Now she wants Emma to be fulfilled in that way as well. This viewpoint in Pym's last novel is not much different from that expressed by women in Pym's first novels. In *Excellent Women*, for example, the widow Allegra Gray wonders aloud to Mildred, " 'What do women *do* if they don't marry?' " (129). Helena Napier cannot imagine what Mildred will do once she and Rocky are gone. When Rocky points out that she had a full life before they came—" 'Very much so—what is known as a *full* life, with clergymen and jumble sales and church services and good works' "—Helena responds, " 'I thought that was the kind of life led by women who *didn't* have a full life in the accepted sense' " (238). Like many others, Helena equates the full life with the married life, despite her own stormy relationship with Rocky. Having failed to marry, Mildred has failed as a woman. Through some fault of her own, she is responsible for her singleness.

In *Some Tame Gazelle*, Belinda Bede weakly attempts to defend spinsters by telling the Archdeacon not to mock them, saying, " 'After all, it isn't always our fault...' " (27-8). But Belinda recognizes the higher status of married women: she is distressed when she imagines Agatha's being crushed and pathetic when it is she herself who has been proposed to by Bishop Grote. She is enormously relieved when Agatha is her old self again at the party celebrating the curate's engagement to Olivia Berridge: "Now she knew that there could never be anything pathetic about Agatha. Poised and well-dressed, used to drinking champagne, the daughter of a bishop and the wife of an archdeacon—that was Agatha Hoccleve" (248). Mildred Lathbury also defends unmarried women, telling Mrs. Morris, her cleaning woman, that many women live alone without husbands because they have no choice. However, Mrs. Morris expresses the more commonly held opinion when she scornfully laughs, " 'No choice!' " and derisively places the blame squarely on women for not being clever enough to get husbands (*Excellent Women* 170). Similarly, Dulcie Mainwaring, wondering if she might become friends with Aylwin Forbes' estranged wife, "realized that Marjorie was in a superior position, for she had at least acquired a husband and been married to him for some years, whereas she herself had only got as far as a fiancée" (*No Fond Return* 225). When Tom Mallow's aunt calls on Catherine Oliphant in *Less Than Angels*, she announces: " 'I am Mrs. Beddoes. I live in Belgravia.' " Remembering that Tom's other aunt is a spinster who lives in South Kensington, Catherine thinks: "Clearly Mrs. Beddoes was the superior one—Belgravia and the married state had raised her up" (132). Because women have traditionally been defined through men and their power limited to the domestic realm, women without men have been relegated to a kind of wasteland where, having failed to establish their worth through marriage, they are expected to dwell meekly and anonymously.

Some clear effects of the lopsided world in which marriage is the desired state are the feelings of inadequacy produced in unmarried women and the way it devalues women's relationships with other women. Mildred Lathbury points out the difference men can make in women's relationships with one another when, shopping one afternoon with her old friend Dora Caldicote, she is able to forget for a while the complications the Napiers have brought to her life: "I was back in those happier days when the company of women friends had seemed enough" (*Excellent Women* 102). Women's friendship is something one must settle for: if it now is something that had once "seemed enough," then something else—in Mildred's case, the excitement of Rocky Napier—is more desirable. Indeed, just a moment later Mildred is thinking nastily of Dora's appearance when Dora wants to choose the same color dress she has always worn for everyday. Similarly, when Emma Howick's mother Beatrix and her mother's friend Isobel visit Emma at Christmas, Emma resigns herself "to a quiet female celebration of the festival...There seemed little prospect of any other form of entertainment" (*Few Green Leaves* 235). The "other form of entertainment," it is implied, is spending the day in the company of a man. Prudence Bates at one point thinks of how husbands always take women friends away and considers herself fortunate that her friend Jane Cleveland has remained fairly independent despite her marriage.

Certainly Letty Crowe's relationship with her longtime friend Marjorie in *Quartet in Autumn* illustrates the ways in which relationships with men supersede women's friendships. While Marjorie had married, Letty had not. But as a widow, Marjorie has gone on several package tours abroad with

Letty, and Letty is planning to share Marjorie's cottage once she retires. On Letty's two-week visit with Marjorie during her summer vacation, however, Letty is once again reminded of her secondary role when Marjorie becomes involved with a man, for David Lydell, the new vicar, gets much more attention than Letty does during that visit. Later, when Marjorie and David become engaged, Marjorie wants Letty to consider retiring to an old people's home, it being impossible now for her to live with Marjorie. Yet not long after, when her engagement is broken, Marjorie naturally assumes that Letty will once again change her plans and move in with her.

In *Excellent Women*, part of Mildred Lathbury's new awareness of the circumscribed nature of her life is a profound deepening of disgust for women just like herself, whom she describes as nondescript, anonymous, and mediocre. Repeatedly she makes disparaging comments about the gatherings of women just like her. While the Napiers seem to have darkened Mildred's attitude toward her predictable and dull friends, she has never been very charitable toward women. When they first meet, for instance, Mildred instinctively dislikes Helena Napier; but she feels an immediate affinity for Rocky before she meets him, leaping mentally to his defense, as it were, when Helena describes her own slovenly ways. She has "an inexplicable distrust of widows" (45) and therefore is not at all friendly to Allegra Gray, though in all fairness to Mildred, Allegra's superior air does not make her particularly lovable. Having lived with Dora Caldicote once, the prospect of living with her again in twenty or thirty years, bickering over trifles, is "a depressing picture" (105). She is in a panic about the possibility of Winifred's living with her, and at the end of the novel, she is not looking forward to the company of the two women who are moving into the flat vacated by the Napiers, even though they are exactly the sort of people one would like to share a house with.

Mildred's low opinion of herself and other women is what comes from living in a society where one's importance hinges on one's attachment to a man: it not only reduces one's sense of self-worth but distorts and embitters one's views of other women. We see this phenomenon in *An Academic Question*, for instance, when Caroline Grimstone feels inferior to Iris Horniblow and Cressida, particularly when she suspects that these women have won her husband's affection. On her way to see Cressida, she feels "a deep sense of inferiority" (127). Certainly Belinda Bede's sense in *Some Tame Gazelle* that Agatha Hoccleve is a stronger woman than she stems in part from her having lost out to Agatha in her bid for Henry's attentions when they were all at university together.

Miss Doggett in both *Crampton Hodnet* and *Jane and Prudence* believes that her advanced age puts her in the same category as married women, whose experience and worldliness place them in a class above lowly unmarried women. Miss Doggett constantly reminds Jessie Morrow of her lack of experience and consequent inability to draw any kind of sensible conclusions from the behavior of others. There is even a sense that unmarried women are not privy to certain knowledge and experiences shared by married women, an opinion rooted in long-held social attitudes. Mildred Lathbury seems to hold this view as well, exemplified by her remark about "the inadequacy that an unmarried and inexperienced woman must always feel" (*Excellent Women* 25). Letty, in *Quartet in Autumn*, goes away from a weekend visit to her widowed cousin feeling that she has failed in a way she had not realized before. Although she had long before gotten used to being without a man and not having children, now she is struck by the knowledge that she has no grandchildren to comfort her in her old age. In contrast to her friend Marjorie, Letty has never had romance in her life. She feels keenly aware of her shortcoming when, over dinner, she knows that Marjorie is keeping her exuberance over her engagement in check in order not to "emphasise the contrast between her own enviable position, that of being a helpmate to a man, and Letty's state of useless retirement" (124). Letty has always felt this contrast, from early on at school when Marjorie had found a husband and Letty had not, to the picnic she goes on with Marjorie and David Lydell, where at one point she feels "in some way belittled or diminished" as Marjorie and David sit on canvas chairs and she on the ground (44). She even defers to Mrs. Pope's opinion at one point when she knows full well that Mrs. Pope is wrong: "A married woman—and she must not forget that Mrs. Pope was that—might very well be able to detect subtle shades of meaning in a relationship which would be lost on the inexperienced Letty" (170). The irony is that Letty's instinct, in this case about the possibility of any special affection between Edwin and Marcia, is correct. It seems more likely to her that there is something between Marcia and Norman, but Mrs. Pope's certainty in her position as a widow causes Letty to feel thoroughly confused about her own judgment.

Despite this superiority attributed to married women, marriages themselves are typically either troubled or boring relationships, disappointments indeed in light of all the energy expended in achieving that state. While it seems that everyone wants to be or thinks people should be married, the marriages themselves are not particularly comforting or loving. Husbands and wives are often sources of irritation to one another, some couples arguing frequently, others having coped by generally ignoring one another. In *Some Tame Gazelle*, for instance, Henry and Agatha Hoccleve argue loudly over her "failure" to prevent moths from getting into his gray suit and often seem antagonistic toward one another. Even passing references to marriages suggest that they are restrictive of women's liberties and largely serve men's interests and needs. When the President of the Learned Society dies in *Excellent Women*, his widow gives all his anthropology collection to the society. Mildred believes his widow must now be experiencing freedom and, when Helena says that she does not have church or good works to keep her busy, Mildred's first response is " 'Oh, did he take even that from her?...Oh, the wicked things men do...!' " (177). Dulcie Mainwaring wonders at her sister's suppressed and unfulfilled desire to live freely, but she understands when she considers her brother-in-law's self-absorbed, annoying habits. In *An Unsuitable Attachment*, Mark and Sophia Ainger are out of touch with one another, Sophia's devotion to her cat Faustina effectively displacing the love Mark thinks ought properly be lavished on him. Furthermore, that novel has a brief but scathing portrait of a truly horrid marriage between Ianthe's aunt and uncle, Randolph and Bertha Burdon. They have made a loveless marriage, for we are told that Bertha Burdon had married because her parents thought the match a suitable one, that she has never loved, and that she *almost* regrets not having experienced it.

Like Mark and Sophia Ainger of *An Unsuitable Attachment*, Alan and Caroline Grimstone in *An Academic Question* are "together yet apart, not exactly incompatible." Caroline sees Alan as "an adequate husband, an unenthusiastic lover, a dutiful father and a son who despised the family he had grown beyond." Add to that the fact that Caroline "had once been in love with him and in a way [she] still was," and the picture of their marriage is complete (28). Her marriage is similar to that of Rodney and Wilmet for most of *A Glass of Blessings*, for the two of them often have little to say to one another, sleep in separate beds, seldom exhibit tenderness toward one another, and find each other boringly predictable. At one point, during tea at Wilf Bason's when Wilf is called out of the room, Wilmet even feels uncomfortable alone with Rodney. Both the Grimstones and the Forsythes manage to work out their difficulties, but only after thoughts of infidelity on Rodney's part and actual infidelity on Alan's. Wilmet and Caroline handle the straying of their husbands in different ways, but both in the end forgive them. One positive example of a successful marriage is that of Jane and Nicholas Cleveland of *Jane and Prudence*, but even they have occasional misgivings, and their relationship is characterized less by intimate sharing and joyous loving as it is by a kind of putting up with one another and having learned to adjust to each other's eccentricities. Jane, for instance, describes marriage as "finding a person boring and irritating and yet loving him" (192), while Nicholas sometimes wonders if celibacy might not have been the better choice.

In addition to the various difficulties of married couples, a further irony is that married women occasionally express envy of unmarried women. Rowena in *A Glass of Blessings*, married and the mother of three children, at one point tells Wilmet she envies spinsters because they still have their dreams: " 'The despised spinster still has the chance of meeting somebody...At least she's *free*!' " (149). Wilmet herself has told us a short time before that April this year was cruel in precisely the way Eliot meant it: "mingling memory and desire. The memory was of other springs, the desire unformulated, unrecognized almost, pushed away because there seemed to be no place for it in the life I had chosen for myself" (148). In *An Academic Question*, Iris Horniblow tells Caroline Grimstone that she envies the unattached their freedom from domestic responsibilities. Belinda Bede, a confirmed spinster, points out in Pym's first novel that one real advantage of being unmarried is the freedom to imagine what might have been or could possibly yet be, and this idea seems to be confirmed by many married women.

Besides simply wanting more freedom, married women find themselves envying single women because they do not have to bother with childish or unfaithful husbands. This matter of husbands' infidelity comes up from time to time. In *Jane and Prudence*, Fabian Driver's affairs are common knowledge. The subject is broached in *No Fond Return of Love* with Aylwin Forbes's alleged involvement with another woman. In *Crampton Hodnet*, Francis Cleveland has an inclination to be unfaithful and goes so far as Dover with his young lover, who abandons him there, much to his relief. His wife, feeling pressured by Miss Doggett to do something about Francis when she would rather just ignore him, finds herself thinking of the freedom of not being married. Sitting in a restaurant puzzling over her husband's presumed infidelity, she equates excellence in women with good sense. Observing a woman in a "sensible hat and costume," Margaret notices that she is not wearing a ring:

> Then, presumably, she hadn't got a husband. She was a comfortable spinster with nobody but herself to consider. Living in a tidy house not far from London, making nice little supper dishes for one, a place for everything and everything in its place, no husband hanging resentfully round the sitting-room, no husband one moment topping and tailing gooseberries and the next declaring that he had fallen in love with a young woman. Mrs. Cleveland sighed a sigh of envy. No husband. (172)

Margaret's envying of unmarried women comes at a time of real strain on her relationship with her husband, of course, yet Margaret has for some time had the sense that Francis is largely someone who gets underfoot, more or less an inconvenience to put up with when he is around.

That the "full life" of married women is not all that wonderful is particularly clear in the case of widows, who enjoy the privilege of their attachment to men but express relief at no longer having to bother with them. Widows of rich or influential men, for instance, are regarded with a veneration that would not be given unmarried women. Lady Beddoes in *Crampton Hodnet* and Lady Clara Boulding in *Some Tame Gazelle* are just such women. Lady Beddoes, widow of an ambassador, is pleased to be invited to perform an opening ceremony at a church garden party. And, like Agatha Hoccleve, daughter of a bishop and wife of an archdeacon, Lady Clara Boulding is doubly important as not only the widow of a former Member of Parliament but the daughter of an earl and is called upon for such distinguished activities as performing the opening ceremony at the vicarage garden party. Like many other widows in the novels, Lady Beddoes and Lady Boulding benefit from their connection to men but no longer have the trouble of them.

Examples of such women abound. In *Civil to Strangers*, for instance, Mrs. Gower's widowhood has been a relief from the pretense of interest in literature and she no longer regrets the death of her husband some eight years before. Cassandra Marsh-Gibbon, whose existence is devoted to the comforts of her egocentric husband, day-dreams of being an old woman: "To have money and leisure to sit in a lovely garden, enjoying the sunshine and doing Jacobean embroidery; to be a comfortable widow, not recently bereaved, but one whose husband had been ten to twenty years in his grave and whose passing was no longer deeply mourned, would not this be a delightful existence?" (91-2). In *Crampton Hodnet*, Lady Beddoes tells Miss Doggett that she has gotten quite used to the absence of her late husband, Sir Lyall, and hints that he was not the great love of her life, much to Miss Doggett's dismay. Mrs. Lyall in *Jane and Prudence* expresses relief that breakfasts are no longer the big meals they were when her husband was alive, while Mabel Swan in *Less Than Angels* refers to her son as being reliable and dull like his late father and is grateful that she is free to prepare salads for the evening meal instead of the heavy, hot meals her husband expected. Finally, in *A Few Green Leaves*, Beatrix Howick's husband "had been killed in the war, and having, as it were, fulfilled herself as a woman Beatrix had been able to return to her academic studies with a clear conscience" (8).

Hence the ideal state for a woman in Barbara Pym's novels may very well be widowhood. She seems to be implying that if the world insists on marriage for women, there is at least one way in which they can have their freedom and still be regarded as worthy human beings. Her tone is not angry nor her vision pessimistic. Rather, Pym treats the self-centerednesss of men with wonderful humor and irony, pointing out the absurdity of their preferential treatment in the way men's importance affects even the most intelligent and admirable of women. In her journal following her breakup with Gordon Glover, Pym at one point wrote: "It is sometimes intolerable to be a woman and have no second bests or spares or anything. I struggled with this feeling" (*Very Private Eye* 119). The result of her struggle was to develop a wisdom about life and relationships that carries over into her treatment of single women in her fiction. Her portrayal of spinsters gives attention to badly maligned human beings who had rarely been treated positively in either literature or life. Pym reveals the ways in which society's view of spinsters can produce feelings of inadequacy in them; at the same time, her unmarried central characters have a resiliency and wry sense of humor that enables them to cope with their particular lot in life.

Thus, Pym creates a character like Belinda Bede, for instance, who might see herself as "dowdy and insignificant, one of the many thousand respectable middle-aged spinsters, the backbones or busybodies of countless parishes throughout the country" (*Some Tame Gazelle* 176), but at the same time, Belinda also good-humoredly thinks that simply recognizing pathos in oneself might mean that it did not actually exist. Like Belinda, many of Pym's other heroines—Mildred Lathbury, Jessie Morrow (of *Crampton Hodnet*), Catherine Oliphant, Dulcie Mainwaring, and Emma Howick—know themselves well. They may be considered by others and even see themselves as being on the periphery of things as spinsters, yet they have developed very clear senses of their own limitations and possibilities. This is illustrated by Pym's archetypal spinster, Mildred Lathbury, who may have resigned herself to a lesser life than she would have liked and may end up married to Everard Bone, performing clerical tasks and cooking for him, but readers are struck by the poignancy, not the pathos, of her life. Indeed, *Excellent Women* is a chronicle of Mildred's struggle to change her life because she knows her own needs very well; at the same time, everyone else in the novel sees her as a source of real strength in times of their own emotional crises.

Pym implies throughout her novels that the characters with real emotional depths and insight into themselves and others are precisely those women who superficially appear nondescript and self-effacing, that is, unmarried women. Catherine Oliphant has considerable inner resources, as do both Emma Howick and Dulcie Mainwaring, who are independent and self-sufficient. While all of these women are intelligent and sensible, they are at the same time drawn to men who are ultimately not their equals. This culturally-shaped inclination in women to subordinate themselves is particularly strong in Pym's spinsterish women, who feel compassion for others and who desire good relationships with men. The problem in Pym's world is that there are no good men, that society defines women's worth in terms of their ability to marry, and that marriages themselves usually turn out to be unsatisfactory.

In general all the men are treated so mockingly, often as caricatures, that, like the women who love them, one can only smile at their pomposities and self-indulgences. Pym's women, compelled as they are to form attachments with these men, are fully aware of the unfairness of such arrangements and regard themselves with a kind of self-mockery for participating in them. When Prudence Bates says scornfully that she has no need of a husband, Jane Cleveland immediately thinks of how useful her husband Nicholas is for such things as telling silly jokes to, carrying luggage, and much more, and when Mrs. Glaze tells her that the previous curate was already married when he came to them, Jane thinks: "Oh, but that was bad! Bad of the Bishop to send them a curate already engaged. It was a wonder the ladies of the parish hadn't torn him to pieces" (*Jane and Prudence* 19). Jane's impression of the silliness of men and the way women flutter about them is refreshing and delightful. Pym implies that this is the kind of balance one needs when weighing the negative social view of spinsters against their real merit. Though the world she portrays requires marriage as ultimate proof of a woman's worth, her real strength, Pym suggests, lies elsewhere, in her self-sufficiency, her self-knowledge, and her ability to adapt to misguided notions of women's value with grace and humor.

Notes

[1] *Women in England, 1870-1950: Sexual Divisions and Social Change*, p. 14.

[2]*Ibid.*, p. 4.

[3]*Ibid.*, p. 3.

[4]For detailed discussions of the portrayals of unmarried women in novels, see Dorothy Yost Deegan, *The Stereotype of the Single Woman in American Novels* (New York: King's Crown Press, 1951), and Merryn Williams, *Women in the English Novel, 1800-1900* (New York: St. Martin's Press, 1984).

[5]For a discussion of single women's ambivalency and married women's disillusionment in five of Pym's novels, see Mary Strauss-Noll, "Love and Marriage in the Novels," in *The Life and Work of Barbara Pym*, ed. Dale Salwak (Iowa City: University of Iowa Press, 1987, 72-87).

Diana Benet in *Something to Love: Barbara Pym's Novels* (Columbia, MO.: University of Missouri Press, 1986) also addresses the subject of marriage as fulfillment or frustration of the need to be loved. Benet observes that Pym's treatment of marriages is unromantic, that marriages may be affectionate and cozy but that they are just as likely to be disappointing and unfulfilling.

Works Cited

Lewis, Jane. *Women in England, 1870-1950: Sexual Divisions and Social Change.* Bloomington: Indiana UP, 1984.

Pym, Barbara. *An Academic Question.* New York: E.P. Dutton, 1986.

———. *Civil to Strangers and Other Writings.* London: Macmillan, 1987.

———. *Crampton Hodnet.* New York: E.P. Dutton, 1985.

———. *Excellent Women.* New York: E.P. Dutton, 1978.

———. *A Few Green Leaves.* New York: E.P. Dutton, 1980.

———. *A Glass of Blessings.* New York: E.P. Dutton, 1980.

———. *Jane and Prudence.* New York: E.P. Dutton, 1981.

———. *Less Than Angels.* New York: E.P. Dutton, 1980.

———. *No Fond Return of Love.* New York: E.P. Dutton, 1982.

———. *Quartet in Autumn.* New York: E.P. Dutton, 1978.

———. *Some Tame Gazelle.* New York: E.P. Dutton, 1983.

———. *The Sweet Dove Died.* New York: E.P. Dutton, 1979.

———. *An Unsuitable Attachment.* New York: E.P. Dutton, 1982.

———. *A Very Private Eye: An Autobiography in Diaries and Letters.* Ed. Hazel Holt and Hilary Pym. New York: E.P. Dutton, 1984.

The Dismembered Couple:
Krapp's Last Tape and *Happy Days*

Mary F. Catanzaro

Coupling and its seeming impossibility are central to the works of Samuel Beckett. That was already apparent in his critical study of Proust in 1931 where we see the full range of broken promise in the separateness and otherness which undermine accord between two people. Beckett speaks of subject and object within the scaffolding of his self-defining term, pseudocouple, which attempts to dissolve the myth of total oneness with another. In the physical impediments and emotional ruptures of the pseudocouple we find a virtual metaphysics of discord. In these two plays, the voice—highly particularized and operating on several registers simultaneously—is the main theatrical device that Beckett employs to show that the subject *speaking* is no more than a succession of always subverted selves.

One of the complications arising from the voice that speaks is that the subject becomes aware of a need for an other whose presence might offer some comfort to the multitude of his changing selves. The impasse, however, is never removed. In *Krapp's Last Tape*[1] and *Happy Days*,[2] Beckett addresses alienation in the realm of voiced memory, where the subjects most often fail to work through prior experiences with others that can be felt, but that cannot be fully articulated. Here, the voice's structure demonstrates finite time within infinity; what it says in effect is that to live is to repeat in succession the fragments of one's past. To speak is to lie, in this case, and as a result both Krapp and Winnie echo the doctrine of guilt and suffering, all the while realizing the insufficiency of memory.

If looked at conventionally, the plain story *Happy Days* portrays a couple who have apparently been married for quite some time. The play is made up almost entirely of domestic banalities exchanged between the two—he reads aloud ads from the newspaper and mumbles vaguely when questioned or addressed. She in turn does her toilette, recites sentimental poetry, and rambles on about her prior youthful "romances." Buried in an earthen mound, Winnie seems to make up for her husband's absence in the first act by rummaging through her pocketbook and examining its contents, which become for her fetish pieces. Like many people who lead extremely orderly lives, she is liable to distressing monologues. She mutters mild abuse of Willie for his shortcomings, and her suspicions of him so reduce her sense of partnership that it becomes harder for her to endure isolation. It appears that her former social networks with Willie have gradually ceased to function. That she suffers because he is absent stems from a need to be witnessed; thus she creates companionship for herself through her voice. Winnie's strategy seems to be based on an inner, voiced narrative, a means at once of denying intolerable contradictions that lie hidden beneath the social surface of their marriage, as intolerable as the necessity that gives rise to relations of domination in their interactions, and of constructing on the very ground cleared by such a denial a substitute truth that makes existence at least partly bearable.

In *Krapp's Last Tape*, the lonely and alcoholic Krapp also manipulates objects, most notably a tape recorder and a reel, which allow him to listen to and to record new material about his past. The information on the tape exposes his past relationships with others, particularly women—his mother, the nurse who attended her, his former lovers, even his favorite fictional heroine. In this play the couple seems to have fallen apart utterly, for Krapp's past affairs (even his present one) are alive only through the voice on the tape. The tape itself seems to play the role of the absent other, and the voice on that tape attempts to reconstruct presence with that other. Combined with Krapp's intellect (he is a stickler for precise diction) and a rare ability to remember minute events from the past, is also a driving will, a determination to welcome sorrow. He unites in his person both inexorable self-will and the capacity for deep attachment, both appalling ruthlessness towards his former trivial errors ("Just been listening to that stupid bastard I took myself for..." [24]) and unswerving fidelity to a beloved who "agreed...it was hopeless and no good going on..." (27). By conventional standards, Krapp and Winnie are not successful as lovers, but their failures there do not diminish their longing for love's continuance.

What Krapp and Winnie become are not as important as the realization that their relationships to others in their memories seem to provide a stable system of coordinates to which the *idea* of permanent companionship may be affirmed. But part of what causes their inability to achieve a sure and confident feeling of coupling is their combative stance towards others, in collision with each other in their consciousnesses, for they have built into them a polarity, a veer toward subject-centeredness.

Krapp's Last Tape and *Happy Days* communicate both mental and physical pain, which is centered in the various guises of love: domestic life, romance, but particularly in sex, where people are most sensitive, where the greatest damage can be done, and where the pain of living is felt most strongly. As a consequence, excruciating and undiminishing pain, which neither Winnie nor Krapp can remedy or alleviate, is one of the inescapable liabilities of human relations that Beckett seems to want to make clear. At the same time, he makes of all the distress of each a never-flagging survival story.

One crucial question stands at the forefront of both plays: what is Beckett trying to say about relationships and coupling in *Krapp's Last Tape* and *Happy Days*? Part of the readers' quandary no doubt stems from the peculiar anonymity of love itself. Where the conscious "forgetting" of past traumas and disappointments erases emotional boundaries and therefore allows us to deal with the here-and-now, the liquid inner dialogue of memory usually permits an unhurried study and detached contemplation of our past affairs.

But there are deeply-rooted sources in the inner voice, whose history is that of a "living" memory and whose nature is quirky and elusively adaptable. The *voice* of memory, moreover, is not easy to dissect, and the agencies responsible for implementing and refining its techniques are not easily accessible. For example, Winnie's strategy as it purports to invest the realm of her personal security is commonly shared by the viewer, far beyond her own voiced memory, whereas Krapp's "reporting" is disadvantaged by his habits of self-selecting in his memories.

What does this suggest about the dismembered couple? To drive the point home, it appears that the contents of the tape and Winnie's monologues are not of such immediate interest here as the *modes* of authentication to which appeal is made, and which consequently inform their various stylistics. The respective drives and dodges of each rely on a variety of groundings in their past experiences. We hear of Krapp's reference to his as yet unfinished masterpiece, and hear the bravura of his "fire," and yet feel skeptical about it because we have seen the dramatic solemnity, the tragic framing of his humanity in the citational mode of his recontextualizing himself on his tape. Plus, of course, the fear of time, lest it run out on him, counterpoised with reason, lest he act unseasonably out of such fear.

These plays present figures who have problems with the idea of romance, with domestic life, and with communication in general. Beckett does not evade the sexual in these plays and it seems to be related in an essential way to the subjects' need to control the feeling of confinement and physical deterioration that partnership and time exact from them. These plays present figures who have very little stage business other than reciting reminiscences, and this dramatic approach poses new critical problems. Beckett seems to be saying that romance has *nothing whatsoever* in common with domestic life, and that the romantic notion of total togetherness is a myth. The aim here is not so much an interpretation of voiced memories as an examination of what the partial or absent figure may yield about the couple. Beckett's concepts of the couple seem to be based on his recognition of the multitude of unknowable and separate selves within the subject, and over against this is posited the reality of suffering within partnerships. The deadly repetitiousness of the voice says one thing only: that the loss of a partner is violent, especially as it surfaces in language. The rhythmic interplay between subject and object is not merely thematic, it is also visual. Thus there is an alternation of light and dark, sound and space, absence and presence. But even when communication appears to fail altogether, or when the partner disappears, the couple, however dismembered, is preserved because Beckett finds a way to bring the other back, either in person, through fetish objects, or the voice. In this way he makes the other visible—an object of sight and experience—in order to stress the pain endured by the other's absence.

Beckett emphatically demonstrates that voiced memory mirrors the instabilities of partnerships, for in his subjects' attempts to triumph over space and distance, to bridge differences in time, and to listen to the inner voice *as it speaks*, it seems as though memory itself has already been implicated in the desire to reconstruct presence with an other. What is ultimately clear is the pain of an absent loved one and sexual impairment. The outright disappearance of the other can be fairly quickly defined—whether or not it can be distinguished fully from memory's recrudescence in the voice is quite another matter. But it is important to have some notion of the complexity of disappearance. It is the relationship to absence which accounts for both Krapp's and Winnie's finding it necessary to substitute for an inadequate relationship the relationship of speech, at the same time that they manipulate objects for the more desired object—the other person. Hence the dramatic need for the tape and pocketbook routines. Winnie and Krapp transfer upon their objects feelings which originally applied to a beloved; thus she kisses her revolver, and he calls his tape by pet names—"rascal" and "scoundrel" (12). The centrality of human relationships in these works is so plain that Beckett seems to be speaking to those who wonder whether life without some sort of tie to another is bound to lack some dimension. But let us examine each play more closely.

Krapp's tape suggests that perhaps the most painful qualities of partnership are alienation and loneliness, and although he is at 69 involved with another woman, Fanny, he still yearns for deeper gratification, something more. His obsessional routines with his tape recorder demonstrate those feelings of separation, for it is on the tape that he experiences regret, self-hatred, and sexual passion. Such mixed emotions, cancelling each other out and resulting in emotional paralysis, characterize Krapp's behavior. From what we hear on the tape, it almost seems as if Krapp's idea of love consists in alternately rehashing romantic memories and anticipating a horrible future. Krapp appears to believe this, for his favorite song is "Now the day is over" (17).

The absence or unavailability of a partner poses an additional sexual problem, which may explain Krapp's reluctance to take on the domestic, and why he clings to romantic ideals. Krapp's disappearance behind the drapes and reemergence is a paradigm of Freud's *fort/da*. In this way he stages his own disappearance, as well as his beloved's; he then brings both back—he on stage and his beloved on tape. This maneuver might also indicate that he needs to control the anxiety that comes from separation with another.

The taped voice says in effect: to be transitory is what we are. There is no new story to tell, nothing new to report. But to *want* it is to be separate, to be apart. Krapp's reproduced voice indicates that he suffers two contrary miseries: to suffer from the other's presence on the tape and to suffer from the other's death (death because she is not united with him in a loving relationship). Krapp is therefore doubly wretched, but feels compelled to remind himself repeatedly of his lost love through the images that the tape recalls. In this way Krapp's taped voice indicates two facts: that he is already distanced from his beloved, and that he has relinquished at least some of his desire for the other's literal presence. For example, the advantage of the tape machine is that Krapp is at once subject and object, actor and audience. With a single object, Beckett eliminates the need for a partner to be present. The tape recorder creates a new perceptual situation, for the open microphone, like the open camera, creates not so much a frame as a window. The tape makes clear several levels of voicing, for the voice on the tape tells one report, while the other voice, at the ready with the microphone, edits and tells another. These vocal processes prime the viewer for closer attentiveness to a work whose action takes place in minute particulars, nuances, overtones that are symptomatic of upheavals in the depths of memory.

The narrative movement of the story on the spool is organized by a series of time disruptions. When we consider to what degree Krapp switches the controls to fast forward, then to play, then to fast rewind, when we realize how much his attempting to rearrange time includes his frustrated sexual desire and yearning for fulfillment, we will perhaps achieve some sense of how much emphasis Beckett is putting on the impairment of coupling and why he causes the voice—here reproduced—to intervene, as though to reawaken the body. Beckett's use of an *amplified* voice to cry out to a lost body suggests even more emphatically than dialogue between pairs, the failure of togetherness.

Krapp does not listen to his tapes to take a realistic stock of himself; it is a mechanical habit, a ritual, a reason to obsessively brood. Little wonder, then, that Krapp's tape only strengthens the huge gulf between the past and the present. He confronts his various selves by means of the mechanical device, and we are eavesdropping on his sexual regrets and conflicts, not his satisfactions. The past anterior—the having done—is heard on the tape and it reveals his resistance to the narrative drive.

Krapp accordingly communicates to a beloved through the tape, which has preserved intact, for thirty years, his passion for the other. But if time cannot close those wounds, can memory do any better? Krapp apparently wants to keep the wound gaping, for at any moment, he can simply reach for the tape and recycle a lost passion. With the punt sequence, Beckett took one of his biggest risks. It is all a subdued hysterical outburst, a scene that must be must be played in three ways: backwards, in order for Krapp to identify himself with his former self; forwards, as a way to anticipate his present, disappointed self; and in real time, in order to comment on both the past and present selves. Like Lacan's notion of *méconnaissance*, the tape reveals that the subject can only be read backwards. But does Krapp ever modify himself from all his re-plays?

Krapp's returning to the punt sequence over and over stresses the negative function of the absent partner. By Krapp's repeated manipulations of the tape machine's advance and rewind controls, what is suggested is that the real point lies in the *gap* that we don't hear. In the interior sequences of the gaps on the tape we can only guess about Krapp's success or failure with the white nurse, or the the girl in the shabby green coat, Fanny, or even Effie.

If anything, Krapp's *stage* voice reveals his lack of will power, an indifference towards the somersaults of his inner life. It consists primarily of primitive sounds—he mimes the syllables of "viduity" (18), curses unintelligibly and with increasing intensity (21), and "clears his throat" (26) before recording. The voice on the current, virgin tape behaves with skepticism, both towards his reasonings and the raving imperatives of his desires whenever it speaks of his memories of women; and his asides, curses, and commentaries only serve to conceal the painful emotions that his present self feels. As he tapes, Krapp's voice is intense, linear, tough, angry, and, in its terrierlike way, impassioned. This voice is far removed from the warmer, grander, more magisterial voice that prevailed on the earlier tape, at age thirty-nine.

Yet the voice on the older tape also seems to be a trauma manifesting itself, with its dramatic intermittences. This vocal plot provides the only opportunity for Krapp to reincarnate himself in the repetitive scheme of the infinite possibilities that the recorder presents—if not of the real world, at least of the world filtered through the device of the plastic tape. In this way, Krapp's inner life is forced to yield his secret, which turns out to be a recurrent one in all his machinations: the illusory nature of any aspiration to authentic action or living with another person—a real woman—in the here and now. Beckett chooses the taped, voiced memory of Krapp as a young man to show the neediness of the forgotten child curled up within the psyche of the grown, and—for all we know—once successful adult. Now, however, Krapp's desire only flows into the flatness of a journalistic memoir.

One could also argue that by the power that Krapp has to duplicate himself in his tape, he can rediscover his other selves and formulate a repository for his love. In such a manner, his voiced memory may be his only means of salvaging partnership. In calling forth his other selves from the machine, Krapp uses speech and memory, edited with commentary, to conceal the painful and corrosive emotions that his present self feels.

But there is something sentimental about the recorded memory of the death of Krapp's mother and the romantic attachments to the nurse and the girl in the shabby green coat. There is something cowardly in the remark that it was "no good going on" (22) with his beloved, that he gave up on love. Here we become aware that Krapp senses that with even the most cautious acceptance of change comes the fear of being cornered, of being inextricably redefined. With choice also comes entrapment. Nothing is forever and some things cannot be undone easily (marriage) and others cannot be undone at all (children). There is a closing off of certain avenues when one moves forward; the arena in which to play out one's fate may not necessarily get smaller when marriage is elected but it undeniably takes on a different form. And then there is the other specter: we all make new choices in the hope that they're for the better; but what happens when they prove to be for the worse? It's as if the bitter and disappointed Krapp prefers his solitary den rather than face what domestic life demands: an other who may *not* always be available. Even the daily newspaper becomes for some, if not many, the very object behind which partners absent themselves from their mates. The dismemberment of the couple often begins with the trivial objects of domesticity.

In *Happy Days*, it *is* from behind that newspaper that Willie must listen to Winnie's dreams of some lovely Victorian romance. There is something embarrassingly adolescent about Winnie's memories of her first ball and her first kiss; and those "memorable lines" are as useless as her prayers to bolster her up, and fail as much as Krapp's bottle. She and Krapp want to compartmentalize their experiences, and his tape and her handbag reflect this desire for containment. Beckett wants to show that life is not like that, that it's impossible to separate or parcel out our experience; that life in fact is a blend.

But "there is so little one *can* do," concludes Winnie (22). Most commentators have expressed more sympathy for Winnie than disapproval at her prudishness. Willie is usually only mildly castigated for his seeming lack of interest in his spouse, but has she, in fact, had something to do with their separation? Is there a need in Willie that she hasn't met? True, she speaks to Willie. But she has also poked him with her umbrella and has cracked his head with her carelessly tossed empty medicine bottle.

Yet Willie *seems* willing enough, as his name and his diversions with the sexually explicit postcard suggest. The connection here seems to be that coupling need not necessarily be hindered by confinement, for the realization of togetherness is primarily in the head. Willie's head rising up from behind the mound achieves two dramatic functions: first we see a literal partial figure, and second, this focus on the head lends significance to the fact that Winnie's sexual parts are buried in this play. Their absence makes a crucial point. (We must remember too that even Krapp's sexuality was alive only on a plastic piece of tape).

Winnie's pathetic repetitions and reminiscences imply a weakening of her ability to recognize another. Winnie accordingly appears to have learned nothing in Act II, as the notes indicate: *"Scene as before"* (49). She does indeed try to get through her day in the present, but she shoots back to memory—"What are those wonderful lines?" (10). Later on we realize that those wonderful lines are a cover-up for something else, namely the cries: "No, no, my head was always full of cries" (56). She does not have the *words* to express her pain, but she has "cries." Beckett sees that trouble with expressing pain is one of the hallmarks of couples who aren't in tune with each other. Winnie's details of little Mildred's "rape" by the mouse, the Cooker story, and her talk of her breasts are suggestive that something has gone wrong with the sexual aspect of their relationship that surpasses her confinement.

It is a measure of how inextricably the visual language of Winnie's past is tangled with that of the present that the viewer does not hear much mention of the present tense. In some part, this is a conspiracy between Beckett and the audience. The viewer is first introduced to Winnie and then to her voiced memories. The title ironically implies this. They *were* happy days and they now have a voice—several voices actually, Winnie's personal, neutral one (a sly deviation from her *real* feelings) and other unspoken voices (the cries in her head) closely embedded in the text of the first, and the former is mute without *them*. If, in fact, the cries had not offered her the problems of various "subjects," she would have nothing to recount and would probably never have emerged into the light of words.

In *Happy Days*, Winnie is restored to herself outside the ordinary dispersion of time, for everything is dismissed except her voice. The intention seems to instill in her the confidence that here, at least, in this walled-up world, she is in the presence of something that might still be called company: God? the future presence of Willie? What we have here is the bedrock Calvinist insistence on the complete otherness of God and the brokenness of humanity, the perfect "couple" in particular. If that gap is to be bridged, it will be done from the other side, by God's gracious act, and not by anything that Winnie can do except acknowledge her own need. Such a frieze is a visual incantation, a hopeful ritual summoned up to restore her crippled faith in her ability to enjoy *real* coupling and to engage in reciprocal love. The visions of the past continue to recur not so much for love of their details as for the security they provide in her loneliness. The past offers a vision of measurable, wrapped-up order. Her life had a place, once upon a time, and its own clear rules. Now, it is all confusion. Small wonder, then, in this perplexing environment, that she should so often be drawn to bizarre tokens for companionship—her "lines" and stories on the one hand, and her revolver, toothbrush, lipstick and hat on the other. The stark tableau of Winnie, buried to the neck, lit in a blazing light against a backdrop of giant silhouetted shadows, emphasizes all the more that she is dressed only in the dramatic coats of her past.

Winnie's failure with her spouse cannot be grasped except through her voice, and the pain that follows is an intrinsic feature of the couple. Her voice is also what agitates her memory. The business with Willie's obscene postcard is a minuscule scene, yet it leads Winnie further along toward the loss of her mate. She takes issue with its contents: *"No but this is just* genuine pure filth! (*Examines card.*) Make any nice-minded person want to vomit!"* (19). This is precisely the sort of activity that Willie "relishes" and seems to crave. Later on she nags at him for picking his nose behind the mound. Her speaking may provide a momentary break with her memory of the "old style," but it is also the stimulus for much of her connection with him. A torrent of speaking reveals the difficulty of love, yet talking heals the disease.

Happy Days is, above all else, the apotheosis of the voice. What is its substance, its deep structure? It is at once complex and polysemic, spreading its subtle configurations everywhere into the text. But the voice's reception and understanding can only take place when an other is present. This voicing is also an endeavor that can be evaluated only through being heard and by listening to oneself. But Winnie feels injured by that newspaper and Willie's refusal to look at her directly. She makes herself attractive—does her nails, hair. Nothing. She wants to generate a little conversation and so inquires about her toothbrush. Winnie rattles on about nothing. She has nothing to say, but she voices on another level in order to tell Willie that she is speaking to him, in order to say I am speaking to you, you exist for me, I want to exist for you. She wants that reciprocity of which Sartre speaks: "To speak is to pass over words in silence. But this invisibility of the Word obviously implies a deep understanding between those who are communicating."[3] Beckett tirelessly records Winnie's nothing and such talk serves a multiple function. Her rattling offers schemes to provide a way out for her. It also permits the discourse to stand without saying anything (by saying *nothing*), and it allows the incontrovertible banality of domestic life to lay bare all its insignificance.

And cruelty. For conversely, when Winnie says, "—so much to be thankful for—" (11); or, "That is what I find so wonderful, that not a day goes by—(*smile*)—to speak in the old style—(*smile off*)—hardly a day, with some addition to one's knowledge however trifling..." (18), all *that* talk also reveals a deepseated and aggressive anger directed at the other. The torrent of talk that speaks the hurt without *saying* it may be more damaging than saying it outright. Already Willie has affirmed her by simply being there and providing information, but he has *not*. Accordingly, *Happy Days* is a work about people coupled in non-affirmation through talk, and this is their shared activity.

Just as Krapp's tape machine and spool were devices that he used to convey his innermost feelings to his loved ones, the objects in Winnie's bag are also symbolic expenditures through which Winnie attempts to communicate to Willie. In *Happy Days*, however, the objects are used with savage irony. Winnie pokes her spouse with her parasol to get his attention as though he were a household pet. On another occasion she hurts Willie's head with her tossed medicine bottle. The revolver "Brownie" is handled with the same absentmindedness as her toothbrush. This behavior casts doubt on her maturity on the one hand, and her sincerity towards her husband on the other. Norman O. Brown observes that Melanie Klein made her discoveries by interpreting the gestures of children playing with toys.[4] Winnie's comb and brush, her toothbrush, lipstick, revolver, even the hat, make her appear as though she's *playing* grown-up. The bag itself looks like a toy. Growing up, Klein observes, consists in finding new toys, new symbolic equivalents. But here the couple seems to be playing a game. What Willie does *not* say is noteworthy, just as the portions that Krapp bypasses on his tape are telling in their silence.

The voice in *Krapp's Last Tape* and *Happy Days* is used as an instrument that follows its own score going through the detritus of memory. The texture is polyphonic, composed of many voices. The "soul" of both works is in a severe declension of light and dark which gives rhythm and structure and allows the voices to live. In this manner, Beckett rescues the couple through the separation and exchangeability that light and voice induce on subject and object, where a controlled and patient knowledge of lost love is acknowledged, which Krapp and Winnie are only capable of understanding in their voices. But this understanding calls for two parties—the self who voices and the self who hears, for if one were missing there would be a lack.

We are given a glimpse into the complicity between Winnie's ramblings, Krapp's self-commentary, and the tedium of memory. A history of desire is revealed rather than truth. The circular movement of Winnie's monologue and Krapp's voice on the revolving tape allow each to find a solution of sorts, but their voices reveal on a deeper level the devices through which we read the tainted, conditioned, and supplementary text of the couple's most basic needs. But one needn't worry that the couple will vanish. What one does worry about, as always, is one's own relationship to the silence of an indifferent universe. Beckett's figures, at once reduplicated and divided, lack autonomy and are ultimately forced to turn to themselves to achieve psychic unity. The peg of identification of Beckett's couples lies in the realization that many people are more comfortable in a familiar but unhappy situation than in a potentially better one.

Notes

[1]Samuel Beckett, *Krapp's Last Tape and Other Dramatic Pieces* (New York: Grove, 1958). Subsequent references will be cited in the text.

[2]Beckett, *Happy Days* (New York: Grove, 1961). Subsequent references will be cited in the text.

[3]Jean-Paul Sartre, *Saint Genet*, trans., Bernard Frechtman (New York: Pantheon, 1963), 43.

[4]Norman O. Brown, *Love's Body* (New York: Vintage, 1966), 37.

Works Cited

Beckett, Samuel. *Happy Days*. New York: Grove, 1961.
———— *Krapp's Last Tape and Other Dramatic Pieces*. New York: Grove, 1958.
Brown, Norman O. *Love's Body*. New York: Vintage, 1966.
Sartre, Jean-Paul. *Saint Genet*. Trans., Bernard Frechtman New York: Pantheon, 1963.

July's People:
She Knew No Word

Stefanie Dojka

Loyalty is an emotion, integrity a conviction adhered to out of moral values. Therefore I speak here not of loyalties but integrities, in my recognition of society's right to make demands on the writer as equal to that of the writer's commitment to his artistic vision; the source of conflict is what demands are made and how they should be met.[1]

Art is on the side of the oppressed.

(Gordimer, *The Essential Gesture* 289, 291)

Nadine Gordimer is a white South African writer of world importance who, between 1937 and 1989, has published several volumes of short stories, innumerable essays, and ten novels. Her work has been translated into twenty languages, and she has been awarded literary prizes of distinction.[2] In Gordimer's work, social and artistic forces combine to reveal truths that are difficult to face and dangerous to confront, for she writes not only about the injustice of South Africa, but also about the injustice of a world system that depends on the exploitation of the many for the benefit of a few.

Gordimer examines, in convincing detail in her novels, the institutions, public and private, that combine to perpetuate the system of exploitation. The institution of marriage, which both reflects and supports the system, is held up for particular scrutiny. The nature of the marriages in Gordimer's novels reveals the nature of the social and economic forces of exploitation. The majority of the novels are set in South Africa, where the only marriages supported by the power structure are bourgeois ones that contribute to the system of racial abuse and economic oppression.

The pivotal novel in Gordimer's exploration of the institution of marriage is *July's People* (1981), a work set in the future that charts the disintegration of a marriage under the influence of revolution in South Africa. The destruction of the traditional middle-class marriage in *July's People* opens the way for a new institution, the inter-racial marriage, that Gordimer develops in her next novel, also set in the future, *A Sport of Nature* (1987).[3]

To understand the significance of *July's People*, it is useful to look briefly at the nature of the marriages in Gordimer's earlier novels. Her first, *The Lying Days* (1953), is important because in it Gordimer sets the type for several marriages to follow. *The Lying Days* is a coming of age story of a young woman, Helen Shaw, who has been raised in the traditional closed value system of a South African mining community. Helen succeeds

155

in escaping these values as she struggles to develop a broader and more just view of the world. Her parents, however, function exclusively in relation to the mine, where Mr. Shaw has, not coincidentally, risen to a management position. The Shaws' is a traditional bourgeois marriage that both reflects and supports the unjust social and economic system which expresses itself overtly in racial prejudice. When Helen asks permission to offer a black friend a room to study for exams, her parents refuse. Later the Shaws disown Helen when she moves in with her white lover, Paul, without the benefit of marriage. This is a typical example of their support for public social norms at the expense of personal relationships.

It is not only the marriages of middle class aspirants like the Shaws that support the system, however; even marriages between well-intentioned liberals are doomed to repeat the pattern. In the same novel, John and Jenny Marcuse, who at first seem infinitely superior to Helen's parents, prove to be different only in style. John's idea of avoiding bourgeois behavior is to refuse to allow his wife to wear a hat (something she very much wants to do—Gordimer's use of a small humorous detail to expose a greater hypocrisy is reminiscent of Jane Austen here). John and Jenny Marcuse's eventual move to the suburbs and Jenny's total preoccupation with her children implies acceptance of the traditional values of the repressive system that both had originally attempted to reject. The Marcuses are motivated by their desire for comfort. In Gordimer's novels, people who attempt to resist the system are never comfortable; people who attempt to reform it are in trouble.

Reformers are separated from spouses and potential spouses by internal pressures imposed by the system and/or by external pressures such as detention.[4] In *The Lying Days*, internal pressures are explored. Helen is unable to marry Paul, the man she loves, because his commitment to justice for blacks in his work has made commitment to her impossible. Helen initially thinks that she can wait for the right time for the marriage, but reality indicates that the wait will have no end: "Yet how can human beings wait?" she muses, "Wait to live until an atom bomb explodes, a government is overthrown, a white man knows a black man to be just such another as himself?" (264). This statement turns out to be prophetic: in Gordimer's world, the system will have to be overthrown before such a marriage can take place.

A continuing refrain in Gordimer's novels is that love itself is not strong enough to effectively challenge the oppressive system.[5] Helen's distress documents the demise of love due to internal constraints:

I loved Paul and part of my loving him was my belief and pride in the work he had chosen: how was it possible, then, that the difficulties of this work, affecting him, should throw our relationship out of balance? What was the matter with me? Why couldn't I manage? Why couldn't I give him what he needed? (271)

Helen eventually comes to accept her disillusionment as a beginning rather than an end.

For others in the novel, however, there is no such possibility. The final threat to the system lies in the idea of inter-racial marriage. The impossibility for one of those to succeed serves in Gordimer's novels as a metaphor for the division between the races.[6] *The Lying Days* documents the external force used to prevent the mixing of the races with a particularly nightmarish account of the arrest of an old interracial couple who had lived quietly together for years, unaware that they were violating any law. The couple, when the arrest takes place, are compared to "hares that get transfixed by the lights of [a] car on a dark road" (236).

Such external force is, of course, employed in the name of laws used to separate not only inter-racial couples. Separation of black marriages is the norm in a country where blacks are legally prevented from living with their families near their places of employment. Gordimer's second novel, *A World of Strangers*, documents the impossibility of maintaining even the semblance of a good marriage when separation is imposed on black couples. That novel also explores the overwhelming constraints imposed upon rare black marriages where the couples actually succeed in living together. Sam and Ella Mofokenzazi, for example, are educated black professionals with reasonably good incomes. Their attempt to live decently, "following a modest taste for civilized things" (133) in Sophiatown demonstrates the barriers that confront any black couple that desires to have a reasonable life together. Sam's friend, Stephen, says simply of Sam and Ella's home, "it costs too much" (132). Stephen is talking about emotional costs, not about money. In the final line of the novel, Sam is being watched by a suspicious policeman while he talks with a white friend at a train station (265). There is no place for a black middle-class marriage in the system. The Mofokenzazis are a curiosity to their own people, a threat to whites.

Whites who challenge the system that places them in positions of privilege over blacks undergo enforced separations of their marriages. In Gordimer's novel, *Burger's Daughter* (1979), external pressure in the form of political detention poses a constant threat of separation to married couples. The novel opens at the door of a prison where a school girl is waiting to drop off some necessities for her detained mother. The girl provides loving support to her father in the mother's absence. The father is soon to be detained, as well, for political activities on behalf of blacks. The only kind of marriage in these novels, black or white, that is not destroyed or threatened by the unjust political system, then, is the white middle-class marriage that depends for its existence on the preservation (by force, when necessary) of the status quo.

II

In *July's People*, Gordimer pushes into the future, into a violent revolution where the structure of white supremacy is being toppled. The novel focuses on the effects of the revolution on the middle-class marriage of two white liberals, Bam and Maureen Smales, and on their relationship with their black servant, July. The Smales would object very strongly to any notion of their similarity to Helen Shaw's parents (*The Lying Days*), although Maureen, like Helen, was raised in a mining town. They would also object to any suggestion that they condoned the use of violence to preserve the status quo. Unlike the Shaws, who support the oppressive system in obvious ways, Maureen and Bam Smales regret their position of privilege in South Africa and have joined political parties and other groups in attempts to slough off that privilege.

However, in the course of the revolution, the Smale marriage becomes a battleground for the forces unleashed by apocalyptic events that leave no assumption unchallenged. As the novel proceeds, the Smales are forced to confront their complicity in a system which they themselves abhor, and to assume responsibility for conditions which they were conveniently able to ignore in their comfortable suburban existence. As power shifts and becomes ambiguous over the course of the revolution, the marriage is shaken. Gender roles are overturned: Bam becomes more like a woman, Maureen becomes more like a man. The universality of moral values is challenged. The forces of revolution undermine the very basis of the white middle-class marriage, uncovering the language of repression obscured by sincere liberal rhetoric.

The story-line of *July's People* is a simple one. Maureen and Bam Smales are residents of suburban Johannesburg, where July has been their servant of fifteen years. Revolution occurs, and when the shooting and burning overtake the city, July saves the Smales and their three children by taking them to his home.

July's home is a collection of mud huts on the veld, inhabited by his wife and family. It is six hundred kilometres from Johannesburg where he lives and works for the Smales. July's is a marriage of separation, like the ones documented in earlier Gordimer novels. To support his wife and family, July must live in Johannesburg; his family, however, is prevented by law from living with him. This is not a natural arrangement, but one maintained by the imperatives of an exploitative system that overrides "the authority of nature" (83).

Maureen and Bam Smales are not aware of their personal roles as exploiters. To them, July is a "decently paid and contented male servant" (9). He has brought them and their children to his home to save them from the violence of the revolution, and he continues to act as their servant, accepting their standards and supplying their needs. He has given them a mud hut to use, one that belongs to his mother.

The novel opens with Maureen awakening in the mud hut. She cries out, "Bam, I'm stifling," thus "raising him from the dead" (1). The cry summarizes the dynamics of Bam and Maureen's marriage: it reveals Maureen's dependence on her husband as well as the responsibility he assumes for her. (By the end of the novel, Maureen will no longer be able to find the words to raise Bam from the dead.) The hut itself, with its dirt and dung floor and vermin infested thatch, is contrasted to the sanitary imitation-huts where Maureen vacationed as a girl. Exposure to the real article is a shock, and marks the beginning of Maureen's education in the novel. The hut is a metaphor for the meager and stifling lives allowed blacks in South Africa, or more broadly, a metaphor for the lives of oppressed people anywhere.

Bam and Maureen's departure from their comfortable suburb becomes a potential source of intellectual and psychological as well as physical change. Their suburban existence, recalled at the beginning of the novel, provides the standard by which change is measured. Revolution destabilizes the lines of power: July, by necessity, becomes the decision maker, and Bam and Maureen become dependent on his decisions. This change in the power structure sets the plot of *July's People* in motion. The plot revolves around the different responses Bam and Maureen have to their experiences in July's home on the veld. Maureen moves from ignorance to understanding of her role as oppressor; she seeks to divest herself of that role. Bam, however, who as a male has more to lose from the shift in power, remains trapped in the past, unable to change.

Initially, both Bam and Maureen are unaware of their ignorance about the nature of their relationship with their black servant, July. Maureen believes that, although Bam has never learned to understand July's broken English, she and July understand each other well. July, however, is not so deceived. He exercises a kind of authority in his own family, for example, in spite of the enforced absences, and he is embarrassed at Maureen's ignorance "of a kind of authority not understood—his" (13). July exercises his greatest authority in the hut of his wife, and when he takes Maureen there to meet his wife and mother, she becomes aware of not knowing where she is "in time, in the order of a day as she had always known it" (17). Maureen experiences, and is aware of experiencing, the unsettling of her old knowledge and its basic structures.

This unsettling occurs at several places in *July's People*. When Maureen tries to read a novel to imagine an escape to another time and place, for example, she does not find the pleasure possible because she already is in another time and place:

She was in another time, place, consciousness; it pressed in upon her and filled her as someone's breath fills a balloon's shape. She was already not what she was. No fiction could compete with what she was finding she did not know, could not have imagined or discovered through imagination. (29)

What Maureen discovers she "did not know and could not have imagined" is the total, unrelieved poverty of July's family. She discovers, that very literally, "they had nothing" (29). This statement, "they had nothing," is a three word paragraph set off in the text between two lengthy paragraphs of description in Gordimer's text. It represents the most significant step in Maureen's movement from ignorance to understanding. It is no longer possible for her to think of July as her "decently paid and contented" black servant.

Questioning her own responsibility for the poverty of July's family, Maureen returns to her memories of the past for guidance. She examines her relationship with her black childhood servant, Lydia, which was one of affection, and now she realizes, also one of ignorance and exploitation. "Why had Lydia carried her case?" (33), she asks, recalling a photograph of Lydia carrying her school books for her.

Like his wife, Bam too returns to the past for help to deal with the shock of the present. Instead of questioning the past like Maureen does, however, Bam becomes stuck in it. Contacts with July's family, for him, do not lead to growth. He drinks good-naturedly with the men, but doesn't understand a word of what is said. As days go by, it becomes difficult for Bam to talk, even with Maureen. The increasing inability of Bam and Maureen to exchange words is an early symptom of the breakdown of the marriage.

Words, especially those that have defined moral values in her past life, lose their authority for Maureen. When she realizes that July, who is "perfectly honest," had stolen things from her long ago, things she has never missed, she redefines honesty: "honesty is how much you know about anybody, that's all" she decides (36). Maureen's discovery of July's stealing is followed immediately in the novel by her acknowledgment of her own stealing. She looted the malaria pills they've been using, she tells Bam when he questions her. Need is the leveler here, and Maureen is courageous in confronting her changed circumstances. The facts become, for her, "a currency whose value has been revised" (58). And she almost chokes on gratitude as she acknowledges that they owe their servant, July, "everything."

Bam refuses to make this leap. Having had more power in their past life than Maureen, he finds it harder to acknowledge his indebtedness to a servant, who seems to be usurping his authority. He lacks the consciousness required to grasp his new position. When Maureen notes that supplies will last only as long as their money, Bam responds with a denial that reveals his diminished sense of reality: "The money! We'll be out of here, with plenty of money," he says. The narrator comments,

Habit assumed the male role of initiative and reassurance—something he always had on him, a credit card or check-book. [Maureen] would not look at him where it had passed from him, and remark his divestiture. (59)

Bam is divested of his male role, and the issue is economic. His power had derived from his place in the economy; without money, he will be powerless. Money is what kept him in South Africa when revolution began to threaten.

The economic issue is really crucial to an understanding of what is transpiring in this marriage. In her early novels, Gordimer dealt with both the economic status and race of married couples as determiners of social status. In *Lying Days*, for example, both conspire to keep Helen's friend,

Joel Aaron's, Jewish parents in their slot in the system, just above the blacks. The Jewishness of this couple places them for Helen Shaw's racially bigoted mother, but they are placed for Helen too. For her the issue is cultural and economic. The Aaron's green leatherette sofa (with shiny portholes for ash trays in the arms) places them for her as surely as their Jewish name does for her mother. And it forms a barrier between her and Joel that cannot really be surmounted in that system.

In *July's People*, Maureen analyzes the impact of economic circumstances on the nature of relationships between human beings. She concludes that, contrary to what she had always understood in her previous life, there are no absolute validities about the sacred rights and power of sexual love. In her old life they were formulated in the master bedroom; here they are formulated in a mud hut. They are different depending on the wealth and power of the people who formulate them. She concludes that,

the balance between desire and duty is—has to be—maintained quite differently in accordance with the differences in the lover's place in the economy. These alter the way of dealing with the experience; and so the experience itself. (65)

This, of course, has profound implications for her relationship with her husband; duty and desire are essentially cut loose from the laws of their past existence because of the shift in their economic status. On a broader scale, there is no aspect of human relations so private that it is not determined by economic circumstances.

III

As Maureen grows in understanding over the course of the novel, her relationship with Bam steadily deteriorates. Bam no longer has the ability to answer her questions. He can only use the language of the past, the dead language of liberal politics. In July's village, Bam attempts to continue the role of white provider, fixing a water tank from "back there" and giving away fish he catches that his own family finds unacceptable. When he first arrives in the village with his family, he seems adaptable: he bathes in the river with no apparent concern for disease; he is the first to observe that his children drink water from the river, and that attempts to boil it for them will be useless. Without his checkbook and credit card, however, symbols of his economic power, Bam's manhood is steadily eroded. This process culminates when he shoots some wild pigs for food and then, "in a moment of hallucinatory horror," (80) sees their blood on his penis. (He has made love with Maureen, and what he actually sees is her menstrual blood).

Bam's fearfulness contrasts with Maureen's developing boldness. Initially, she too had been fearful. She felt stifled, not just by the hut, but ironically, by the vast space that surrounded her, space she found "confining in its immensity" (26). She was afraid to "walk out into the boundlessness" (27), afraid even to go to the river very often, the place where so much of the village activity took place. The bush seemed to her like a growing "mould," its inhabitants, like fungus.

But freed of the restrictions of her role as middle class wife, Maureen gradually develops confidence and begins to act spontaneously. When Bam quakes with fear when the family is required to visit the district chief, for example, Maureen laughs, decorously (as it turns out) in the chief's face. There is a poignancy in Bam's awareness of his inadequacy and in his inability to speak to Maureen during the visit: "he did not know to whom to speak these days when he spoke to her" (104). For Bam, Maureen is no longer "his wife," no longer "Maureen," or "the woman to whom he was 'my husband'" (105). Just who the partners are in this marriage is no longer clear. Bam has awaited the chief's presence like he once awaited surgery for piles; in contrast, Maureen "plonks" herself down in comfort. Bam notes "how everything came easily to her now, if she didn't know what was expected of her she did as she liked" (114).

Things do not come easily to Bam. With his checkbook and credit cards no longer of use, there are two remaining symbols of his power: his gun, and the bakkie, the vehicle that brought him and his family to July's village. When July departs from the village in the bakkie without explanation, Bam is helpless to respond. He is capable of making himself understood to the villagers when he asks where July has gone, but he cannot ask them what he is thinking, what really is on his mind. He cannot "get an answer out of anyone" (40). With the car gone, there is "nowhere to run to. Nothing to get away in" (40). In this state of vulnerability, Bam feels humbled toward Maureen. He is aware, however, that she does not share his feeling and is preoccupied with her own thoughts. Essentially these two exist in isolation with their identities suspended by events beyond their control.

Maureen, with the removal of the car, has undergone another shock of recognition:

She was someone handling her being like an electrical appliance she has discovered can fling one apart in a wrong touch. Not fear, but knowledge that the shock, the drop beneath the feet, happens to the self alone, and can be avoided only alone. (41)

To avoid falling, Maureen has no choice but to act independently. The repetition of the word, "alone," emphasizes her division from Bam. In his isolation, Bam thinks of his gun, comparing himself to a boy with a pea-shooter. Fantasies of safety in Canada are followed by angry thoughts about Maureen. Is it her fault he stayed in South Africa? Bam feels that Maureen has twisted herself around him, that he is both split open and held together by her. The narrator comments that as Maureen and Bam bicker, Bam rotates his head as if his neck were in a noose. When Maureen taunts him, the rope seems to be in her hand. The imagery here is harsh. These two do not stand together in adversity: each seeks to blame the other for their mutual predicament; each exposes the other's weaknesses and accuses the other of distorting facts.

Gordimer does not engage readers' sympathies for one partner in this marriage at the expense of the other. Although Maureen is the one experiencing growth, she is actually a less sympathetic character in many circumstances than is Bam. When Maureen sees July return with the vehicle, she does not relieve Bam's anxiety by telling him about it, for example. "Each one for himself," she thinks.

As she becomes the tougher of the two, Maureen takes on the role of protector. It is she who battles with July over the keys to the vehicle. Gordimer uses the battle to expose the lies at the heart of the supposedly trusting relationship between master and servant. The weapons in the battle are words. July confronts Maureen with her distrust of him; in response, Maureen lies to him. July, however, will no longer accept lies. He rejects the polite but dishonest communication that has been a staple of their relationship for the fifteen years she and Bam have been married. And then he uses his weapon: he calls himself Maureen's "boy." The word falls on her like the strokes of a whip. "Where had he picked up the weapon? " she asks:

The shift boss had used it; the word was never used in her house; she priggishly shamed and exposed others who spoke it in her presence. She had challenged it in the mouths of white shopkeepers and even policemen. (70)

July, recognizing the efficacy of his weapon, continues to use it, "You good madam, you got good boy." And he compels Maureen to understand that he has never felt trusted by her. She has walked behind him, looking to make sure he does as he is told.

Because she has genuinely believed that she has had a good relationship with July, Maureen experiences another shock. Wounded, she wants to hurt July as much as he has hurt her. Maureen's weapon is another word, this time a name, "Ellen." Ellen is the woman July lived with in town because the law prevented him from living with his real wife. Maureen asks him what his wife thinks about Ellen, knowing full well that Ellen is July's guilty secret. Again the imagery of battle is employed:

They stepped across fifteen years of no-man's land, her words shoved them and they were together, duellists who will feel each other's breath before they turn away to the regulation number of paces, or conspirators who will never escape what each knows of the other. (72)

Maureen triumphs in this battle, but it is a triumph that leaves her only with a burning pain.

July's refusal to live by the old lie, that Maureen trusts him, has compelled Maureen to confront the unjust and exploitative nature of her relationship to him. She would never call him "boy," and she had never allowed others to do so, but July has been her boy, nevertheless. Gordimer, in her essay, "Living in the Interregnum," has written that "the South Africa in which white middle-class values and mores contradict realities has long become the unreality" to her (*Essential Gesture* 278). In *July's People*, she exposes

the unreality perpetrated by liberal middle-class myths, through Maureen's
awakening to her role as oppressor.

The truth is that the comfort of Maureen and Bam's marriage has been
achieved at the expense of July's marriage. Prevented from being with his
own wife, July has been with Bam and Maureen since the date of the wedding.
He awakens them in bed in the morning and closes the house at night.
Certainly he has spent as much time with Maureen as Bam has. Together
they have managed the household, detail by detail. It is not surprising that,
although Bam cannot talk to Maureen because he no longer knows who
she is, July knows very well who she is and can force her to speak words
that describe reality. July and Maureen have no difficulty communicating.

In fact, July has better communication with Maureen than he does with
his wife, Martha. Given the time he has spent with each, this is not surprising.
Martha and July's conversations have an oblique quality. Often Martha will
begin speaking to July and conclude by speaking to herself as if he were
not there. This happens because he is gone so much that she is sometimes
inclined to forget his existence. Her letters to him are written by another
because she has not much practice writing. They follow the conventions
that have been developed by the generations of black couples that have been
separated by the system. These marriages have been denied in favor of white
middle-class marriages that depend on black labor to keep them functioning.

As Maureen becomes aware of her exploitative role, she seeks to depend
on her own labor when possible, even for unpleasant tasks. While (in
stereotypical terms) Bam has become less man-like, she has become more
like a man. When Maureen drowns some kittens in a bucket of water to
prevent their suffering starvation, it is Bam who experiences disgust and
distaste on her behalf. She, however, experiences none of the horror he felt
when he killed the pigs and had the illusion of their blood on his penis.
Indeed, when Bam expresses his sympathy over her deed, Maureen pulls
off her shirt and asks him what he is making a fuss about. The castration
imagery began earlier with the pig episode is complete here: "The baring
of breasts was not an intimacy but a castration of his sexuality and hers:
she stood like a man stripped in a factory shower" (90). Bam remarks to
himself that Maureen's neck has become her father's neck. She seems to
grimace at him and become ugly; he thinks of her as his "poor thing"
(90). "Why didn't you get one of them to do it?" he asks.

By "them," Bam means the blacks. For him, all blacks are servants,
and servants do the unpleasant work. His attitude is not shared by Maureen,
who begins to work with the village women in the fields. Maureen studies
the women's behavior and learns to gather greens for her family, working
as a team with July's wife. This behavior bothers July, who tells her that
the work belongs to the other women and that she doesn't need to work
for them in their place. The word, "place," confuses Maureen. Does July
mean role or location? Is he implying she has no claim to the earth?[7] Maureen
is no longer where she was in either role or location, and July's attempt
to force her into the "place," in the sense of "role," that she occupied in

the other "place," "location," draws her ire. This time Maureen feels fear within herself that originates from July, although he has not threatened her. The humiliation he experienced as her servant was something she could not understand until she came to his home. "Place" and "place," although separately defined, are indistinguishable in a system that allows for no distinctions where blacks are concerned. Not ever having entered into a relation of subservience with Bam, Maureen struggles to avoid one with July.

Her responses to Bam are now divided between those she feels for the man of the past and those she feels for the man of the present. When Bam comments on the hard work it takes to gather greens, Maureen has an impulse to embrace him, but it is only to "touch someone recollected, not the one who persisted in his name" (93). Her battle with July over her work with the women clarifies for Maureen the nature of her relationship with her husband. The architect lying on a bed in a mud hut, this "man without a vehicle" is separate from the man left behind in the master bedroom, she senses. The narrator is careful to state that Maureen does not feel disgust for the diminished Bam, that she recognizes their commonality in the same mud hut. And yet Maureen has gone on a long trip and left Bam behind. This alienation is the product not of choice, but of botched circumstances outside of the marriage (98).

Maureen has also, in her journey, left her children behind. Bam (who sees parenthood as a paradise from which he will someday, resentfully, be expelled, [76]) takes over for Maureen here as she has taken over the more aggressive activities for him. His fatherliness stands in for the listlessness toward the children that tension produces in Maureen (47). The effect of their father's less strictured care (Bam points out that it is good that they are learning to wipe their behinds with stones, for example [35]) is positive. At several places in the text, the narrator documents the children's increasing self sufficiency. They drink river water, eat the villager's food, form close friendships, learn the language, and move in and out of the village huts with ease. Gina even makes herself at home in the huts of the chief's village. The children's need for traditional middle-class mothering decreases over the course of the novel. Maureen notes that she no longer has to worry about them: "she fed them; they knew how to look after themselves like black children" (125). When she sees them leaping in the river she speculates that they may have become immuned to water-born diseases like the black children have. "They had survived in their own ability to ignore the precautions it was impossible for her to maintain for them," she thinks (138).

Not only have the children become more self-sufficient as they have merged with the black culture, they have become more fully developed human beings. In their old lives, they had only taken pleasure in the acquisition of new possessions. Nothing else had made them as happy or excited. They did not take pleasure in even the debased contact with nature available to middle-class children, the feeding of rabbits (6). Their selfishness in dealings with other children and each other is amply documented. They are already exercising proprietary rights over natural resources; they believe that they own the rain water collected in the tank Bam has repaired, for example, because their father has harnessed the resource. They own it and do not intend to share it. The children mimic in private life the exploitation and cultural exclusivity that the white middle-class evinces in public life.

Gordimer has pointed out that when the black majority takes over in South Africa, which it surely will, the whites will have to redefine themselves in a new collective life with new structures. "It is not a matter of Blacks taking over white institutions," she writes, "it is one of conceiving of institutions...that reflect a societal structure vastly different from that built to the specifications of white power and privilege" (*Essential* 265). If Maureen and Bam's marriage represents a white institution that cannot survive in its current form (dependent as it is on white power and privilege), then the children of that marriage offer a contrasting hope for the development of new institutions. Subject to new specifications in child-rearing practices based on a blend of black and white, male and female influences, the children become generous, adaptable, happy human beings, whose fulfillment is not dependent on material possessions. Moreover, they have learned to show proper respect and gratitude to blacks: when July gives Royce some fishing-line, Royce bobs obeisance, receiving the gift with cupped palms (157).

July's People is about an explosion of roles (117), the blowing up of public institutions (the Union Building), and the burning of private institutions (the master bedroom). Bam senses, occasionally, the great drama that is being enacted around him. He struggles hopelessly to find words that are not phrases from "back there,...words that would make the truth that must be forming here, out of the blacks out of themselves" (127). Here he articulates the essential problem of the liberal, and in the process, documents Gordimer's reason for rejecting liberalism in favor of radicalism: Bam wants to *make* the truth with words for the blacks. In *The Essential Gesture*, Gordimer quotes Bishop Desmond Tutu:

The leadership of the struggle must be in black hands. They must determine what will be the priorities and the strategy of the struggle. Whites unfortunately have the habit of taking over and usurping the leadership and taking the crucial decisions.... (266-7)

She adds a line from the black South African poet, Serote, "Blacks must learn to talk; whites must learn to listen" (267). Blacks will *make* their own truth, and the white liberal predilection to articulate it for them must fail.

This is what happens to Bam. Bam, in fact, cannot even articulate his own truth. The words will not come because they are locked by the old vocabulary of liberal politics: "the words were not there; his mind, his anger, had no grip" (127). He is, as Maureen perceives, "the man who had been left behind" (126). Bam sees himself moving along a track after Maureen and losing her. The division of the radical segment of white South Africans from the liberals is a painful one, and Gordimer documents it in the anguish of this divided marriage.

Bam's final humiliation in the novel is cruelly ironic. The family has gathered in the hut because the village is having a celebration, and Maureen does not want the children to see the women squatting to urinate in public when they have had too much to drink. The humiliation involves Bam's loss of his gun, and it is ironic because Bam has never valued guns, except for the pleasure of shooting small birds. True to his liberal values, he had never kept a gun under his pillow to defend his family or property in his suburban house (6). In the hut, however, his gun has become the last remaining symbol of his declining power. When it is stolen, Bam lies defeated in front of his family:

He lay down on his back, on that bed, the way he habitually did; and at once suddenly rolled over onto his face, as the father had never done before his sons...[Maureen] looked down on this man who had nothing, now. There was before these children something much worse than the sight of the women's broad backsides, squatting. (145)

It is left to Maureen to confront July about the gun. Once again these two are locked in verbal combat. Maureen has triumphed in their previous battles because words were the weapons, and the language her own. This time July, taunted by Maureen, speaks in his own language, but because of her new consciousness, she understands his meaning:

She understood although she knew no word. Understood everything: what he had had to be, how she had covered up to herself for him, in order for him to be her idea of him. But for himself—to be intelligent, honest, dignified for *her* was nothing; his measure as a man was taken elsewhere and by others. She was not his mother, his wife, his sister, his friend, his people. (152)

Here Maureen and July at last speak the truth, and their words are like spilt blood. Maureen's relationship to July is not one of family or friend, but of a cheap commercial nature. The "death's harpy" pose she strikes at the end of their battle is that of a vulgar call girl. The relationship between white madam and black servant cheapens both.

July, in spite of his dramatic confrontation with Maureen, never becomes the actual subject of this novel. Aware of the white people's diminished role, he continues to think like a servant, waiting for someone to tell him to destroy his passbook. His use of his own language with Maureen demonstrates some growth, but generally he, like Bam, remains trapped by the past. Gordimer shows him to be, like everyone else, confused by events that are not clearly defined. That blacks are no more prepared for the revolution than the whites is illustrated by July's old chief who is prepared to fight with the whites against other blacks, if he thinks his territory is threatened.

It is Maureen who breaks free of the past. A helicopter flies over, and she runs after it, although there is no way to know whom it is carrying, friend or enemy. She crosses the river to meet the future, whatever it may be. Having been "shut up" in a hut like a "prison," Maureen has become aware of herself as one "confined" (126). As she runs, she escapes confinement and abandons fear. She does not abandon Bam—he remains in the master bedroom of the past. In the hut on the bed is a different man, one whose blue eyes are closed. Maureen's lips move to speak to him, but the words do not come. She looks for a long time at the closed eyelids (155). This is the sleep of death, not of rest, and it recalls the first page of the novel, where Maureen cries out in fear of stifling, and wakes Bam from the dead. She can no longer awaken him. Better to confront the possibility of death across the river than succumb to the certainty of death in the hut, stifled by the past.

The marriage in *July's People* reveals important things about power— about what happens when it becomes ambiguous: men become like women (Bam cares for the children, responds passively, lies face down on the bed in depression); women become like men (Maureen leaves the children, battles aggressively with July, runs toward the helicopter). It reveals the economic basis of power and uncovers its influence in even the most private aspects of human relationships.

The disintegration of Bam and Maureen's marriage reveals the necessary demise of institutions that support oppression. The old must be abandoned before the new can be born. When Maureen runs, she runs,

trusting herself with all the suppressed trust of a lifetime, alert, like a solitary animal at the season when animals neither seek a mate nor take care of young, existing only for their lone survival, the enemy of all that would make claims of responsibility. (160)

Maureen has divested herself of husband and children. That she is not to be judged for this is clear from Gordimer's use of the animal imagery. Her state is temporary and natural; it is compared to a season.

Rebirth results, and with rebirth, fear is shed. Maureen, when she runs out of boulders crossing the river, "does as she has seen done"; she immerses herself in the water as the black people do. The experience is compared to a baptism. The water is "tepid and brown and smells strongly of earth." This is a new kind of baptism, the kind found in the novels of Tony Morrison and Margaret Atwood. It works against a separation of body and spirit. Birth imagery is strong. The sense of gravity is removed: Maureen is "righted" like a newborn at delivery. She is physically and spiritually made "right," and she arrives at a "landmark" of a bank she has "never crossed to before."

Shedding fear opens the way for growth. There is a potential for a new kind of order (orderly clumps of daisies) to replace the "tidiness of cupboards" which Maureen leaves behind when she begins to run. The new order coexists with freedom: running through the bush, Maureen finds that orderly varieties of flowers stand side by side with undergrowth and airy knob-thorn trees.

> 'The old is dying and the new cannot be born;
> in this interregnum there arises a great
> diversity of morbid symptoms.'
>
> —Antonio Gramsci
> *Prison Notebooks*

The words Nadine Gordimer chose to introduce this novel describe what is to come: morbid symptoms of a state between death and birth. The old liberalism with its genuinely kind impulses (Bam) has words only for the past, not the future. It leads to death of the spirit. Escape is necessary (Maureen), but to what and at what cost? The old institutions of exploitation (the white middle-class marriage) must give way to new ones, but the new institutions are not yet developed. It is essential to shed fear and enter the uncertainty of that immense space, but what is out there is yet to be determined. The conclusion of this novel is about a positive change.[8] The morbid symptoms that accompany that change are threatening, and what the change will lead to is uncertain. But Maureen runs, and if what she runs toward is only the possibility of the ideal, that is, perhaps, the best that can be hoped for.

In her essay, "Living in the Interregnum," Gordimer writes about the possibility of an alternative left, "a democracy without economic or military terror." "We must continue to be tormented by the ideal," she writes:

Its possibility must be there for peoples to attempt to put into practice, to begin over and over again, wherever in the world it has never been tried, or has failed. This is where your responsibility to the Third World meets mine. Without the will to tramp towards that possibility, no relations of whites, of the West, with the West's formerly subject peoples can ever be free of the past, because the past, for them, was the jungle of Western capitalism, not the light the missionaries thought they brought with them. (*Essential* 284)

Like the missionaries, Bam and Maureen were well intentioned but deceived. Through their marriage in *July's People*, Gordimer challenges all privileged peoples to 1) recognize their responsibility for oppression, and 2) end the exploitation of the many for the benefit of a few.

Notes

[1]Gordimer defines her role as writer in terms of what she calls "the two presences within—creative self-absorption and conscionable awareness." The writer, she says, "must resolve whether these are locked in a death-struggle, or are really foetuses in a twinship of fecundity" (*The Essential Gesture 299*). Gordimer has seized these two presences and engaged them together on the side of life. To be consciously aware, for her, is to enter "the brotherhood of man which is the only definition of society that has any permanent

validity" (296); to be creatively self-absorbed is to freely employ the imagination to transform human experience in order to reveal its "full meaning and significance" (298).

[2]Clingman's introduction to Gordimer's collection of essays, *The Essential Gesture*, provides a good summary of her accomplishments.

[3]*A Sport of Nature* centers around a white woman who is exiled from South Africa. She marries two black men. The first, an exiled South African revolutionary, is killed before her eyes; the second, a general who regains rule over another African country, returns with her to South Africa to celebrate a new rule by the black majority. Gordimer's thinking on the acceptance of inter-racial marriage by newly liberated blacks may possibly have undergone a shift since her 1959 essay, "Where Do Whites Fit In?" In that essay, she speculated that black Africa would frown on such relationships due to a stoked up nationalism.

[4]Gordimer examines the pressures brought to bear on a marriage in which a reformer is not "good enough" for the revolutionary role he undertakes, in *The Late Bourgeois World*.

[5]This is a major theme of *Occasion for Loving*, which centers around a love affair between a black man and white woman. The affair does not end in marriage due to "the distortion of laws and society" (296). An observer concludes at the end of this novel, that as long as the law forbidding inter-racial cohabitation exists, nothing can "bring integrity to personal relationships" (296).

[6]*A World of Strangers* discusses a marriage between a white woman and Indian man that ends in divorce due to pressures caused by the system. The woman, Anna Louw, describes the difficulty:

It's terribly hard to keep a marriage like ours personal; it starts off like an ordinary marriage but then everything else, outside it, forces on it the onus of a test case. If you quarrel, you can't simply be a man and wife who don't get on, immediately you're the proof that mixed marriages don't work. You've no idea how this influences you, in time. (176)

[7]The issue of who owns the earth is dealt with by Gordimer in *The Conservationist*, where a black corpse lays claim to a white farm.

[8]There is a debate in the literature about this. Cooke asserts that the conclusion is negative. He makes observations like the following about Maureen and Bam's lives in July's village:

The Smales want to fit in. *They* try hard. *They* want to do their share of the work, make friends, be honest about their motivations. *Theirs* is the most conscious attempt in Gordimer's fiction to make the transition to an alien landscape.

   They fail. For all their good will and effort, the Smales remain bound by the conceptual system of the privileged urban world they have been forced to flee...
(164, emphasis mine)

The problem with Cooke's interpretation is that he considers Maureen and Bam as a unit with Bam as the determining voice of the unit. Bam fails; therefore, the *Smales* fail. However, Maureen and Bam are not a unit, and Bam certainly does not speak for them both. They are two individuals whose bonds with each other deteriorate as the novel progresses. Maureen succeeds in breaking out of her old conceptual system; Bam does not.

   Clingman, in his reading of *July's People*, avoids some of Cook's difficulties simply by refusing to submerge Maureen's identity beneath her husband's. Consequently, he sees Maureen as a character who, having been historically entrapped, runs "from old structures and relationships...toward her revolutionary destiny" at the novel's conclusion (203).

Works Cited

Cooke, John. *The Novels of Nadine Gordimer: Private Lives/Public Landscapes*. Baton Rouge: Louisiana State University Press, 1985.

Clingman, Stephen. *The Novels of Nadine Gordimer: History from the Inside*. London: Allen & Unwin, 1986.

Gordimer, Nadine. *The Burger's Daughter*. New York: Viking Press, 1979.

_____ *The Conservationist*. New York: Viking Press, 1975.

_____ *The Essential Gesture*. New York: Alfred A. Knopf Inc., 1988.

_____ *A Guest of Honour*. New York: Viking Press, 1970.

_____ *July's People*. New York: Viking Press, 1981.

_____ *The Late Bourgeois World*. New York: Viking Press, 1966.

_____ *The Lying Days*. New York: Simon and Schuster, 1953.

_____ *Occasion for Loving*. New York: Viking Press, 1963.

_____ *A Sport of Nature*. New York: Alfred A. Knopf, 1987.

_____ *A World of Strangers*. New York: Viking Penguin, 1962.

Contributors

Katherine Anne Ackley is a professor of English and Women's Studies Coordinator at the University of Wisconsin at Stevens Point. She has published articles and presented papers on a variety of women's issues. She is editor of *Women and Violence in Literature: An Essay Collection* and author of *The Novels of Barbara Pym.*

Patrick Bizzaro is an associate professor of English at East Carolina University. He has published poetry, articles on composition and literature, and essays on nineteenth-century British authors in addition to several texts.

Christopher K. Brooks is an assistant professor of English at The Wichita State University. He is an eighteenth- and nineteenth-century British literature specialist and Goldsmith scholar who has published articles and presented papers on Goldsmith and, recently, the field of popular culture films and sports. His article on Goldsmith's view of war appeared in the *Dayton Review.*

Laurie Buchanan is an assistant professor of English at Marshall University. She has presented papers and published articles and book reviews on feminist psychoanalytic literature and theory and on nineteenth-century women and fiction. She is currently working on a book analyzing the feminist themes in Elizabeth Gaskell's novels.

Patricia Prandini Buckler is an assistant professor of English and Director of Composition at Purdue University, North Central. Her research interests include Chaucer's audience and the rhetorical context in which he wrote, humorous writing, composition theory and pedagogy, and antebellum popular culture. Her conference papers and publications cover such topics as medieval rhetoric, comedy in Chaucer, teaching the humorous essay, and the antebellum woman's scrapbook as rhetorical composition.

Mary F. Catanzaro teaches in the English Department at Marquette University. She has presented papers in the U.S. and abroad on the works of Samuel Beckett and has published in the *Journal of Dramatic Theory and Criticism, Modern Drama, Critique,* and *Analecta Husserliana.* She is interested in the psycho-dynamics of couples and is preparing a book on Beckett's couples.

Stefanie Dojka teaches English at Lakewood Community College in Minnesota. Conference papers and publications include work on the novels of Jane Austen and Nadine Gordimer, as well as research on collaborative learning and the authority of the personal in student writing. She is currently writing about the integration of feminism in the curriculum.

Thomas H. Fick is an assistant professor of English at Southeastern Louisiana University. He has published articles on Mark Twain, James Purdy, Toni Morrison, Charles Reich, Ken Kesey, Catharine Sedgwick, John W. De Forest, and various aspects of nineteenth- and twentieth-century popular culture. He is currently working on a book on antebellum realism.

Richard D. McGhee is professor of English and former head of the department at Kansas State University. He has published articles on Romantic and Victorian poetry, drama, and fiction. He is author of *Marriage, Duty and Desire in Victorian Poetry and Drama* (1980), *Henry Kirke White* (1981), *Guilty Pleasures: William Wordsworth's Poetry of Psychoanalysis* (forthcoming), and *John Wayne: Actor, Artist, Hero* (1990).

JoAnna Stephens Mink is an assistant professor of English at Mankato State University. She has presented papers and published articles on nineteenth- and twentieth-century fiction and authors as well as on aspects of the composing process and tutor-training. She is interested in the changing role of women in the nineteenth century and has an essay on the emergence of woman as hero in *Heroines of Popular Culture*.

Mary R. Reichardt is an assistant professor of English at the University of St. Thomas in St. Paul, Minnesota. A specialist in American literature, she is especially interested in women's writing of the late nineteenth century. She has presented several papers on Freeman at M/MLA and has published articles on Freeman in *Legacy* and in *American Literary Realism*. Currently, she is preparing a critical study of Freeman's short fiction.

Pamela S. Saur is an assistant professor at Lamar University, where she teaches German, English, and ESL. She is presently Chief Editor of *Schatzkammer*, a journal primarily for German teachers at all levels, and Business Manager of the *Lamar Journal of the Humanities*. Most of her publications and presentations have been in twentieth-century Austrian literature, but she has also published articles on pedagogy and American popular culture.

Janet Doubler Ward is an instructor of English at Illinois Central College. She has presented conference papers on composition theory and teaching methodology as well as women in literature. She is interested in women's roles in society and how those roles are depicted in literature that shapes current thinking about issues involving women.

Joyce W. Warren teaches in the English Department at Queens College, CUNY. She is the author of *The American Narcissus: Individualism and Women in Nineteenth-Century American Fiction* (1984). She edited *Ruth Hall and Other Writings* by Fanny Fern (1986) and in 1987 received a grant from the National Endowment of the Humanities to work on a biography of Fern (pseud. of Sara Willis Parton), which will be published by Rutgers University Press. She has also authored numerous articles and papers on nineteenth-century American literature, particularly on literature by women.